Making socialists

MANCHESTER
1824

Manchester University Press

Making socialists

Mary Bridges Adams and the fight for knowledge and power, 1855–1939

JANE MARTIN

Manchester University Press
Manchester and New York
distributed in the United States exclusively by Palgrave Macmillan

Published by Manchester University Press
Oxford Road, Manchester M13 9NR, UK
and Room 400, 175 Fifth Avenue, New York, NY 10010, USA
www.manchesteruniversitypress.co.uk

Distributed in the United States exclusively by
Palgrave Macmillan, 175 Fifth Avenue,
New York, NY 10010, USA

Distributed in Canada exclusively by
UBC Press, University of British Columbia, 2029 West Mall,
Vancouver, BC, Canada V6T 1Z2

British Library Cataloguing-in-Publication Data is available

Library of Congress Cataloging-in-Publication Data is available

ISBN 978 0 7190 8994 7 paperback

First published by Manchester University Press in hardback 2010

This paperback edition first published 2013

Printed by Lightning Source

Contents

List of illustrations

Acknowledgements

I wish to acknowledge the help and support I have received from numerous people in writing this book. However, I owe a special debt of gratitude to the late Mr Nicholas Bridges-Adams and his wife, Jenifer, for their warm support, advice and encouragement during the research on Mary Bridges Adams. I also wish to acknowledge the British Educational Research Association, whose award of the Brian Simon Educational Research Fellowship for 2004/5 made much of this research possible and to express my appreciation to Manchester University Press. In addition, I thank Elizabeth Burn, David and Mandy Nutton, Elaine Unterhalter and Ruth Watts for comments on earlier versions of particular chapters. A special debt of gratitude is due Richard Aldrich, Bernard Barker, Dennis Dean and Tom Woodin for the time and care they took in making suggestions and offering feedback on an earlier draft of the manuscript.

I wish to thank the librarians and archivists at the following libraries: Birmingham City, British Newspaper Library Colindale, Calgary University, Columbia University, Greenwich Local Heritage Centre, Greenwich University, the House of Lords, Hull University, Lewisham Local History and Archives Centre, London Metropolitan Archive, the London School of Economics, Marx Memorial Library, Newcastle Local Studies Centre, the People's History Museum at Manchester, National Library of Ireland, Northamptonshire Record Office, Royal Holloway University of London, Tyne and Wear Archives Service, the University of London and Warwick Modern Records Centre. My particular thanks are due to Chris Coates at the TUC Library Collections at London Metropolitan University for her support and lively interest over the years and the Hon. Oliver Soskice for giving me permission to consult the Soskice Papers at the House of Lords.

A number of other people have been particularly encouraging, especially Kevin Brehony, Rosemary Deem, Carol Dyhouse, Joyce Goodman,

Gordon Kerr and Marion Whiting. More recently, Chris Lynch and Roger Smalley helped raise my awareness of the writings of Ethel Carnie.

Closer to home, I would particularly like to thank my mother, who helped with the proof reading and Paul, who has provided support and practical assistance over the many years of research leading to this publication. I am most grateful to them all. The book is dedicated to the late Emeritus Professor Brian Simon and Mrs Joan Simon. It was my privilege to know them.

Abbreviations

BLPES	British Library of Political and Economic Science
BSP	British Socialist Party
CUBM	Columbia University, Bakhmeteff Materials
HL	House of Lords Record Office
HUA	Hull University Archives
ILP	Independent Labour Party
LA	Lewisham Local History and Archives Centre
LCC	London County Council
LMA	London Metropolitan Archive
LRC	Labour Representation Committee
LSB	London School Board
LTC	London Trades Council
NLI	National Library of Ireland
NRO	Northamptonshire County Record Office
NUT	National Union of Teachers
RACS	Royal Arsenal Co-operative Society
RACSP	Royal Arsenal Co-operative Society Papers
SDF	Social Democratic Federation
SDP	Social Democratic Party
TNA	The National Archives, London
TUC	Trades Union Congress
TUC Lib.	TUC Library Collection, London Metropolitan University
TWA	Tyne and Wear Archives Service
UCal.	Calgary University Special Collections/Archives
UCL	University College London, Special Collections
WCG	Women's Co-operative Guild
WEA	Workers' Educational Association

Introduction: biography and history

> Socialism is going to govern the world! Labour is going to rule the world! Labour is going to own the world! Capitalism cannot prevent it! (Mary Bridges Adams, 1920)[1]

> If ever the history of the Socialist movement comes to be written, it will be in the main a history of the labours of obscure and unknown men and women. (William Stewart, 1900)[2]

Recovering forgotten voices

Making Socialists will revisit the history of British socialism in the late nineteenth and early twentieth centuries in the light of the life and work of Mary Bridges Adams. Although traditional narratives pay little attention to women, Mary's activities within the Labour movement, and as a campaigner for improvements in working-class education, challenged established elites in ways that are important for our understanding of this watershed period. The intention of the book is to recover voices that have been discounted or forgotten, to recapture a 'world we have lost', without losing touch with its spirit.[3] I have tried to steep myself in a landscape and a mindscape whose forgotten interconnections, ideas and multitude of activities have a continuing relevance. In re-examining the link between various interpretations of socialism and different views of education within the Labour movement, I have found myself writing about an everyday world of social practice in which socialist politics, the co-operative movement and the trade union movement combined.

Mary was among the thousands of women recruited to teach in the nineteenth-century elementary school system. She objected to the capitalist model of society that she saw strengthened by the educational process, and a vision of a better society carried her out of the classroom and into political action. In her late twenties, she decided to 'cross the river of fire' and enter the socialist movement. This was how William Morris (b. 1834) characterised the life-changing experience that becoming a socialist represented in the 1880s and 1890s. Eager idealists borne along by an almost millennial ethical fervour, the men and women who made up the 'pioneering' generation of British socialists spent much time and energy spreading the word.[4] In common with other early converts, Mary was inspired by the example of Peter Kropotkin (b. 1842), the intellectual leader of anarchist communism, and Morris himself, founder of the short-lived but influential Socialist League. During the 1880s she moved from Newcastle to London, where she was amongst many luminaries drawn into networks of radical doers and dreaming radicals that made the Labour movement a living reality. Throughout her life she carried forward a belief in the possibility of revolutionary socialist transformation, as well as its inherent rightness.

Politically, she aspired to change the world. At a local level, Mary spent seven years as a member of the London School Board (LSB), where she supported the extension of the public elementary system for all working-class children and specifically attacked the elitist idea of a 'ladder of opportunity' for the exceptional. Her own education biography shows that she valued the acquisition of knowledge very highly. She was firmly committed to 'common schools' rather than selection and tried to move the Labour movement toward a clear, unified view about education priorities and policies. Creating the National Labour Education League in 1901 represented a transition in Mary's political journey, putting her on a trajectory of moving between local and national activities at several levels. Against a backdrop of mounting tensions in the education world, the League heralded a new step forward – the closest thing to a Labour education policy then in existence. For her, the advance of education and political progress were part of a single programme.

However, this is not a story of a career in the Labour movement. Mary remained faithful to the extra-parliamentary Labour Left when the Conservative government's 1903 London Education Bill became law. This piece of legislation abolished the School Board and invested its authority and the control and management of elementary schools in the education committee of the London County Council (LCC), to which women could not be elected. With the financial support of her remarkable friend the aristocratic Countess of Warwick (b. 1861), she used her training in street-corner meetings and outdoor agitation to continue the fight for free school meals and medical inspection. A charismatic speaker and increasingly prolific writer, Mary advocated political action by trade unionists in all her journalism, prioritising education as part of the socialist vision of a better society. Having lost the battle to save the school boards, and suspicious that the government might want to use schools to make future workers more compliant and obedient, she would pin her faith to the socialist education programme as practised by the National Labour College on the eve of the First World War.

Mary became a political correspondent for the *Cotton Factory Times* as the militancy of the industrial workers and the suffragettes gained momentum, with the overt intention of appealing to working women in Lancashire's mill towns. Deeply suspicious of the strategy and tactics of Labour's parliamentary leaders, she would resist and challenge the assumption that manoeuvre and compromise were essential to the furtherance of Labour's position. Mary belonged to a small minority of socialists who looked forward to a revolution, with a strong attachment to 'class conflict' and opposition to capitalism. In common with the critics and opponents of the 'politics of Labour' that Ralph Miliband describes in *Parliamentary Socialism*, she would condemn the parliamentarians as class collaborators.[5] By the time of the anti-war struggles in 1914, she took it for granted that she should intervene in public debate and, if necessary, criticise those responsible for the implementation of what she saw as unjust and discriminatory policies. In the interwar years, she handed the struggle over to a new political generation. It would not be easy, she warned the youth of the Red International. 'All the indications go to show that the young proletarian students in Britain, who "see straight" on the paramount necessity of working-class education in Social Science will have a tough fight before them. But, after all, the fight is THE thing.'[6] In his memoirs comrade Harry McShane (b. 1891) referred to her as 'the outstanding woman fighter for socialism'.[7]

The friend who wrote Mary's obituary for *The Times* claimed that she had William Morris's blessing when she became involved in popular educational politics.[8] For Mary, as for Morris, education was a completely dominating, central concern and making political propaganda was more important than the particular organisation through which one worked for the Cause. As the years passed and circumstances changed, Mary joined and left the Social Democratic Federation (SDF), formed in 1884 and renamed the Social Democratic Party (SDP) in1908; the Fabian Society, established in 1884; the Independent Labour Party (ILP), which dates from 1893; and the British Socialist Party (BSP), formed in 1911. This to-ing and fro-ing was not unusual, but the literature on English socialism in the 1880s and 1890s has a tendency to present a clear-cut contest between stances and assumptions that fall neatly on one side or another of the split between ethical (humanitarian) and Marxist materialist socialist belief systems.[9] The reality was much more complex, and biographies provide the clearest evidence that political thought is not so neatly distributed. As Denis Lawton points out, 'organisations are made up of individuals who usually vary considerably in their beliefs'.[10]

Then, as now, momentous events like socialist unity negotiations reveal as much about the personalities of the individuals involved as they do about questions of doctrine, strategy and style. Geoffrey Foote suggests that by the time the Labour Representation Committee (LRC) was established in 1900, the three main (overlapping) groups within it were the ILP, the Fabians and trade union representatives, with three different but overlapping sets of beliefs or ideas.[11] The first group articulated a vision of a better society based on a more moral, principled way of life, often of a semi-religious kind. The second group were more concerned with economic efficiency and a programme for the good state, rather than with social justice and the dignity of human beings. Many of the third group, the trade unionists, remained loyal to the radical wing of the Liberal Party. They tended to be more pragmatic and more specific, prioritising a list of changes to achieve better working conditions and wages for their members, as well as making specific pronouncements on education policy, among other things.

Mary's activities intersect with a grand historical narrative about the origins of the British Labour Party. However, she never appears in standard histories of the organised Labour movement. Harry McShane first raised the issue of the neglect of Mary's significance in correspondence with historian Raymond Challinor in the 1970s, saying, 'It is nothing short of a scandal that she seems to be forgotten. I am certain that a probe into her work would reveal valuable history long overlooked'.[12] John Saville, who wrote her entry for Volume 6 of the *Dictionary of Labour Biography*, published in 1982, agreed. At the time of writing, the histories have not been reworked and his conclusion still stands: 'Her life is hardly noticed even in the footnotes of works about the labour movement in the twentieth century – a melancholy illustration of how easily memories become dimmed and reputations are lost.'[13]

Perhaps Mary was seen as part of a past generation by those who played an important role in the consolidation of Labour, as a parliamentary party, after 1900. Unable to pose an effective challenge to the electoral strategy pursued by the Parliamentary Labour Party, in common with other rebels from the Labour Left she shared a weakness to which

Miliband draws attention: 'The critics were a threat to unity. They were rocking a fragile boat. They were letting down the team. They were not playing the game.'[14] A problem as far as those trying to 'work' the political system were concerned, they seemed obsessed with the need to distance 'them' (the impractical socialists) from 'us' (who can really take power). However, this does not mean we should adopt a view of the past as a foreign country or neglect to consider some significant inhabitants. The residue of ideas would find new political forms, and the historian acts as mediator, seeking to do justice to the past while speaking to the present. As Peter Cunningham and Philip Gardner point out, history teaches us that 'in the work of creating a better future, the past holds out much more to us than we may at first imagine'.[15]

Women in the making of socialist history

Historians make history through the production of knowledge, explanations and interpretations of what has gone before. As Carolyn Steedman puts it, 'The place where what is found may be put, is History. It is in this way, and outside the walls of the Archive, that History has become the place where quite ordinarily and by remembering, we can find things where we have already put them.'[16] The problem is that the politics of history deny some voices the occasion to speak. Witness the testimony of two authoritative males.

Our first is Scottish essayist, satirist and historian Thomas Carlyle, with his self-confident assertion that 'history is the biography of great men', still a reputable dictum when E.H. Carr was Craven scholar at Trinity College, Cambridge. Completing the first draft of his reflections on historical theory in 1960, Carr's imaginary historian is male, the function of history to enable '*him* to understand the society of the past and to increase *his* mastery over the society of the present' (my emphases).[17] Similarly, when E.P. Thompson famously insisted that class was not a 'thing' but a relationship occurring historically, he did not examine the gender dimension. In contrast, feminist historians took the need to reclaim 'herstory' as axiomatic. For example, Leonore Davidoff and Catherine Hall showed how 'the consciousness of class always takes a gendered form',[18] adding an appreciation of gender relations, theorised as a variable social organisation of sexual difference that must itself be explained, as a division of power.

The early socialist organisations were unusual, compared with the Conservative and Liberal parties in the 1880s, in permitting women to be full members. This meant there were crucial connections between socialist aims and feminist aspirations. Socialist groups included a commitment to sexual equality in their programmes, but rhetoric could be one thing and reality another. In political practice, the experience of relations between the sexes might be rather different. The proposition that women's place is in the home was at its height in mid-Victorian Britain. The doctrine of separate spheres strongly influenced views on women's potential as political activists, with ideas about gender-specific roles complicating women's independent aspirations within socialist groups. Acceptance of the domestic ideal meant the structure of gender-based job segregation became more pervasive, and this in turn framed the narratives through which the category 'working class' was understood. The end result was a tendency to idealise and then take as normal the experiences of white male workers. This is the approach that skilled engineer and trade union organiser Tom Mann (b. 1856) took when he characterised the typical socialist as 'a workman who through youth and early manhood had been battling against long hours in order that he might attend the institute, listen to lectures, and read the works of able men, and who by these means has succeeded in having a mind worth owning'.[19]

As June Hannam and Karen Hunt and others have pointed out, male labourism has been the dominant perspective constituted by the discipline of labour history.[20] Therefore, the question of gender remains under-researched in the socialist tradition as a whole. In seeking to understand why socialist women have rarely been the subject of systematic historical enquiry in their own right, Hannam and Hunt note the neglect of women and gender in histories of individual socialist organisations as well as the construction of historical texts which move beyond an institutional framework. As an example of the latter, they cite Stephen Yeo's pioneering article on the 'religion of socialism', in which 'he fails to discuss whether or not women's experiences were different from those of men and whether there was a gender dimension to "new life" socialism or the process of becoming a socialist'.[21]

With regard to conventional wisdoms underpinning the rhetorical practices of historians, a few generalisations are possible. For instance, Hannam and Hunt suggest that when histories of the pioneering days of British socialism *do* mention women they invariably highlight the role of Katharine Bruce Glasier (b. 1869), Caroline Martyn (b. 1867), Margaret McMillan (b. 1860) and Enid Stacy (b. 1868), who helped to build up support for the ILP. A focus on these middle-class women (dubbed the 'Famous Four'), reinforces the orthodox view that the ethical, non-Marxist socialism of the ILP was friendly to women, which, in turn, relies on the Marxist SDF being seen as unfriendly to women. Hannam and Hunt challenge the characterisation of the ILP as feminist and the SDF as anti-feminist. To support their view, they cite a distorted focus on the opinions of particular male leaders and a representation of each organisation in terms of its leadership, which they argue is equally misleading. Biographical approaches enable them to dismantle the dichotomy, suggesting the friendly/unfriendly to women dualism is probably an exaggeration. Political journeys of individual socialist women expose it as a false distinction which forms a chain with other simplified polarities implicit within constructions of British socialist women 'as either national propagandists or local tea makers'.[22]

Reflecting on the history of British feminism, Hannam and Hunt show also how the sex/class equality binary has supported an approach to the history of the women's movement characterised by a tendency to marginalise socialist women. Among suffrage historians this yielded a general assessment which was deeply affected by the emphasis on divided loyalties with regard to sex, class and party, principally because it was assumed that material inequalities polarised demands for rights to political equality. Consequently, socialist women who adopted an adult suffrage position are often overlooked in mainstream studies of the suffrage movement, especially when their positions resist easy categorisation as feminist.

The case of Mary Bridges Adams may help to illustrate this point. There were crucial connections between socialist aims and feminist aspirations in Mary's political practice. In 1899, for example, she took part in the International Council of Women which was held in London. The ILP's newspaper, *Labour Leader*, highlighted her contribution. Significantly, she expressed reservations at the apparent privileging of sex over class and said that 'the emancipation of women was doomed to failure unless it ceased to be a sex movement and became part of the great effort on behalf of adult suffrage'.[23] In common with many socialist women, Mary did not view her socialism primarily through the lens of suffrage. Mary's political identity was shaped by questions of class, and education remained the focus of her activities. She wanted to open up possibilities for struggle and placed great emphasis on the involvement of working-class women in political life and trade union organisation. Therefore, her labour movement activism cannot be considered in isolation from the growth of the Edwardian women's suffrage campaign.

Most histories of the Labour movement have tended to focus on high politics and well-known people at the centre. This has tended to obscure the activities of people like Mary who neither joined successful organisations nor became part of successful leadership and ideologies. Crucially, the established canons of political history have concentrated on political parties and the realm of the state. This has resulted in a general neglect of local government, where women played an active role in the development of policy, especially around the politics of educational reform. Paul Thompson's *Socialists, Liberals and Labour: the struggle for London 1885–1914*, which was published in 1967, contained a long section on the origins of Woolwich Labour Party, with no reference to Mary. More recently, Kim Yoonok Stenberg produced a study of working-class women in London local politics in the period 1894 to 1914 concentrating on the boards of the poor law guardians, and leaving Mary out.[24] The exception to this is Patricia Hollis's *Ladies Elect*, an outstandingly detailed account of the work of women in English local government in the period 1865–1914. Hollis has four references to Mary, noting her past as a head teacher, involvement in social settlement work, promotion of the ILP programme and support for integration as opposed to segregation for children with special educational needs.[25]

Mary's activities do grace the footnotes of the history of education. For example, Brian Simon's acclaimed 4-volume *Studies in the History of Education* is rooted in the concept of a class analysis of society. Volume 2 follows the interventions of organised Labour in pressing for education reform in the British context. The book presents the reader with the radicals' optimism regarding the formative power of education – defined as radical by virtue of their association with the long struggle of the working-class, first for democracy and then for socialism. She hardly appears, but Simon does name Mary by association with the Labour movement's political position on the hustings at school board elections, saying, 'Mrs Bridges Adams was elected for Greenwich as an "Independent and Labour candidate" on a clear policy of equal educational opportunity'.[26] So, too, does Kevin Manton in a study designed to investigate the crucial importance of education to the early socialist movement in Britain.[27]

Hilda Kean goes further, however, by examining the educational strategies of British feminists and the Labour Left in the period 1900–30. She pioneers a distinctive analysis which shows that these political and intellectual groupings played a crucial part in the development of what was to become, in a new form, the dominant educational orthodoxy of a much broader political settlement under the influence of the Second World War.[28] Studies by Annemarie Turnbull and, more recently, Joyce

Goodman and I, have also explored the experience of women active on the separately elected boards of education since their formation in 1870.[29] In this spirit, *Making Socialists* will take Kean's analysis a step back in time.

Mary's social action troubles a social, cultural and political landscape which validates and values the accomplishments of male workers/would-be citizens. A truer picture of the past requires an appreciation that British women, like British working men, played an active role in politics in the years before they obtained the national vote. Some ambitious, highly motivated middle-class and elite Victorian women accessed the public realms of social life through involvement in correspondence networks, personal philanthropy, voluntary societies and women's organisations, while the Co-operative movement was one of the routes through which working-class women became politicised. By the mid 1890s, British women could vote for and be elected to school boards, the boards of the poor law guardians, parish councils, rural district councils, urban district councils and London vestries. In these circumstances, British socialist women helped to put social welfare on the political agenda, negotiating traditional ideas about gender roles to affect the lives of many through their achievements in community politics, poor law administration and municipal government.

Therefore, a more spacious idea of context is needed, a social, cultural and political landscape that is unconstrained by traditional emphases on institutional histories and conventionally itemised labour leaders and people. This requires a more 'open' conception of politics and the political world to better accommodate specific forms of activity that did not take place within the parameters of parties and/or in the electoral arena. For example, Gillian Scott examines visions of citizenship in the Women's Co-operative Guild (WCG).[30] Revising the conceptual divide of private-female/public-male, Scott looks beyond class to reveal the significance of other sources of social identity and social imagery as actively constituted by language. She argues against stereotyping working-class housewives as hidden from sight in the home and provides an emotional portrait of the feelings and beliefs of working-class women caught up in an outstanding women's organisation. In a major assault on Victorian domestic ideology, the early Guild leaders repositioned working women as entitled to and capable of public work. Scott argues that the model of militant proletarian femininity evolved as the organisation developed in the period up to 1920 and projected empowering images of the ideal guildswoman as an agent of her own emancipation.

Writing feminist biography

Mary is of particular interest as a socialist woman from a working-class background. Working people, especially working women, leave few traces for the historian to work with, and the autobiography of Hannah Mitchell (b. 1871), who went into service, worked as a dressmaker and as a shop assistant, is a rarity.[31] Most published autobiographies are by socialist men, and the subjects of biography are almost invariably male.[32] Forged from below in strong grass-roots organisations, Mary's story and perspectives bring a new dimension to the political lives of working people. Long unheard, her voice merits incorporation in historical policy stories as a way of rethinking the history of the Labour Left.

Various claims have been made for the place of the personal in academic study and historical research, and my starting point is Barbara Finkelstein's rather poetic suggestion that 'biography is to history what a telescope is to the stars'.[33] Feminist history tells us of the heightened awareness of the politics of women's situation that can be found in the discourses of feminism's second wave. Collective memory, rooted in women's understanding of past struggles, was crucial to establishing a legitimating tradition, a heritage to impart. In the years intervening between the women's liberation movement and the present, collecting women's lives has become a staple of feminist scholarship amid calls for the study of 'concrete cases' to investigate what it means to be a woman situated in a particular time and space.[34] Given this, it is hardly surprising that the interaction of personal and historical pasts involves an engagement with the politics of history that operates on two levels. In the first place, it offers a challenge to mainstream accounts through recognition that those overlooked by posterity partook nonetheless in the making of history. In the second place, the task of recovering hidden female voices is to contribute to the project of making history through the production of gender knowledge.[35]

The wider sense of context and action that this study explores lies in C. Wright Mills's vision of the 'sociological imagination' that enables the researcher to reflect critically upon the moment at which individual lives and social structures intersect. For example, Carolyn Steedman's groundbreaking study, *Landscape for a Good Woman*, is a subversion of central cultural norms where the traditional historical class perspective validates and values the accomplishments of men.[36] Interweaving elements of her own and her mother's biography, she recasts the interpretative devices of working-class autobiographies to find a place for working women's lives in the male narratives. Deconstructing the particular circumstances of 1920s Burnley and South London in the 1950s enables her to illuminate aspects of wider social history and develop a political perspective on women's private lives. Using the lens of gender to explore history's representation of the past she offers a classic exposition of how to avoid the pitfalls of an 'add-on' approach in the production of knowledge about sexual difference.

In turning her childhood memories into texts, Steedman brought a methodological self-consciousness to the study of women's lives. Liz Stanley similarly is concerned with analysing accounts in connection with wider social structures and processes. She uses the analytic idea of auto/biography to encompass a range of methods drawing on individual memory, both biographical and autobiographical. Far from claiming the ability to gain access to the 'real' person through the accumulation of data, Stanley likens auto/biographical work to looking through a kaleidoscope – with each shake you see something different, even if the configurations remain the same. To my mind, the insertion of the 'slash' serves to remind us that this is not a question of either/or, not the individual or the social, but both. Stanley and Steedman both emphasise the need to pay close attention to the social contexts in which the speaking and writing and picturing of 'selves' takes place. The ways in which the self is framed and created by the social can be seen in the concept of intersubjectivity. As Stanley notes, 'no person is an island complete of itself; and an approach informed by feminist sociology and cultural politics should recognise that social networks are a crucial means of enabling us to get a purchase on other lives'.[37]

Interweaving individual and collective biography, I assemble a series of fluid contexts of social power and resistance which attend to popular culture as well as a subject. To map this terrain involves a process of historical retrieval that allows room for the interpretation of a less familiar tributary in the struggle for socialism, a way of thinking about the politics of place, corresponding to the spaces in which Mary constructed a political identity for herself. Drawing on a wide range of documentary sources (archive collections, official papers, newspapers, books and articles) as well as oral testimony, the account offers a perspective on the pattern and character of the support she received and the everyday world in which she sought both to embed and differentiate her ideas and practices. At the same time, I have kept in mind the significance of patterns of conflict and forms of association at several levels when considering influences of kinship, neighbourhood, work, religion and political association which tend to reinforce each other.

This representation of the past is produced with self-consciousness that the conventional genre of historical narrative creates the illusion of inevitability. Researcher's plots are grounded in empirical fact while employing imaginative reconstruction around momentous events which provide a purchase on the research being carried out. For example, autumn 1894 constituted what Norman Denzin calls a personal epiphany of life-changing proportions.[38] This was the moment when a delegation representing sixty labour organisations invited Mary to contest the triennial elections for the LSB. Locality is important in understanding her engagement in socialist politics because of the focus on community issues, as well as workplace struggles, in the early years of the Woolwich Labour movement. Unsuccessful at the polls the first time around, in autumn 1897 she defeated a serving member and she was able to serve her political apprenticeship on the most powerful organ of local government then in existence.

Mary took an active part in the making of the history of working-class educational politics during this period. Putting her energy into a particular policy arena, she championed the cause of equal opportunities for workers' children in a number of ways. First of all, she reasoned that you cannot educate a hungry child. On moral and ethical grounds she argued that the cost of providing free school meals should be borne by the community. Secondly, she encouraged an expansion in the Board's building programme, arguing for increased expenditure to achieve a maximum class size of thirty children. Finally, she objected to the organisation of education along the lines of social class. Mary never became a national figure in the Labour Party but she was consummately well networked within the Labour movement. Her socialism grew in the context of an alternative way of life that she discovered as a young married mother, living in an isolated enclave of socialist politics.

After the strike of militant worker-students at Ruskin College, Oxford in 1909, Mary was deeply involved in the Plebs League, launched to argue the case for an independent system of working-class adult education. Its members published the educational journal *Plebs*, and in 1912 she established Bebel House, a College for Working Women, set up in connection with the full-time Labour College for men in London's Earls Court. Aiming to win over the Labour movement to a class perspective on learning and education, her interest in educational questions was firmly situated within the broader contexts of the exploitation and oppression which class politics challenges. Unlike those twentieth-century proponents who developed a carefully considered doctrine of Labour socialism and sought intellectual respectability for their views, she did not moderate earlier attitudes. In the spirit of the self-taught worker intellectuals and the communist supporters who found a home in Britain's 'Little Moscows' in the South Wales coalfield, she eschewed 'the men who organised, lobbied, waited on Royal Commissions and finally were admitted to office'.[39] Further to the left than those who tried to negotiate and manoeuvre from within parliament, she presented rather different views. Her preference was for direct action mounted by rank-and-file agitators and Marxist pedagogues.

During the First World War, Mary was in close touch with the anti-war movement and threw herself into Russian émigré politics at the invitation of George Chicherin (b. 1872), a well-known figure in London socialist circles, responsible for the creation of the Russian Political Prisoners and Exiles Relief Committee. When he and other Russian revolutionaries were arrested and interned she emerged to hound officials and campaigned ardently for their release.

Constructing the narrative of Mary's life

Of course, as Michael Erben points out when writing on biographical research and biographical theory, lives have to be understood as lived within time (both biological time and clock time). Narratives of the relation between past, present and future time are the means by which biographical experience is given meaning.[40] Nonetheless, the term 'social career' is put forward to indicate important developments within biographical writing: the emergence of a spiral form that moves away from the life-course approach. It is accepted that a life-story may pass through a combination of interrelated social careers, intersected by transitions, reversals and leaps forward. Therefore, Mary's life is not presented as a linear narrative culminating in 'old age'. It records the experience of a woman who never was prepared to sink her whole being in home and family. Each chapter has been designed to interweave the personal with the political, the life with the woman – both public and private. The framework relates to Raphael Samuel's brilliant depiction of the 'lost world' of British Communism and the writing sets out to champion the value and importance of 'thick descriptions', detailed accounts of behaviour that serve as a starting point for understanding.[41] We have only a tiny knowledge of Mary's early life, which makes it difficult to place Mary in her social context. My history making becomes the work of producing a historical ethnography of oppositional cultural worlds, used as a vehicle to conjure up and try to understand mentalities from another place and another time.

Reflecting this, the biography's structure is shaped around central events in Mary's political life as well as in her personal life, rooted within the wider socio-political and cultural context. Mary's left-wing political activism provides an entry point for exploring the meaning of oppositional networks in a social history which connects rather than separates the domains of education and labour and shifts our understanding of the Left and educational politics itself. The focus is on the character of socialist commitment, combined with an appreciation of issues of language and representation and the making of selfhood, captured through the relations of discourse, subjectivity and power.

By 'subjectivity' is meant the constructed quality of memory and experience. The term is used to convey a sense of the struggle and contest over identity, and the formation of an unstable, shifting subject as mediated through the workings of a structural relationship (such as gender) occurring historically.

Steedman's pointed emphasis on gender and her foregrounding of a tension between coming in from the margins and not wanting to see the hitherto neglected voices 'absorbed by the central story'[42] are of special relevance to my study as a whole. I will follow Toril Moi, writing of the French philosopher and feminist Simone de Beauvoir (b. 1908), and use her category of 'lived experience'[43] in calling for the study of 'concrete cases' to investigate what it means to be a woman situated in a particular time and place. Mindful of the fact that lives and experiences are shaped by material forces, I make notions of radical working-class subjectivity the point of entry for my historical analysis.

From the point of view of Pierre Bourdieu's theory of social practice, the individuals profiled here are similarly located in terms of their common experience of a specific 'field' of action constituted by their shared participation in labour politics.[44] Bourdieu understands the social world – depicted together with the concept of the 'habitus' and, most centrally, 'capital', as made up of different but overlapping fields of power which function according to their own tacit logic or set of rules which may explain specific forms of reproduction by successive generations through historical time. Learned more by experience than by teaching, 'habitus' is social practice linked to, for example, linguistic competence, lifestyle, politics and prestige, combined with particular habitual acquisitions, attitudes and tastes. 'Habitus' is a system of durable, transposable dispositions that predispose individuals to do certain things.

Biographical approaches can be used to reconstruct the acquisition of the activist habitus historically, to the extent that it inscribes the individual with a repertoire of practices that facilitate the taste for contention. A combination of cultural and political capital and geographical and social mobility enabled Mary to take up a variety of subject positions to challenge a landscape of male public space. Following Joan Scott, one way to map the transitions and trajectories of her political journey is to frame the individual in history as a 'site' on which 'political and cultural contests are enacted'.[45] In this I am influenced by Gareth Stedman Jones, who made the same point in relation to political parties, seen as discursive 'sites' controlled by different social and political groupings at different times.[46]

Such cartography would delineate the ways in which constructions of gender, generation and social class frame both collective political practices and Mary's own autonomous agency at certain key moments. Since the narration of a life cannot be confined to a single, isolated subjecthood, the ways in which the self is framed and created by the social can be seen in the concept of intersubjectivity, reflecting how the structural and the interactional are intertwined. A study of community defined as 'a fluid network of social relations that may be but are not necessarily tied to territory'[47] enables me to reconstruct her 'escape' from the classroom into the complexities of social action through the production of herself as a worker intellectual. Self-education opened up opportunities for her to write and act in the developing working-class 'public', despite its growing organisation around masculine conditions, conventions and space which cast wives in the role of full-time home makers. Unravelling classed and gendered political journeys can be the key to deepening our knowledge and understanding, to show that there was fluidity and that family life did not always become the depoliticised haven some assume.

Sources

The sources are a problem here. Much of Mary's evidence is missing because her son destroyed the letters written by her to him and all photographs of her.[48] As a consequence, her personal papers are only fragments and her surviving letters are mostly short. The politics of historical survival mean archival gaps, and we do not know where she was educated, where she taught or what kind of classroom teacher she was. Yet she was a prolific writer of articles and her national reputation as a speaker meant that her political activities were regularly reported, and some of these spoken words were relayed in local newspapers. This means that an account of her life can be constructed from a wide variety of different kinds of evidence, including her own published letters and articles culled from the newspapers of the day; reports in the socialist and educational press; official records; memoirs and other autobiographical writings; present-day books and articles.

Accordingly, the works of other historians, political writers and journalists of different hues, biographical writings of fellow travellers and contemporaries have been used to contextualise Mary's experience of maturing in the 1870s and 1880s. Add to this the diaries, letters and press cuttings that have been excavated from personal papers and local history collections to reinsert her presence into the social and political landscape from the 1890s to the middle 1930s. Mindful of the risks of formlessness, I seek to make use of what Virginia Woolf calls 'this loose drifting material of life' in ways that allow the reader to understand complexity rather than force her experiences into an oversimplified pattern.[49]

Visual remains have been very hard to come by. There are the passport-sized studio photographs of the newly elected LSB which take up several pages of the *Illustrated London News* in December 1897. Mary is shown in profile. Luxuriant, almost pre-Raphaelite-styled hair frames a strong, attractive face and she fixes the camera with a commanding gaze. This is in stark contrast to her female colleagues, their hair scraped off their foreheads and pulled behind their ears.[50] A decade on, there is a *Daily Mirror* photo of two ladies in hats – Mary and the Countess of Warwick – resplendent in an open carriage, alongside a report on the 1907 Trades Union Congress (TUC). In what must have been a staged photo shoot, they both look directly at the camera with panache.[51]

Mary's life shows greatness of spirit and endeavour. Ten years ago I was warned that it might be too hard to recover, since no first-hand account exists and she did not write an autobiography. Gradually the historical detective work paid off and it has been possible, but not easy, to piece together an integrated picture from the surviving fragments. More optimistic than the writer A.N. Wilson, I neither consider myself the arrogant liar he proposes all biographers to be, nor do I believe that I 'can play at the recording angel and tell the whole truth about another human life'.[52] I have struggled with contingency and done much more than 'survey a few boxes full of letters, diaries, bank statements and photographs', not all of which were available to me.[53] As Mary's biographer, it is my duty to tell her story with integrity, to try to elucidate her lived experience insofar as I do 'know' her through my research. My interpretation is provisional, but I offer it to you in the spirit of 'a reading *of* the past *from* the present *for* the future'.[54]

Mary's life is historically placed. As such, the scope of my study becomes the cultural milieu of which she was a part, the history writing a synthesis which combines the use of biography to show the interactive nature of politics organised around specific chapters with highly focused thematic or community studies on relatively restricted chunks of time. My motivation is the impulse to recover lost lives and my aspiration is to try to show what it was like to be there, from the point of view of participants who shared her commitment to a wider vision of the future.

Chapter 1 contains an overview of Mary's life with a focus on her route into the socialist movement. Chapters 2 and 3 are both micro-histories and use prosopography, a historical method involving the examination of a number of lives in a given place, to show that socialism is both lifestyle and a form of organised political activism. Chapter 4 puts these elements together to provide a bridge between the social, political and education history. Here discussion of the issue of parental choice, considered in relation to her son's education biography, acts as mediator between the personal and the political, to examine the importance of education to the pioneering generation of British socialists. Chapters 5 and 6 contain a discussion of different aspects of Mary's political practice, in an attempt to formulate a new interpretation of the making of the British welfare state. Chapter 7 injects a gendered dimension into the analysis of the independent working-class education movement and chapter 8 examines Mary's social action and milieu in the First World War.

Although largely forgotten today, my leading figure has value for me because of her lifelong concern for class justice. If she had emerged victorious from the political battles she fought at a crucial turning point in English education, my mother's family would not have felt the sting that came from having to leave school at thirteen or fourteen. It was a hot July afternoon when I first read her passionate speech in support of free school meals in the *School Board Chronicle*, effectively telling the upper-middle-class membership of the LSB that they could not possibly imagine what it was like to be poor.[55] She hooked me then, and she hooks me now. I fervently wish I could recapture more of her personality and early life, and her activism shames me when I live in a different time where the impact of some of her achievements has made possible wider education and expanded political participation by women. She made history, but in rediscovering her story I am making history, restoring my neglected subject to her rightful place in the histories of British socialism.

Notes

1 M. Bridges Adams, *The Socialist*, 8 July 1920.

2 William Stewart, writing in the *Labour Leader* c.1900, quoted in L. Thompson, *The Enthusiasts: a biography of John and Katherine Bruce Glasier* (London: Victor Gollancz Limited, 1971), p. 14.

3 R. Samuel, *The Lost World of British Communism* (London: Verso, 2006).

4 S. Yeo, 'A new life: the religion of socialism in Britain, 1883–1896', *History Workshop*, 4, pp. 5–56.

5 R. Miliband, *Parliamentary Socialism* (London: Merlin Press, 3rd impression, 1979).

6 M. Bridges Adams, 'Education and the youth of the Red International', *Socialist*, 8 July 1920, p. 222.

7 H. McShane and J. Smith, *Harry McShane: no mean fighter* (London: Pluto Press, 1977), p. 32.

8 *The Times*, 16 January 1939.

9 See the discussion in K. Manton, *Socialism and Education in Britain 1883–1902* (London: Woburn Press, 2001), pp. 4–9.

10 D. Lawton, *Education and Labour Party Ideologies 1900–2001 and Beyond* (London: RoutledgeFalmer, 2005), p. 15.

11 G. Foote, *The Labour Party's Political Thought* (Basingtoke: Macmillan, 1997).

12 HUA, DLB/6/2, H. McShane to R. Challinor, c. 1976.

13 J. Saville and J. Bellamy (eds), *Dictionary of Labour Biography*, Vol. 6 (London: Macmillan, 1982), p. 5.

14 Miliband, *Parliamentary Socialism*, p. 32.

15 P. Cunningham and P. Gardner, *Becoming Teachers: texts and testimonies 1907–1950* (London: Woburn Press, 2004), p. ix.

16 C. Steedman, *Dust* (Manchester: Manchester University Press, 2001), p. 83.

17 E.H. Carr, *What Is History?* (Harmondsworth: Penguin, 1987 edition), pp. 45, 49 and 55.

18 E.P. Thompson, *The Making of the English Working Class* (London: Victor Gollancz, 1963); L. Davidoff and C. Hall, *Family Fortunes: men and women of the English middle class 1780–1850* (London: Hutchinson, 1987).

19 Quoted in D. Torr, *Tom Mann and His Times1856–90* (London: Lawrence and Wishart, 1956), p. 217.

20 J. Hannam and K. Hunt, *Socialist Women Britain, 1880s to 1920s* (London: Routledge, 2002).

21 Hannam and Hunt, *Socialist Women*, p. 17.

22 Hannam and Hunt, *Socialist Women*, p. 34.

23 *Labour Leader*, 8 July 1899.

24 P. Thompson, *Socialists, Liberals and Labour: the struggle for London 1885–1914* (London: Routledge & Kegan Paul, 1967); K. Yoonak Stenberg, 'Working-class women in London local politics, 1894–1914', *Twentieth Century British History*, 9:3 (1998), pp. 323–49.

25 P. Hollis, *Ladies Elect: women in English local government 1865–1914* (Oxford: Clarendon Press, 1989), pp. 14, 66, 123, 125.
26 B. Simon, *Education and the Labour Movement 1870–1920* (London: Lawrence and Wishart, 1980 edition), pp. 151–2.
27 K. Manton, *Socialism and Education in Britain 1883–1902* (London: Woburn Press, 2001).
28 H. Kean, *Challenging the State? The socialist and feminist educational experience, 1900–1930* (Lewes: Falmer Press, 1990); Centre for Contemporary Cultural Studies *Unpopular Education: schooling and social democracy in England since 1944* (London: Hutchinson, 1981).
29 A. Turnbull, 'So extremely like Parliament: the work of the women members of the London School Board, 1870–1904', in The London Feminist History Group (eds), *The Sexual Dynamics of History* (London: Pluto Press, 1983), pp. 120–33; J. Martin, *Women and the Politics of Schooling in Victorian and Edwardian England* (Leicester: Leicester University Press, 1999); J. Goodman, 'Women school board members and women school managers: the structuring of educational authority in Manchester and Liverpool, 1870–1903', in J. Goodman and S. Harrop (eds), *Women, Educational Policy-Making and Administration in England* (London: Routledge, 2000), pp. 59–77.
30 G. Scott, '"As a war-horse to the beat of drums": representations of working-class femininity in the Women's Co-operative Guild, 1880s to the Second World War', in E.J. Yeo (ed.), *Radical Femininity. Women's self-representation in the public sphere* (Manchester: Manchester University Press, 1998), pp. 5–56.
31 H. Mitchell, *The Hard Way Up* (London: Virago, 1977).
32 Exceptions to this would include Dora Montefiore's autobiography: D.B. Montefiore, *From a Victorian to a Modern* (London: Edward Archer, 1927), and the biography of Charlotte Despard A. Linklater, *An Unhusbanded Life* (London: Hutchinson, 1980).
33 B. Finkelstein, 'Revealing human agency: the uses of biography in the study of educational history', in C. Kridel (ed.), *Writing Educational Biography: explorations in qualitative research* (New York: Garland Publishing, 1998), p. 45.
34 T. Moi, *What is a Woman? and Other Essays* (Oxford: Oxford University Press, 1999).
35 See, for example, J. Scott, *Gender and the Politics of History* (Columbia: Columbia University Press, revised edition, 1999).
36 C. Steedman, *Landscape for a Good Woman* (London: Virago, 1986).
37 L. Stanley, *The Auto/biographical 'I': the theory and practice of feminist auto/biography* (Manchester: Manchester University Press, 1992), p. 10.
38 N.K. Denzin, *Interpretive Biography* (Newbury Park: Sage, 1989).
39 S. Macintyre, *A Proletarian Science. Marxism in Britain, 1917–1933* (London: Lawrence and Wishart, 1986), p. 3.
40 M. Erben (ed.), *Biography and Education: a reader* (London: Falmer Press, 1998).
41 Samuel, *Lost World*, p. viii.

42 Steedman, *Landscape for a Good Woman*, p. 144.
43 Moi, *What is a Woman?*, p. 256.
44 Economic capital refers to income, wealth, financial inheritances and monetary assets. Cultural capital, defined as high culture, can exist in three forms: embodied cultural capital, objectified cultural capital and institutional cultural capital. The last is the product of investment in formal education. Social capital is the product of sociability, which speaks of investment in culturally, economically or politically useful networks and connections. If and when the different forms of capital are accepted as legitimate they take the form of symbolic capital. See, for example, P. Bourdieu, *Practical Reason* (Cambridge: Polity Press, 1998).
45 J. Scott, *Gender and the Politics of History*, p. 32.
46 In this I am influenced by Ralph Miliband's contribution to the study of the Labour Party, beginning with *Parliamentary Socialism*; see also D. Coates and L. Panitch, 'The continuing relevance of the Milibandian perspective', in J. Callaghan, S. Fielding and S. Ludlam (eds), *Interpreting the Labour Party* (Manchester: Manchester University Press, 2003). This paragraph is based on G.S. Jones, *Languages of Class: studies in English working-class history, 1832–1982* (Cambridge: Cambridge University Press, 1983), p. 243; J. Lawrence, 'Labour – the myths it has lived by', in D. Tanner, P. Thane and N. Tiratsoo (eds), *Labour's First Century* (Cambridge: Cambridge University Press, 2000), pp. 341–66.
47 L. McDowell, *Gender, Identity and Place. Understanding feminist geographies* (Cambridge: Polity Press, 1999), p. 100.
48 Just one letter seems to have survived the cull.
49 Quoted in H. Rosen, *Speaking from Memory: the study of autobiographical discourse* (Stoke-on-Trent: Trentham Books, 1998) p. 171.
50 *Illustrated London News*, 4 December 1897, p. 796.
51 *Daily Mirror*, 3 October 1907, Tuckwell Collection, Trades Union Congress (Bath), press cuttings 1907. Sadly, the image quality was too poor to reproduce in this text.
52 A.N. Wilson, *Incline Our Hearts* (Harmondsworth: Penguin, 1988), p. 20.
53 Wilson, *Incline Our Hearts*, p. 20.
54 R. Hennessy, *Materialist Feminism and the Politics of Discourse* (New York: Routledge, 1993), p. 102.
55 *School Board Chronicle*, 18 December 1897, pp. 677–8.

1

Being Mary

> Let me beg of my opponents to reveal their identity, I hope N.D. will set the others an example, and let me know precisely who he is. Being a Welsh-woman I do not shrink from a fight, but I like to see 'my foe man's face'. (Mary Bridges Adams, 1915)[1]

Beginnings

Mary Bridges Adams was a forthright and strong-minded woman. The quotation with which we start, taken from one of her many letters to the editor of the *Cotton Factory Times*, captures these qualities. She prosecuted enmities with ferocity, and this side of her character prevailed more frequently in her later years. Because she was so convinced of her own right inspiration, her actions, stories and words could create tremendous controversy and make people exceedingly angry. At the same time, others walked away feeling they had encountered something quite out of the ordinary. She excelled as a speech maker and this was evident in George Bernard Shaw's (b. 1874) remark, in his letter of condolence to her son, 'what an orator'.[2] She had fervour and energy and a personal desire for education that helped her to construct and articulate an empowering identity, providing a route out of the classroom into sustained political activism. This chapter traces the trajectory of Mary's private life. By using vignettes of those most closely associated with her, we can distinguish elements operative in her journey into revolutionary political agitation.

She was born in the Monmouthshire hamlet of Maesycwmmer, in south Wales, on 19 October 1855.[3] Mary's father, William Daltry (b. about 1825), listed on her birth certificate as an engine fitter, was the son of a Welsh farmer named Benjamin. However, Benjamin Daltry left the land and the family moved to Monmouthshire, where he became an innkeeper. Sometime after that, William's parents separated. Benjamin emigrated and William's mother, Elizabeth (b. about 1797), settled in Aberystruth, in a new boom area of iron and coal industry.

Industrial development of the South Wales coalfield drew on indigenous raw materials – iron, coal and clay ironstone. From mid century onwards, the application of steam power, the inflow of financial capital from England and the impact of war triggered a maelstrom of change, with phenomenal economic growth based on the latest technology and industrial organisation. Having grown up in rural Pembrokeshire, William Daltry and his siblings joined an influx of migrant workers willing to provide the labour force. In 1801, Aberystruth's total population was 805. In 1851, it was just under fifteen thousand. William's two brothers were working as blacksmiths and their sister, Jane, worked as a house servant.[4] From 1835 to 1848, the population of Monmouthshire trebled, leading historians to draw a ready comparison between the nascent Welsh industrial towns which were sprouting up, and the frontier settlements of the American west.[5]

Following in the wake of this social and economic change came the growth of radicalism and Chartism, which dominated British domestic politics in the later 1830s and 1840s. Disgust at the provisions of the 1832 Reform Act, a corrupt political establishment and the harshness of the 1834 Poor Law Amendment Act intensified popular unrest. Mary's inheritance, therefore, included the use of collective action to transform society. Within living memory, her birthplace had been a meeting point in the Newport Rising of 1839, when mine owners reputedly hid themselves down the pits. Newport was a well-established Chartist centre and Maesycwmmer was one of the points from which a contingent of Chartists joined a social insurrection, which ended in tragedy with more than twenty people killed by the militia. The three principal Chartists were arraigned for high treason and sentenced to death. A public outcry ensued and the punishment became transportation for life 'without even the opportunity to bid their wives and children farewell'.[6] Two decades later, the anonymous author of *Murray's Handbook for Travellers in South Wales* noted the good, civilising work of education and the influence of religion: 'The character of the mining section of the Welsh population has wonderfully improved in the last 10 or 15 years, which must be a source of congratulation to those who remember the lawlessness and ignorance which characterised Chartism, and the fearful riots to which it gave birth'.[7]

It is not known how or where Mary's parents met, but her mother was born Margaret Jones and probably came from very much the same milieu. The couple had three children. Thomas, the eldest, was born in

1 Crumlin Viaduct, Ebbw Vale

Bedwellty in 1854, followed by Mary a year later. Then, in May 1858, there was Benjamin, who lived only seven days, born in the mining village of Crumlin a few miles south of Aberystruth. But Margaret was 37 years old and childbirth in the 1850s carried far greater risks than it does today. William was present when his wife, who had been unwell with chronic pneumonia for many weeks before and since Benjamin's birth, died after eleven days, leaving two small children. On 4 November 1860, Mary's father married again. His second wife was Margaret Thomas, the daughter of a Welsh farmer, eleven years his junior. They solemnised their wedding at Panteg parish church and Margaret became stepmother to Thomas and Mary during a union that lasted thirty-four years.[8]

The reconstituted family resumed living in Crumlin, in the straggle of workers' housing and shops close to the Viaduct Inn.[9] Their neighbours consisted of railwaymen and their families. Built to carry the Taff Vale extension of the Newport, Abergavenny and Hereford railway, over the river and valley of the Ebbw, the Crumlin viaduct was the latest addition to the physical landscape. Twenty thousand people travelled to see its opening on Whit Monday, 1 June 1857. Organisers decorated locomotives on the Viaduct line and the Western Valley line below with flags, flowers and evergreens. Beer booths and shows were set up in fields, whilst two ballad singers strolled about singing a song they had composed and selling song sheets at a penny a time. The magnificent wrought iron structure remained the highest railway viaduct in Britain throughout its working life. By 1900, the contractor who built it had established a company school, shops, a hotel and a mutual improvement society with library and reading room. However, this was not the setting in which Mary grew up. As a girl, she moved with her family to North East England, where she became a pupil teacher.

Formative years

Mary's father had taken a post as a boilermaker at the Elswick factory established by Sir William Armstrong (b. 1810), solicitor-turned-engineer, who sprang from the close-knit Newcastle oligarchy of commercial and professional families. The story continues in 1871, with the Daltrys living at the Robin Adair public house on the Scotswood Road, mentioned in the Tyneside anthem 'Blaydon Races'. This was in the village of Benwell, which then consisted of a pub, and a track leading past cottages to an old coal shaft and a row of miners' homes. The family's neighbours included blacksmiths, labourers, a factory foreman, a painter, a plumber, a tanner, a teacher and their families.[10] Initially producing huge hydraulic cranes, Armstrong's diversified into arms manufacture, notably the revolutionary breech-loading rifle-barrel 'Armstrong gun', which was superior to existing field ordnance. Sales rocketed during the Crimean War but the company was shrewd enough to seek out alternate work before demand dried up, and went on to dominate the field of naval shipbuilding. Armstrong's wages were good by contemporary standards, especially for the skilled trades. When Mary's father died aged 69 in 1894, the workforce had grown from one hundred to close on thirteen thousand.[11]

The remarkable increase in economic activity that transformed the landscape just west of Newcastle ensured a ready market for houses, so the families who made a fortune out of industrialisation subsequently diversified into property development. Compared with what it had been before, the pace of change was rapid. Plans for the South Benwell Estate, developed at great profit by Sir William Armstrong and his business partner, show 'a clear intention to surround and contain the smaller working class housing with higher status houses on the main grid roads'.[12] The social distance between different streets and types of house, including the ubiquitous Tyneside flats which combined two separate dwellings in one building, reflected the status accorded different jobs at factory level. A local building boom followed and rows of terraced streets appeared on the slopes above the river Tyne, among them George Road, a street on its own and possibly a bit superior to its immediate neighbours, where Mary's parents lived at number 25. It was emphatically a labour aristocratic residence, part of the social landscape of the most militant and politically active sections of the working class.

If her early life in the South Wales coalfield vitally informed Mary's later politics, they were also a product of popular radicalism on Tyneside. As an adolescent, she saw the campaign by the Nine Hours League to reduce the traditional working week for engineering workers in 1871. The men met with determined resistance from William Armstrong, who had planned carefully for just this contingency. He signalled his ruthlessness when he refused to negotiate and tried to break the strike by recruiting foreign workers from Belgium, France and Germany. Subsequently, he housed blacklegs inside the Elswick Works, in the works school, so they need not become involved with pickets. As one past pupil was to say of the strike, they all 'felt the influence and noisily supported the strike', yelling the doggerel 'Ye men upon the Banks of Tyne, Aa think thors little fear, But ye'll get the nine oors movement if ye'll only persevere'.[13] Besides closing the school, Armstrong urged the authorities of Newcastle Lying-in Hospital not to admit the wives of strikers.

North East workers led the agitation. However, the paucity of sources means we can only speculate if Mary's father and brother, the latter now working as a factory draughtsman, ceased work. Mary may have been a pupil teacher in the Elswick Works Girls' School attached to Armstrong's, but the records are only available from 1888. There are no school records for the locality of the Robin Adair public house before 1910. In addition to this, the names of pupil teachers first appear in the Newcastle School Board Minutes in the late 1870s and there is no clue either there or in the Newcastle directories.[14] It is possible that she did not serve her apprenticeship in the embryonic state system, because the Newcastle School Board did not show itself a particularly effective body. By the autumn of 1874 it offered only temporary accommodation for 700 children, in contrast to neighbouring North Shields, where the newly built Western Board School, opened in 1872, had accommodation designed to house 582 children, plus 284 infants. On the other hand, the Daltry family were used to industrialists providing education, because it was a common practice in the industrial areas of South Wales in the early part of the nineteenth century. Backed by ample funds, company schools enjoyed a number of advantages in the period before 1870. Greater financial security meant they could pay better salaries and attract and keep a full quota of pupil teachers. This made it easier to maintain curriculum variety and provide advanced instruction, as opposed to other elementary schools, which had to confine themselves to teaching the three Rs, and needlework for the girls.

Elementary school teaching must have been an obvious choice for an intelligent young woman from a skilled working-class family. Teaching was a suitable and acceptable occupation at a time when many well-paid craft and industrial jobs excluded women and wider opportunities (such as clerical work) had not yet opened up. Accordingly, Mary's counterparts who became teachers in the years 1907–50 felt that teaching offered a 'special claim to recognised professional status without entirely losing the comfort of a traditional and well-understood cultural identity'.[15] In addition to a good school record and physical strength, female candidates had to be skilled with a needle, and it is worth noting that, in 1867, Mary worked a beautiful sampler depicting 'Solomon's Temple'.[16] Beyond that, one might conclude that, like many of her generation, she received her teaching certificate on the grounds of qualification by experience. Many of the early training colleges applied denominational tests, rejecting trainees with the highest marks in the scholarship examination in favour of those who had done less well. This was particularly true of girls. Mary became head teacher at a Board school by the age of 30. Thereafter, she worked in a Woolwich high school, which was unusual for a woman from her social background.[17]

In between working in the North East and in London, Mary had a teaching post in Birmingham, although it has proved impossible to ascertain where. While there, she may have met local artist and sculptor Maria Matthews, a builder's daughter whom her brother, Thomas, married in the local register office on 23 September 1880. Mary witnessed the marriage, along with Maria's father. Now working as an editor in Manchester, a national centre for labour journalism, Thomas was 27 years old; Maria was 25. Opportunities for freelance writers were expanding, offering what Jonathan Rose calls an 'escape hatch' for workers with a literary flair.[18] Tragically, Thomas died in Chorlton-upon-Medlock, of apoplexy, in January 1890. He was just 36 years old, leaving his wife as the sole supporter of their two young sons, William (b. 1882) and Robert (b. 1884).[19]

Initially Mary continued her learning through participation in the University Extension Movement, which took higher education to those excluded from the universities. The battle for self-enlightenment was a mark of a female dissident and she succeeded in matriculating from the College of Science in Newcastle. From the start of campaigns for women's education, this college took women students.[20] In May 1880 Mary won a prize copy of Herbert Spencer's (b. 1820) *Study of Sociology*, and in January 1882 she travelled to London to enter Bedford College for Women, which placed much emphasis on making up deficiencies in its students' education. She enrolled for two terms. Her fees came to £10 10s for each term and she took classes in history, mathematics, English language and literature, French, Greek and Latin. With respect to women, classics remained a largely taboo subject because the contents of the literature brought Platonic love to the attention of all its readers, so Mary's choice of subjects was 'advanced' even to liberals. In June 1882 she passed the Intermediate London B.A. examination in the Arts, second division.[21] She wanted to obtain her B.A. and got a helpful response from assistant Latin mistress Rachel Notcutt (b. 1841), who gained a reputation for taking an interest 'in the students, their interests and their societies'.[22] Although she did not graduate from Bedford College, the qualification Mary gained did open up her promotion prospects.

Mary kept up her studies with the help of Thomas Whittaker (b. about 1856), a graduate of Exeter College, Oxford, who earned a living as a tutor and writer for the *Westminster Review*, founded in 1823 as a journal for philosophical radicals.[23] She may have been part of a Newcastle-based reading group that worked on British philosopher John Stuart Mill (b. 1806), a favourite author of the first large cohort of Labour MPs elected in 1906. Thomas, who was the son of a mechanical engineer, usually charged 5s a lesson but he refused to charge Mary, saying:

> The review I found time to write will more than pay my railway fares, so that the journey to and from Newcastle has cost me nothing. If I was to make any charge from the small sum that was spent in actual working I should be getting more in proportion from you than I do from my pupils in Accrington … This of course is to be understood as a statement made from the pecuniary point of view. The time I spent in Newcastle was the

> pleasantest episode of my life within the last two or three years at least. But if I had said this when you asked me to say what my charge would be for coaching you would have replied that has nothing to do with the question. I quite agree that it has not. But you must at the same time see that on impartial consideration (looking at the coaching simply as work done for payment – a mode of consideration which the Hegelians call 'abstract') it becomes perfectly clear that I could not make any charge without punitive unfairness.[24]

Back home in Accrington, lost luggage played havoc with Thomas's time management. Anxious and unable to concentrate, he fell back on his sister's holiday reading, including the fantasy novel *Vice Versa: a Lesson to Fathers*, of which several popular film versions have been made. He closes his letter with a light-hearted description of his brother's preparations for a night at the theatre. As usual, said sibling was making 'a series of often-prolonged discordant sounds', he wrote, occasionally recognisable as 'fragments of comic songs'.[25]

There is no way of knowing Mary's sexual history, but there are signs of male admirers besides Thomas Whittaker. Witness the words of John Stokes who wrote to Mary from Gateshead in June 1886, speaking of his sorrow at her recent severance of relations with a mutual friend called Arnold. 'I thought – as who would not who knew you both? – That the world – Humanity itself – man – would benefit by the intimate co-mingling of the ideas of two thinking beings such as yourself and Arnold; I had even built "Chateaux en Espagne" of your future.' He promised to offer Arnold what emotional support he could and ended by asking Mary to 'write to me often for I feel the want of some such sympathy as only a sympathetic and intellectual woman can bestow'.[26] When Mary's grandson Nicholas (b. 1930) spoke to me about her in 1997, he remembered his father saying that she was 'extremely beautiful'. He also pointed out that she was an intellectual. Quite when she met his grandfather, Walter Bridges Adams (b. 1858), is uncertain.[27] Perhaps their paths crossed at a Fabian conference on Land, Capital and Democratic Policy which took place the same month that John Stokes wrote to her. Mary certainly had a ticket. At any rate, Walter was among the diminutive band of socialists, British and European, settled in London who signed the Socialist League's manifesto, *To Socialists*, issued on 13 January 1885.

Marriage

Walter's father was the railway engineer and radical Unitarian William Bridges Adams (b. 1797). The son of a coachbuilder, William showed an early aptitude for engineering. In 1819 he went to South America because he experienced problems with his lungs, and was very probably a consumptive. While there, he looked after the estate of a former frigate captain in the Napoleonic Wars. In 1825, he returned to England a widower, with a son, William Alexander Adams (b.1821).[28] In 1843 he opened his own factory at the Fairfield Works, Bow, where he manufactured railway vehicles. In financial terms, William Bridges Adams gained little from his improvements in and writings on carriages and rail travel, including the invention with which he is most associated, the fishplate joint for railway track, patented in 1847. That same year he joined the council of the People's International League, closely associated with the capital's Italian community.

In London, William's friends and acquaintances included parliamentary reformers, radical novelists, journalists and poets. Taken collectively, their ideas and thinking were republican, democratic and fiercely anti-aristocratic. In the late 1820s and 1830s he joined the coterie of radical Unitarian intellectuals who congregated at South Place Chapel in Finsbury, which Ruth Watts describes as a focal point for 'eager, liberal reformers, autodidacts and free-thinkers especially from the fringes of the middle and working classes'.[29] Under the pen name Junius Redivivus (meaning reborn, a reference to a political letter writer of the previous century), he produced many articles for the radical Unitarian newspaper *The Monthly Repository*. Committed to improving the social, sexual, educational and political status of women, he promoted the idea of associated housing schemes where all living arrangements would be fully collectivised, allowing housework to be transformed from a private service into a social activity, with shared access to kitchen provisions, fires and libraries. He thought the elimination of personal dependence in social communities provided the key to improved living conditions and the emancipation of women. Writing about the conjugal ideal in 1834, he stressed that marriage 'ought not to be, a lifelong commitment, but should be terminable by mutual consent in cases of grave incompatibility'.[30] In fact, his feelings may have been a reflection of what close friends considered an unhappy first marriage to the daughter of radical tailor, ex-trade unionist and autodidact Francis Place (b. 1771).

It was said of his second wife, the Unitarian hymn writer Sarah Flower

(b. 1805), that she was 'manifestly too ethereal for a normal marriage relation'.[31] With her husband's encouragement, Sarah pursued a career on the stage, but had to give it up because of ill-health. His third wife, Ellen Rendall, outlived him. They had two children – Hope (b. 1855) and Walter. The children grew up in London, leaving Walter's birthplace in Croydon for homes in Hampstead and suburban Lewisham. The family lived in some style. When the children were young Ellen instructed other mothers in childcare, while employing a nurse and servant/cook.[32] Poor health in the form of a weak chest meant that Walter was educated at home, whereas Hope went to the junior school attached to Bedford College, founded by a wealthy Unitarian widow and feminist. The death of their father was a significant turning point in the education of the two siblings. Ellen took them to Dresden, where they had private tuition, before Hope progressed to study medicine, eventually receiving her doctorate from the University of Bern. Although she came home to England to put her name on the British Medical Register, Hope returned to Germany shortly after. She was able to set up a medical practice in Frankfurt because the commercial code of the new Reich allowed anyone to practise the 'healing arts' provided they did not claim to be a certified physician. A divorcee, both her marriages were to socialist physicians.

All her adult life, Hope was an active member of the German Social Democratic Party and in the early 1880s she completed the first English translation of August Bebel's *Woman in the Past, Present and Future*, published during 1885. Walter adopted the name John H. Liddel around this time, presumably to lessen the chance of his falling foul of the Anti-Socialist law when visiting his sister. In 1896 Hope published a best-selling 2-volume medical handbook dedicated to caring for women. She and her second husband moved to Munich, where she worked in general medicine and gynaecology.[33] Here, in violation of German law, she helped women to control their fertility and terminate their unwanted pregnancies. In March 1914 a midwife denounced her, and Hope's trial in 1915 is probably the most famous abortion case involving a doctor in Germany during this period. It resulted in her acquittal, but Cornelie Usborne notes an aspect of her medical practice downplayed both at the time and since, namely a tendency to sterilise her abortion patients. She did not obtain informed consent before the operation and many of her patients remained in ignorance afterwards. Most were working class and poor, and Usborne suggests that Hope's decision making 'was not just informed by medical or social but almost certainly by eugenic considerations'. She quotes evidence from Hope's medical notes, which show that her recommendations for sterilising patients were 'findings such as "extreme nervousness" (*Nervenschwäsche*) or "intelligence deficit" (*Intelligenzstörung*), both deemed to be hereditary and leading to "inferior" children'.[34] The revelation that she sterilised the 23-year-old wife of a manual worker with only one child is a shocking example.

How long Ellen and Walter remained in Germany is a mystery. Their names appear in the 1881 census for Kensington, London where they were residents in the same lodging house as the suffragist poor law guardian Henrietta Frances Lord, who translated Henrik Ibsen's *A Doll's House* from the Norwegian in 1882, and *Ghosts* two years later.[35] The plays had a personal significance for her, and the issues they raised – including middle-class convention and women's role in society – appealed to socialism's more bohemian wing in the 1880s and 1890s. Now an undergraduate at London University, in 1884 Walter got an intermediate examination in Arts, while he was denied a prize in German on the grounds of his age.[36] Some time later he became mathematics tutor at the Royal Military Academy, Woolwich, established in 1741 for officers joining the artillery.[37] He lived in Ripon Road in West Plumstead, where the population was growing rapidly. Walter appears as a freelance socialist propagandist in the columns of the *Commonweal*, the newspaper of William Morris's Socialist League. However, there was family opposition to his marriage plans. Nicholas Bridges-Adams mentioned his father's having told him that, as an 'ambitious businessman', William Alexander Adams 'did not want a member of the family to take a sideways or downwards step'.[38] Nonetheless, Mary and Walter were married at Woolwich registry office in October 1887.

Mary was over 30 and well aware of the risks of childbirth, but her marriage was not childless. On 1 March 1889 she gave birth to her only child, William, born at home at Wealdstone, near the north London suburb of Harrow.[39] In the 1891 census the Bridges Adams family home was at 'Fairfield', a recently constructed property in Mycenae Road, East Greenwich. Living with them in this house, and without the help of servants, were Walter's mother and a single male lodger, Donavan Camden, a 48-year-old electrical engineer. Walter worked as a tutor and schoolteacher of languages and mathematics, Mary as a teacher, and Ellen had a private income large enough to give her financial independence.[40]

In his old age, William confirmed that his was an ardently socialist home, 'much more I.L.P. and S.D.P. than Fabian, where the word Bourgeois ... was held to be outmoded, silly, and taboo; we laughed at people who used it', he told a theatrical friend. William heard his mother speak on socialist platforms and remembered his father, whom he described as 'a devotee of German opera', singing *Don Giovanni* at their piano. Walter ran a choir between bouts of ill-health, introducing his son 'to *Der Freischutz* and leading him on to the *Meistersinger*'. Consequently, Bridges, as his family and friends knew William, was always 'more at home with Wagner than with Verdi, and on easier terms with a *Totentanz* or a *Walpurgisnacht* when he met them north of the Alps'.[41] All the family were voracious readers, but Dickens and Shakespeare were especially to their taste. In later years, Mary described the atmosphere to the novelist Storm Jameson (b. 1891). 'She told me a great many stories of her young married life in a small community of other young well-bred social revolutionaries', Storm wrote in the first volume of her autobiography, *Journey from the North*. Apparently, 'the husbands travelled to London to work (not as conspirators) and the wives met the evening train, hoping to hear that the revolution they expected daily had broken out'.[42]

Some time in the 1890s, Mary and Walter sent their son to a boarding school in Cromer, Norfolk. Perhaps they thought the sea air would be palliative, since William suffered from the consumption that dogged his father's side of the family. William's childhood letters show he was sometimes mutinous. In May 1895 he wrote to his Granny Ellen, asking her to give the letter to his mother, whom he nicknamed 'Muma'. A female pupil had lost his rubber:

> Miss Clark like a blooming *damnable* old Pig sent me to bed before tea and I was in such a temper that I stamped and raved and tore my hair, and after that I took my knife and took a bit of wood off nearly every piece of furniture in the room and then started scratching at the wallpaper, and then I threw my knife at the wall a little bit of silver came off and then I tore my hair again and tried to put it in again but still it is loosed and bent. The knife is too good to have here, so I send it so you glue the silver. Don't tell Miss Clark else she'll kill me. Give my fare to go home because I'll leave the school!!![43]

It would be wrong to exaggerate. However, William's early years may have been somewhat unsettled. In October 1899 he wrote to Muma from Coombe Hill School at East Grinstead, Surrey. Mary had not been to visit and he wanted to come home very much. Provided she had no political engagements, he mused, might they go to the National Gallery or the British Museum 'or nicest of all a theatre'?[44] Busy at the time building stage scenery for a school production of Don Quixote, he may have been a contemporary of the actor Athene Seyler (b. 1889) who appeared in *As You Like It* as a pupil there.[45] William signed off with a winding circuit of kisses, drawn between railway track-like parallel lines from East Grinstead to London and back.

Home happiness may have been absent at about this time. In 1898 disaster struck after the family moved to the neighbouring Coleraine Road, part of the same 1881 development as their previous house. There, they suffered two shattering emotional blows. On New Year's Eve 1898, Ellen Adams died of injuries sustained in an accidental fall down stairs. In 1900 Walter died, very probably of tuberculosis, possibly in Europe.[46]

Now that Walter was dead, Mary's recourse was to throw herself into her political work. The financial implications of this decision were profound, since contemporary policies prohibited serving teachers from being members of the school board that employed them. Mary was reduced to a public appeal for funds through the socialist press; there is no suggestion of a legacy or that she had a private income of any sort. Early Labour politicians like Keir Hardie (b. 1856), himself a former miner, were all too familiar with the financial constraints arising from a political career. 'Surely the Labour organisations of Woolwich and district must have fallen from their high estate when they permit so capable and energetic a representative as Mrs Bridges Adams … to bear the cost of her own election,' he expostulated to his readers.[47] In these circumstances, Mary became a housemother in a women's settlement house and allowed relatives on her husband's side to pay for her son's education. Between 1901 and 1907, William went to Bedales, a co-educational boarding school enlivened by the principles of William Morris. Set in spacious grounds near Petersfield in Hampshire, the school had a progressive, secular ethos, making it popular among Unitarians and intellectuals belonging to the pragmatic Fabian Society, an association explicitly committed to political change. The Bedales centenary history notes William's contribution as a 'star' of its merry evenings, impromptu social events initiated by the Old Bedalian Club in the 1900s.[48]

In July 1902 William wrote his mother a long letter, in answer to one from her which does not survive. It gives a more vivid impression both of his character at the age of 13 and of their relationship at this stage than can be gleaned from any other source and it is worth quoting at length:

> Darling Mater,
> Thanks awfully for the lovely letter. What an awfully fine time we'll have. It would be lovely to get a voyage on one of those upping little cargo-steamers that Newcastle is so crowded with. Do you think that we might be able to spend a night on board one of them? You see I have been reading a lot of W.W. Jacobs's sea stories … they are all about the sailors on these

> small cargo boats. He describes them in a way that really makes one love them, and I should so like to see my favourite stories acted over again on such a fitting stage. Besides, there is always a charm about those not too beautiful or commodious cargo boats. Shall we risk the over-crowding and go by the 'Tyneside' or the 'Londoner'? That would be great fun, too, and would help to strengthen you a lot, which would be necessary, considering the huge numbers of meetings you will have to speak at. In the summer nights we could sleep on deck. Also, it would come cheaper to go by boat. Please think about it. I suppose I could bathe at Tynemouth, sometimes couldn't I? … Now, please, please, let me come home at once on Tuesday. It would be miserable to be even alone for a *day* at Bedales, to hear my own footsteps echoing over the house would be simply vile, so please let me come home on Tuesday. I can't forget that summer at Miss Clarke's. It would be fine to go down a coal-mine. Green has been down a coal-mine and says that it is fine. Do you think we could go to the Hippodrome these holidays? They have a new water sensation called the Bandits. Do let's have some copies of the play printed in our own book! If we are in Scarborough next holidays, we must visit Mr Rowntree. Tons of love to you, Peter and the League from yours ever, W.B.A.[49]

William left an account of a childhood visit to Newcastle, when he travelled by boat from Tower Bridge. Whether the trip happened that summer is impossible to say. If it did, he probably saw his cousins on his mother's side, apprentice engineers William and Robert Daltry, then living with their paternal grandmother in Elswick.[50] Peter's identity remains tantalisingly unverifiable. The League was Mary's National Labour Education League.

Growing up in quite unconventional circles, William met most of the leading figures in the socialist movement, from SDF leader Henry Hyndman (b. 1842) to George Bernard Shaw. Perhaps he absorbed some of the political lessons he had learned in adolescence. There is a letter, undated, which survived William's destruction of his mother's private correspondence, from internal evidence, written some time in the spring of 1909, when she was lecturing for the Scottish council of the SDP. Each line that she pens is eager, warm and alive as she tells her son of a new book by H.G. Wells (b. 1866) called *New Worlds for Old*. 'I feel as I always feel when reading a book which stirs me that I must tell you of the great delight that it is giving me', she confides, urging that he 'tell everyone who has time to spare to read it', besides making it his 'starting point for serious study'. Commenting on three women who were at one of her public meetings, she notes the attitude of a suffragette of Calvinist stock who 'really believed it was the will of God that Mr Asquith should be "removed"!' The then Liberal premier would not give votes for women and Mary asked the militant feminist how she would remove him. 'Kill him' she proclaimed, 'with the delicious Scotch enunciation of the "kill"'. Yet, Mary observed, the woman looked incapable of 'smacking her children for playing truant from Sunday school at the Kirk. It is a funny world!'[51]

Friendship with Lady Warwick

After Walter's death Mary formed a warm friendship with the Countess of Warwick, which opened up possibilities for her continued political involvement. As 3-year-old 'Daisy' Maynard, Lady Warwick had inherited the family estate, Easton, from her grandfather, making her one of the greatest heirs in the land, with an annual income estimated at £40,000 a year. Subsequently, she met and married Lord Brooke, heir to the Earl of Warwick, and became notorious for her affairs, particularly her very public liaison with the Prince of Wales. According to novelist Elinor Glyn (b. 1864), 'Easton in the nineties was the centre of all the most intelligent and amusing in the society of the day. Its host, Lady Warwick, was literally a Queen, the loveliest woman in England, of high rank, ample riches, and great intelligence. Her immense prestige made every invitation a great honour'.[52]

Lord Brooke succeeded his father in 1893 and the spectacular celebration of his succession, Lady Warwick's *bal poudre*, became a legend. Portraying herself as Marie Antoinette, Daisy wore a dress of rose-tinted brocade with woven pink and blue flowers, and roses embroidered in gold thread, all studded with diamond stars. Having wowed all the society journals, she was upset to see the ex-army sergeant Robert Blatchford (b. 1851), editor of the socialist weekly the *Clarion*, attack her extravagant lifestyle.[53] Unable to turn a blind eye, she travelled to Blatchford's London office, whereupon he gave and she took a three-hour lecture on the labour theory of value. Her attentiveness may have come as some surprise to Blatchford, but in an age when charity work was fashionable, campaigning journalist W.T. Stead (b. 1849) tuned Daisy Warwick's interest in social questions. As a trustee and local Poor Law Guardian, she sought to convey her flickering social awareness to the Prince of Wales, whom she escorted round the Warwick workhouse. With philanthropic ventures like the Easton Needlework School already eating into her vast fortune, in 1897 she opened a co-educational technical school for disadvantaged children, to which her lover Joe Laycock, the father of her two youngest children, provided three scholarships. She also set up an agricultural college for women, originally based near Reading, with Edith Bradley (b. about 1860) as its first warden. Her biographer, Sushila Anand, argues that Daisy's socialist credentials were strongest in the field of education and 'her involvement deepest'.[54] She was incontestably kind, generous not only with her money but also with her time.

The Countess of Warwick drew people from all walks of life towards herself. She had much to discuss with Mary, since she was toying with the idea of seeking election to the LSB and joined Mary's campaign against the 1902 Education Act. In 1903, she installed Mary in a flat in 48 Carlisle Mansions, where she bankrolled a London salon, which she furnished exquisitely. Writing from Palermo, Sicily, Daisy asked, 'can you wait for curtains till I get back? I am <u>sure</u> there will be some at Warwick or Easton – but I don't like to trust to what the <u>housekeeper</u> might send you as I agree the rooms ought to be in good taste and cosy ... on April 1st you will receive cheque for next quarter.' Buoyed up with enthusiasm, she relied on Mary to transform the flat into what she hoped would become 'the headquarters of the movement and a <u>real</u> "centre of light"!'[55] The atmosphere was luxurious, and visitors included trade unionist and politician Will Thorne (b. 1857). Will remembered that 'the advanced thinkers of the Labour Movement' congregated there and might find themselves rubbing shoulders with radical Victorian gentlemen like Sir John Gorst (b. 1835), a prominent if unorthodox Conservative politician.[56]

Mary replaced Edith Bradley as Daisy's political secretary and collaborator as the Countess was gradually facing a great personal crisis. In the spring of 1902 she put herself through an abortion in Paris, but even then she could not truthfully apprise Joe Laycock of her situation. Still, she clung to the belief that their future lay together, even though Joe had now married her rival, with whom he had a baby son. Repeatedly she begged him to meet her, until he caved in. In 1903 she fell pregnant for a second time with him and he distanced himself once again. Daisy was now 42 years old and friends feared she might die, but she recovered well following her daughter's birth and began fulfilling the political engagements that Mary organised on her behalf. Together, Daisy and Mary attended the Amsterdam Congress of the Second International in August 1904, where the Countess first met Henry Hyndman.[57] In the second volume of his reminiscences, Hyndman recalled the 'almost startling' impression the Countess made. 'For Lady Warwick, apart from her natural advantages, was extremely well-dressed, looked full of animation and vigour, and appeared as if she had not a care in life.' He also noted her 'real devotion' and commitment to 'downright revolutionary Socialism'.[58]

Daisy's tolerant and kindly husband did not bat an eye when she joined the SDF, but the reaction of her family circle was more predictable. Her son and heir thought her ideas 'idiotic' and her mother was deeply shocked. In a chatty letter written to accompany a cheque for Mary's wages, Daisy asked, 'Did I tell you that I found my mother gasping over what you said about the Church …? I don't think she will ever meet you again!!! And she thinks I have sold my soul to the Devil!!! I did laugh'.[59] In another note she commented: 'the King is again at my feet! I spent two hours last week telling him of Socialist ideals – he said, "I have never thought of it (the subjects) in that way before". I have promised to write him once a week. I tell him anything of interest. My table is suddenly crowded with invitations to dinner from people who have looked on me for three years as plague stricken!'[60]

On the eve of the opening of parliament in February 1905, she and Mary hosted a dinner party at Easton Lodge for trade unionists, Labour MPs, party candidates and their wives which ended with the singing of 'The Red Flag'. Ramsay MacDonald (b. 1866), the secretary of the Labour Representation Committee, summarily refused his invitation to dine. The 'ideal apologist', as portrayed by David Marquand, he expressed doubts over 'the permanent good which can be done to a democratic movement by the exploitation of an aristocratic convert'. Ramsay also told the Countess that he regretted 'some of the methods which you have thought fit to adopt'.[61] Of course, the truth of the matter was that she had followed Mary into the SDF and he was chair of the ILP.

As they were of a similar age and both lacked emotional fulfilment, Mary's spirit may have enthused Daisy across the barriers of class. Perhaps her female patron recognised and took pride in Mary's struggle to gain professional and academic qualifications, her skills as an orator, her solid organisational effort, her remarkable courage and enthusiasm. One of Daisy's early letters to Mary gives a good indication of what the nature of their relationship may have been. Her secretary required not only drive and organising ability, but also tact and understanding. She wrote:

> Dearest Friend,
> Kettering was awful. You ought to have stayed the night – as it was absurd to ask an audience to pay for such a meeting as that! Gribble – the worst and most absurd tub-thumping style of socialist street orator I have yet heard! You were not even half as good as you were at Lincoln – in fact you were bad. (For the first time in my life I've thought that!!) Your speech was flat and had no sequence in it. Though some of your inimitable 'points' saved it! When we found that those fools had no-one but two tired women

> to make a 'meeting' with, you ought to have stayed … I had no idea we should be asked to address a middle-class audience quite unsupported, except by that awful choir. (Two good socialist hymns would have helped us warm the atmosphere.) For the first time in your life, you left them cold and unconvinced. *I* – as always happens when I speak late – was pitiable – there is no other word … I have never been to such a meeting and hope I never shall again!

On occasion, a careless aside from the Countess could spark an unpleasant tiff. During one such contretemps the Countess raged that the male leadership were going to bring 'charges' against another socialist in her name and asked Mary to act as her representative. All the personal antipathies smoothed over, Daisy exclaimed, 'I think the SDF are hopeless spitfire … In future, I shall only tell you when Comrades' [*sic*] disgust me!! Best love yours Evelyn Warwick'.

Daisy's patronage made an important difference to Mary's life. She now enjoyed a degree of economic security and, with William at boarding school, could devote herself to socialist politics and propaganda. Freed from the practical worry of financial survival, Mary became what her son later described as the 'educational mentor' of trade unionism.[62] When exhausted by strain and overwork she went to Easton for the respite it offered. Daisy would put the 'motor and children's pony carriage' at her disposal, urging her to 'sit in garden … and rest'. Sometimes William accompanied her to restore his own fragile health, sometimes he convalesced with family and friends in Germany. As his son Nicholas remembered years later, 'my father frequently stayed with Hope in Munich until the outbreak of World War I, particularly close to that branch of the family'. Here is an extract from a letter William wrote to 'Dearest Daisy' on 28 May 1907 while convalescing at the home of a friend near Dresden. He believed he might attend the upcoming Congress of the Second International, 'but not as a delegate. Clara Zetkin who is always so ill that she cannot do any work at all, had still influence enough to hinder with the lowest means my delegation'.[63] One of Hope's closest friends, Clara (b. 1857) co-edited *Die Eleichheit*, the newspaper of the Social Democrats.

However, William would survive to face an uncertain future after Bedales. Sacrifices were necessary, and Hope condemned William's extravagance. On 26 December 1907 he wrote a long letter of explanation, in answer to one from her which does not survive. Hope had insisted on being kept informed of his expenditure, saying she regarded 'him alone as responsible for this' and admonishing that he 'must try to be businesslike'. In response, he admitted that his allowance had gone on Oxford entrance exams, train fares, overnight accommodation and a university 'fine' for late registration. All because he had overspent in Germany and then bought 'new clothes; for my Bedales stock, always very low, had to be to some extent renewed if I was to make the impression it is as well to make in cases such as mine'.[64] Gentility of this kind was expensive, especially for someone without the money to match his aspirations to status. Fortunately, William had a rich friend to foot the bill. The Countess of Warwick stepped into the breach and her kindly, impulsive voice is almost audible. 'I love you much,' Daisy wrote Mary. 'I want you and Willy to have a real happy time – and Willy and his university career shall be quite settled – and hang the Adams.'[65] In May 1907 she pledged £1,000 to help meet the cost of William's education. William 'must think out with you the very best way of getting to the University, and what he most wishes to work for', she said.[66]

Meanwhile, William matriculated as a non-collegiate student at Oxford. Presumably, he was blissfully unaware that after years of personal extravagance and enthusiastic social projects Daisy's large debts were piling up. In February 1908 she wrote to Mary about the need for financial retrenchment:

> 1. Flat This is done with in 6 weeks time, viz March 25th – have you made other plans? You are welcome to all the facilities of mine but should think you will have too much to move to a new abode? If so, best sell what you don't want. Money more useful. Will you see to this?
> 2. You know how greatly I appreciate your brave work, no one more so – but for some time I shall have to be careful over resources. I can pay you £300 a year – quarterly, regularly – or in advance if you want it. Out of this, you would have to keep yourself I fear, for two years anyhow until I should be in a position to do more. For Willie I hope to pay the £500 I promised in instalments if not in a lump beginning in April. But this is all I can see my way to do for some time to come. You are perfectly at liberty to choose your own place and manner of abode and I should fall in, as ever, with what you think best.
> 3. If you lecture at great distances or anywhere, they must pay your expenses as any other lecturer – except when you and I go together and you are my guest … Much love, I hope Willie is well and happy![67]

Shortly after, one of Daisy's creditors resorted to legal action and bailiffs seized portable property from Carlisle Mansions.[68] Mary returned to a mixed labour aristocratic/lower middle-class community in suburbia – first in Herne Hill, then in Battersea Park. The £300 a year Daisy paid her was equivalent to that earned by London's top women elementary school head teachers under the scale adopted in 1899. Daisy still thought Mary was 'wonderful!' In October 1908 she promised she would keep paying for 'Battersea – but nowhere else – you shall have my sympathy and love and money and individual help to comrades but platforms I can't do!'[69] There Mary stayed until an anonymous donation from a 'friend of the cause of women and of Labour' enabled her to buy the lease of a house in the new West London suburbs. From 1912 onwards she lived at Bebel House, the college she founded to provide political education for working women.[70] In becoming resident principal, she also generated a job for herself.

Nevertheless, this is to look forward. In the summer of 1908 Daisy Warwick kept her promise of financial assistance to help pay for William's education and he entered Worcester College, Oxford in the autumn. While there, he played Leontes in *The Winter's Tale* and Prospero in *The Tempest* for the Oxford University Dramatic Society. During his final year he was involved in a local stage production, and William's son remembered that his paternal relatives were angry when his father left Oxford without taking a degree. Still seriously ill with consumption, William failed the army medical and did not fight in the First World War. Mary worried, and her feelings are recorded in wartime letters from one of her oldest friends in politics, Lyulph Stanley (b. 1839), the leader of the Progressive Party on the LSB. 'I feel very much for you in the gloomy prospect that is hanging over your family affairs. As I grow old I feel that apart from public interests to see the young who are linked with me grow up is a great pleasure for old age,' Stanley wrote in July 1918. At the beginning of November, worried by her silence, he begged her to let him 'know if only a postcard that you are all right'. Days later, he expressed his joy at hearing she had 'better hopes' of her son's health.[71]

William went on to an illustrious career as a theatre producer. In 1915 he married the actor Muriel Pratt, with whom he directed the Bristol and Liverpool repertory theatres. He was Director of the annual Shakespeare Festival at Stratford upon Avon from 1919 until his resignation in 1934, by which time his first marriage had been annulled and he had married Marguerite Coote (nee Wellsted). She had substantial independent means and they spent fifteen years in Suffolk with their only son, Nicholas, before settling in Ireland. In 1936 William directed *Oedipus Rex* at Covent Garden and the following year he started work as honorary dramatic adviser for the British Council. During the Second World War, he became a full-time member of Council staff. Towards the end of his life, he saw his career and achievements honoured by the award of a CBE.[72]

Final years

The costs of a peripatetic political life were high for Mary. This was a woman whose outlooks and ways of life sharply transgressed the feminine norm. She lived almost entirely by her wits and her pen, supporting herself through school teaching, working as a political secretary, her own writings for socialist newspapers and lecture tours. Outside genteel notions of social refinement, she found herself desperately poor. The economic circumstances of her final twenty years or so have come down to us in the published autobiographies of Storm Jameson and the Russian political émigré Ivan Maisky (b. 1884) both of whom came to London in 1912.

A graduate of Leeds University then studying at Kings College, Storm responded to an appeal for someone to give free tutoring to the students at the Working Women's College. She 'went there, and found a large house in one of those solid yellow terraces built in not the worst manner in the world, its rooms almost bare of furniture, unheated, and with two or perhaps three young women living on heaven knows what scratched-up food'.[73] Ivan Maisky, Soviet diplomat and historian, Ambassador to Britain from 1932 to 1943, recalled 'a big desert of a house … which by some miracle had survived from the wreck of Mrs Bridges Adams' previous life. Because its owner had not the means to keep it up the inside was cold, dusty and uncomfortable'.[74] Storm, whose memory was of the pre-war period, recollected: 'She lived as Spartan a life as her protégées, in a room of which I recall only the bed and a chest of drawers with a spirit lamp on which she made tea for herself, and fried kippers: I doubt if she troubled to eat meals'.[75] Her grandson's memories transport us to the same space in the 1930s, a setting made distinctive for him by its lack of carpet. 'She seemed formidable to a small boy. She seemed not to have a lot of time for small boys'.[76]

Several years after his return to Russia, Mary appealed to her friend Georgii Chicherin, who had become People's Commissar for Foreign Affairs. Letters in the Bridges Adams papers suggest that Mary confided she was experiencing financial problems and sought his help in arranging a travel permit. 'My possibilities are very limited,' he told her in April 1921. 'Hard necessity reigns. Nothing personal, state and business prevail … I look upon your personal needs as being urgent the delegation knows about it, I hope all will be well – I am extremely pained if you misunderstand us. The better days dawn – Be hopeful!' A few months later, he complained:

> I have received some letters from you by post and some letters by courier. You speak of an 'impudent' letter but you do not send its copy, so I can't say anything about it. It was a collective official decision to propose to you personal sustenance of living, but taking as granted that you cease to forward your so-called claim. We can never recognise such transformation of judetarian action based on principle into money claims. Help to feminine movement or to student movement is a thing to be considered in itself not on ground of a bill. We present a bill for principles or for devotion. We have all given our life energies, our whole life-time, our heart-blood, those who had fortunes all their fortunes, and we present no bills ... We work for our ideals, and not for money. If somebody replaces ideals by money claims, he is against the proletarian ideal.[77]

The cause of the wrangling was Georgii's offer of a pension, which she presumably declined, since her impecunious state continued. After the First World War was over, she had serious health problems and never fully recovered her old vitality.

Mary felt her age in her later years and the perennial struggle to keep the wolf from the door sapped her strength. Shortly after her eighty-third birthday, she crossed swords with Ivan Maisky over a suitcase of papers that the now deceased Georgii Chicherin had left in her care when, following the intervention of the new Soviet government, he was deported to Russia in January 1918. What, she wanted to know, would the Russian Embassy pay her for the safe return of his private letters? The sum of £25 had been mentioned but she had not heard back and wondered if she needed to visit the Embassy once more?[78] Alert and cognisant, albeit frail, she hoped to avoid another call, given her infirmities.

This portrait of Mary's private life is necessarily fragmentary and impressionistic. Nuggets of biographical sketches survive in apocryphal family stories. Her grandson, Nicholas, considered her a 'lady of strong independent views with an ironic sense of humour'. For instance, he said, his father once told him that he had found her standing in the kitchen at Lexham Gardens 'with a hand dripping blood, to which she retorted: "I'm not going to be told what to do by a sardine can."' Another time, she asked William to accompany those attending a meeting on education issues to Earls Court tube station. 'On the way they asked each other about the credentials which enabled them to speak on education. One said he was a professor, one said he was a civil servant and another said he had assassinated a Minister of Education.'[79]

Nonetheless, William had been growing more and more alienated from Mary. Nicholas confessed that his father 'didn't get on very well with her in her old age, which saddened my mother. He didn't visit her much. She would send telegrams asking him to carry out political tasks for her when he was busy with work at Stratford. He felt that she was making unrealistic demands given his work commitments and this caused tension between them.'[80] In the 1970s William's daughter-in-law, Jenifer, acknowledged that:

> She was regarded with strong disfavour by her son, who seldom spoke about her and who destroyed all photographs of her and all letters from her. The impression that remains is that of a hot-headed idealist who, in her anxiety to set the world to rights according to her ideas, disrupted the lives of others and made a mess of her own life. Her main problem was lack of money. She had a formidable personality that made her an unpopular companion to her relations.[81]

Mary's world was shrinking. As her network of friends and acquaintances contracted, she must have yearned for the heady joy of working together in a cause that seemed indubitable. The feelings were articulated by miners' leader Will Lawther (b. 1889) in a letter he wrote to her in January 1913: 'we get plenty of kicks, but there is a joy experienced in ploughing the straight furrow that compensates for the hardships undergone.'[82]

For the moment, we leave Mary as observed by her son at the time of her final ordeal. William gave Nicholas to understand that she stamped on an exposed, rusty nail in a fit of temper (something he shared, if his childhood letters are anything to go by). She made no secret of the fact that she was bitterly anti-Catholic and camouflaged her feelings with irony. Unable to stand or walk, she reputedly said that 'having opposed Catholicism all her life she was now suffering from mortification of the flesh'. Towards the end, the doctors amputated her leg. Her understanding became clouded and she thought she was seeing men in black, and asked William to 'make them go away'.[83] On 14 January 1939, Mary died in her hospital bed of senile gangrene and hardening of the arteries.

Working-class by social origin, middle-class by occupation, for many years Mary had to fend for herself. Mary was a thorn in the side of the nascent Labour Party in the House of Commons; her heart remained with the millennial utopianism of the 1880s. She appealed to the grass-roots movement across the generations to articulate her rejection of Labourism and her growing conviction that 'making socialists' through the creation and consolidation of a radicalised proletariat could achieve socialism more quickly. To understand her political work, it is necessary to qualify the meanings underpinning her networks. Therefore, the purpose of chapters 2 and 3 is to unravel the political affiliations and the groupings and regroupings of alignment that enable us to follow Mary's footsteps from reform to revolution.

Notes

1 M. Bridges Adams, *Cotton Factory Times*, 30 July, 1915.
2 Private information received from Mr Nicholas Bridges Adams, 29 May 1997.
3 Birth certificate Mary Jane Daltry, 19 October 1855.
4 1841 Wales Census Record, hamlet of Manmoel, parish of Bedwellty; 1851 Wales Census Record, township of Aberystruth, Monmouthshire.
5 See D. Gareth Evans, *A History of Wales 1815–1906* (Cardiff: University of Wales Press, 1989).
6 See the discussion of the Newport Rising in Evans, *A History of Wales*, p. 150; M. Chase, *Chartism: a new history* (Manchester: Manchester University Press, 2007), pp. 109–16, 126–33.
7 Quoted in D. Smith, *Aneurin Bevan and the World of South Wales* (Cardiff: Cardiff University Press, 1993), p. 47.
8 Birth certificate Benjamin Daltry, 25 May 1858; death certificate Benjamin Daltry, 1 June 1858; death certificate Margaret Daltry, 6 June 1858; marriage certificate William Daltry to Margaret Thomas, Panteg Parish Church, 4 November 1860.
9 1861 Wales Census Record, Parish of Llanhilleth, Crumlin.
10 1871 England Census Record, Parish of South Benwell, Robin Adair.
11 N. McCord, *North East England* (London: Batsford, 1979), pp. 133–5; death certificate William Daltry, 13 November 1894.
12 Benwell Community Project, *The Making of a Ruling Class*, Final Report No 6 (Newcastle Upon Tyne: Benwell Community Project, 1978), p. 43.
13 J.R. Hall, *The Elswick Works Schools 1869–1871: some recollections and impressions* (Newcastle-upon-Tyne: Privately published by the Schools Committee, 1912), p. 11.
14 TWA, records relating to Armstrong's Elswick Works, Newcastle school records, Newcastle School Board Minutes.
15 P. Cunningham and P. Gardner, *Becoming Teachers: texts and testimonies* (London: Woburn Press, 2004), p. 120.
16 Private information received from Mr Nicholas Bridges Adams, 29 May 1997.
17 Greenwich Heritage Centre, 'Vincent's Cuttings', Volume 6, p. 108.
18 J. Rose, *The Intellectual Life of the British Working Classes* (New Haven and London: Yale Nota Bena, 2002), p. 418.
19 Marriage certificate Thomas Lewis Daltry and Maria Arabella Matthews, 23 September 1880; death certificate Thomas Lewis Daltry, 11 January 1890.
20 C. Dyhouse, *No Distinction of Sex? Women in British universities 1870–1939*

(London: UCL Press, 1995), p. 13.

21 Bedford College, Student Register, Lent, Easter terms 1882; College Calendar.

22 M. Tuke, *A History of Bedford College for Women* (Oxford: Oxford University Press, 1939); R.L. Notcutt to Miss Daltry, n.d. All letters addressed to Mary Bridges Adams are in the possession of Mrs Jenifer Bridges-Adams.

23 1881 England Census Record, Accrington, Lancashire, St John's district; 1891 England Census Record Accrington, Lancashire, St John's district.

24 T. Whittaker to Miss Daltry, 9 September 1884.

25 T. Whittaker to Miss Daltry, 9 September 1884.

26 John Stokes to Miss Daltry, 22 June 1886.

27 Birth certificate Walter Bridges Adams, 20 September 1859; marriage certificate Mary Jane Daltry to Walter Bridges Adams, 22 October 1887.

28 Private information received from Mr Nicholas Bridges Adams, May/June 1997; UCL, A597, William Adams, 'The Record of a Busy Life', 1891; H.T. Wood, 'Adams, William Bridges (1797–1872)', *Oxford Dictionary of National Biography* (Oxford: Oxford University Press, 2004; online edn, May 2007) [www.oxforddnb.com/view/article/129, accessed 20 March 2007].

29 R. Watts, *Gender, Power and the Unitarians in England 1760–1860* (Harlow: Longman, 1998), p. 203.

30 S.K. Ratcliffe, *The Story of South Place* (London: Watts & Co., 1955), pp. 24–5.

31 Ratcliffe, *Story of South Place*, p. 25; V.H. Blain, 'Adams, Sarah Flower (1805–1848)', *Oxford Dictionary of National Biography* (Oxford: Oxford University Press, 2004; online edn, May 2007) [www.oxforddnb.com/view/article/129, accessed 20 March 2007].

32 1861 England Census Record, 4 Hollymount, Hampstead.

33 M. Krauss, *Die Frau der Zukunft* (München: Buchendorfer Verlag, 2002); J.C. Albisetti, *Schooling German Girls and Women* (Princeton: Princeton University Press, 1988), see pp. 122, 128–9, 137.

34 C. Usborne, *Cultures of Abortion in Weimar Germany* (NewYork, Oxford: Berghahn Books, 2007), pp. 84, 92.

35 *Englishwoman's Review*, 14 April 1883, 15 May 1884.

36 Part 2 of the University of London Register, 1899.

37 Greenwich Heritage Centre, 'Vincent's Cuttings', Volume 6, p. 108; W.T. Vincent, *The Records of the Woolwich District* (London: J.S. Virtue and Company Ltd, 1890), p. 407.

38 Interview with Mr Nicholas Bridges Adams, 29 May 1997.

39 Birth certificate William Bridges Adams, 1 March 1889.

40 1891 England Census Record, Greenwich, London.

41 William Bridges-Adams to John Moore, 5 March 1965, 1 April 1949, 3 May 1963, cited in R. Speight (ed.), *A Bridges-Adams Letter Book* (London: The Society for Theatre Research 1971), p. 11.

42 S. Jameson, *Journey from the North Vol. 1* (London: Virago, 1984), p. 67.

43 UCal., W. Bridges Adams Papers, William Bridges Adams to Dear Granny, 11 May 1895.

44 UCal., W. Bridges Adams Papers, William Bridges Adams to Muma, 31 October 1899.
45 With thanks to M.J. Leppard for supplying me with this information.
46 Death certificate Ellen Bridges Adams, 31 December 1898; interview with Mr Nicholas Bridges Adams, 29 May 1997.
47 M. Bridges Adams, 'London School Board Election: An Appeal for Aid', *Labour Leader*, 21 September 1901, p. 303.
48 R. Wake and P. Denton, *Bedales School 1893–1993* (London: Haggerston Press, 1993), pp. 57–8.
49 William Bridges Adams to Darling Mater, 20 July 1902.
50 1901 England Census Record, 59 Warrington Road, Newcastle.
51 CUBM, Mary Bridges Adams to Darling Boy, Dunfermline, n.d.
52 Quoted in S. Anand, *Daisy: the life and loves of the Countess of Warwick* (London: Piatkus, 2008), p. 54.
53 M. Blunden, *The Countess of Warwick* (London: Cassell, 1983), pp. 98, 119.
54 Anand, *Daisy*, p. 96.
55 Evelyn Warwick to Mary Bridges Adams, 21 March 1903.
56 W. Thorne, *My Life's Battles* (London: George Newnes Limited, 1926), p. 199.
57 Evelyn Warwick to Mary Bridges Adams, 21 March 1903; Thorne, *My Life's Battles*, p. 153.
58 H.M. Hyndman, *Further Reminiscences* (London: Macmillan & Co., 1912), pp. 83, 84, 89.
59 Evelyn Warwick to Mary Bridges Adams, 26 March 1903, Palermo, Sicily.
60 Evelyn Warwick to Mary Bridges Adams, 6 March (possibly 1906).
61 Quoted in D. Marquand, *Ramsay MacDonald* (London: Jonathan Cape, 1977), pp. 70, 72.
62 W.P. McCann (1960) 'Trade unionist, co-operative and socialist organisations in relation to popular education, 1870–1902', PhD thesis, University of Manchester, p. 423.
63 CUBM, Willy to Dearest Daisy, 28 May 1907.
64 William Bridges-Adams to Hope Bridges Adams, 26 December 1907.
65 Evelyn Warwick to Mary Bridges Adams, 3 March 1907.
66 Evelyn Warwick to Mary Bridges Adams, 5 May 1907.
67 Evelyn Warwick to Mary Bridges Adams, 1 February 1908.
68 CUBM, receipts the Right Honourable Frances Evelyn (Countess of Warwick), 27 February 1908, inventory of goods seized by George Rolfe, 123b Pentonville Road, London.
69 Evelyn Warwick to Mary Bridges Adams, 9 October 1908.
70 BLPES, Fabian Society Papers, record of subscriptions paid to the Fabian Society 1907–1909; *Cotton Factory Times*, 23 April 1913.
71 Lord Sheffield to Mrs Adams, 28 July 1918; 5 November 1918; 12 November 1918.
72 R. Speaight, 'Adams, William Bridges- (1889–1965)', Rev. Stanley Wells *Oxford Dictionary of National Biography* (Oxford: Oxford University Press, 2004;

online edn) [www.oxforddnb.com/view/article/32068, accessed 20 March 2007].

73 Jameson, *Journey from the North Vol. 1*, p. 67.

74 I. Maisky, *Journey into the Past*, translated from the Russian by Felix Holt (London: Hutchinson, 1962), p. 75.

75 Jameson, *Journey from the North Vol. 1*, p. 67.

76 Private information from Mr Nicholas Bridges Adams, June 1997.

77 Chicherin to Mary Bridges Adams, 26 June 1921.

78 Drafts of letters to Mr Maisky, 14, 17 and 28 December 1938.

79 Personal information from Mr Nicholas Bridges Adams, June 1997.

80 Personal information from Mr Nicholas Bridges Adams, June 1997.

81 HUA, Jenifer Bridges Adams to Dr Bellamy, undated.

82 W. Lawther to Mrs Adams, 14 January 1913.

83 Personal information from Mr Nicholas Bridges Adams, June 1997.

2

Rebel communities

I'd forgotten the peculiar quality of my Uncle Robin. He was an atheist. He was a socialist; he was a vegetarian; he was a physical culturist; he was – in short, he was a crank. 'A crank,' quoted he, not long after this, 'is a little thing, but it makes revolutions.' (Jack Common, 1991)[1]

She was a dedicated Fabian and looked the part, with her serious grey eyes, wide intellectual forehead and her air of a pained saint always looking for the good in people and not finding much. Such a woman is not likely to provide a good table and Mrs Jones, for that was her name, was no exception. I had early observed that people of idealistic left wing tendencies did not seem to enjoy food much, let alone provide it for others. They drank a great deal of tea and ate shop buns at their gatherings, and at home, they were often lentil and bread-and-jam people. (P.Y. Betts, 1991)[2]

Mary's socialist milieu

Mary's social action took place in what the generality of people considered a rather bohemian setting, the kind of habitat mapped out in the extracts with which we start, taken from memoirs of growing up around the time of the First World War. As Mary nursed her own schemes for social revolution, her horizons ranged wider than educational debates at local government level. This chapter sets Mary in a network of comrades at a particular time and place. A matrix of tiny tributaries of dissent that coalesced because of shared political convictions and a shared political vision. From the mid 1880s onwards, the trajectory of her political activities drew her into the orbit of trade union and Labour leaders, prominent radicals, socialists in the British adult education movement and the revolutionary activists from the Russian Empire who sought refuge in London. In middle age, she formed deep and lasting associations with a new generation of socialist recruits, including miners' leader Noah Ablett (b. 1883), former mill worker and writer Ethel Carnie (b. 1886), Harry

McShane and John Maclean (b. 1879), the most successful Marxist educationalist of all. The reconstruction of a living milieu will bring us closer to Mary, helping to furnish the story and plot of her life.

All political movements are as much the history of social and intellectual networks as they are of campaigns and lobbying, organisations and institutions. Making sense of Mary's political career, her circle of influence connects us to leftist counter-cultures in Glasgow, Lancashire, London, the Rhondda and West Yorkshire. Although casual comparison is potentially flawed, my purpose is a graphic encapsulation of political space presented as a relationship between the individual and the community of believers to which they belong and relationships within socialist organisations.

This is not the place to examine the complex histories of earlier movements, but the socialist evangelism of the 1880s had its roots in the dissenting protest tradition of left-leaning activists. For example, the radical Unitarians who congregated at South Place Chapel discussed the social and moral questions that Mary and her comrades posed, the dilemmas they sought to resolve. Mary's educated father-in-law felt that he had a direct duty to help those less fortunate to see the light of a better life. Written against the backdrop of a rising organised working class, his essay on *The Rights of Morality: state of society in England* (published in 1832) fused the duty of social cohesion with the rights of citizens. Connecting education and politics, he wrote: 'Let all those who love their kind – who prize beneficence more than selfishness, spare no efforts to ensure, as far as may be, to the greatest possible number, that species of mental training, whose fruit is wisdom, and which alone is worthy to be called – Education.'[3] These attitudes were not typical of the middle class as a whole. However, the basic egalitarianism was handed down from father to youngest son. Affected by the radicalism of the first half of the century, Walter Bridges Adams was among the first few hundred recruits to socialism, attracted by William Morris's combination of creativity and agitation.

The insights of Mary's father-in-law rested on very specific conditions. You must conceive of a moment when mass schooling was in only the early process of construction, dominated by the care and consideration of faith-group motivations and/or philanthropic persons of respectable social standing. Politicians were moving around to the idea of state involvement, initially in the form of parliamentary grants and a weak form of inspection and, after 1846, of control over teacher training. At the same time, substitutional activity was the favoured radical strategy for those seeking to challenge the orthodox method and content that characterised schools supported by state subsidy. For instance, radical educators of the Chartist and Owenite movements chose to concentrate on establishing their own educational media to make workers understand the exploitation underpinning their economic condition. What was different about the late-nineteenth-century revival of the radical education tradition was a heightened sense of the ideological resources of authority. For Mary, as for Noah Ablett, Ethel Carnie and John Maclean, a strategy of independent working-class adult education to secure a majority in favour of socialism, as a prelude to workers' control, made sense in the 1900s. This was a political project harking back to the counter-cultural Chartist and Owenite experience of the 1830s and 1840s. Once again, there was no one organisational focus. The adult education movement included the weekly branch life of socialist groups and the classes organised by the Plebs League and the National Labour College before and after the First World War.

Socialist experience varied by class, culture, gender and generation. Witness the words of Will Thorne, recalling the spread of New Unionism. 'It was a great and thrilling period for any one to live in; it was still greater to be part of, and in the thick of, the struggle.'[4] Mary was operating, in the early stages of her political career, against this background. As a member of the Gas Workers and General Labourers' Union, she moved across organisational boundaries, becoming prominent in the London ILP but forming alliances with Social Democrats on the London Trades Council (LTC). Chief among them was the West Country-born compositor Fred Knee (b. 1866). After the loss of her elected status on the LSB and the collapse of the National Labour Education League, Mary's unyielding advocacy of Marxist education classes knit her together with Noah Ablett, Ethel Carnie and John Maclean. With her faith in Parliamentary Socialism eroded, she campaigned for independent socialist MP Victor Grayson (b. 1881). Her polemic for the cause helped to inspire Harry McShane, with whom our story continues, before our trail takes us back to pre-war London and Russian revolutionaries George Chicherin, Alexandra Kollontai and Prince Peter Kropotkin. The chapter will conclude with the single case of dissident Liberal Edward Lyulph Stanley, fourth Baron Stanley of Alderley. We start with the narrative of Gas Workers' leader Will Thorne.

Social Democrats

As a group, the New Unions arose in the course of a series of massive strikes in 1889 and 1890. Among them was Will Thorne's Gas Workers' and General Labourers' Union, formed in March 1889, initially around the demand for a reduction in gasworks shift hours from twelve to eight. Will was a sharp-witted organiser who knew how to win over a crowd, and the gas workers' strike involved semi- and unskilled, casualised workers who, in conditions of good employment, scored a momentous victory. Will's belief was simple. The union's motto was 'Love, Unity and Fidelity', and by creating unions that were inclusive, unlike the old craft unions, he hoped that the wages of the lowest-paid would rise. 'One Man, One Ticket, and every Man with a Ticket' became the union's slogan. With a policy of low dues, membership soared. Mary knew several of the key organisers, including Eleanor Marx (b. 1855). By the autumn, the Gas Workers' Union had twenty thousand members with forty-four London branches and over twenty provincial ones.

Born in Birmingham, Will Thorne had had an unhappy childhood. Financially, the family were very poor. Will had his first job when he was 6, helping at weekends in his uncle's barber's shop. His alcoholic father died in a pub brawl a year later and Will's work for a local rope maker supplemented the family's meagre income from his mother's home sewing work and the weekly poor relief from the local guardians. Every Wednesday, at the end of a twelve-hour working day, Will walked four miles to collect the 4s and four loaves of bread. His memoirs stress the politicising effects of his mother's revulsion at the way one boss exploited her son's labour, making him hunchbacked.

> It is the rebellion that I feel, and will continue to carry on. Just think for a moment. Here was I, a boy of nine years of age, that should have been in school, getting up in the cold of early morning, leaving home at about 4.30, walking four miles to work, and then, after a long twelve-hour day, walking back again, a fifteen-hour day by the time I got home, dead tired, barely able to eat my scanty tea and crawl to bed.[5]

In the 1870s Will drifted from job to job, generally gas stoking during the winter season and brick making in the summer. A keen boxer and one of the best runners in the Midlands, in his youth he was 'slight and fine-drawn … straight from the retort house with the mark of the fiery place burnt into his features. Round his eyes were dark rings of coal grime'.[6] This was a time when the practice of 'tramping' to find work was general, and Will worked with the navvies on the construction of the Burton and

Derby railway line. The outlook of 'these big-hearted carefree men … an independent type, with the spark of rebellion growing bright within them'[7] proved influential. By the age of 18, he had come out on strike five times and was readily dismissed as a militant worker.

In 1879 Will married the daughter of a fellow worker at the Saltley gasworks. Neither party could sign their own name, so they made their 'mark' on the marriage register. Several times, as a strike leader he lost work, forcing him to tramp to London to seek employment, the second time for good. Will's last job was at the Beckton gasworks, and he found lodging in Canning Town. The area has been industrial and residential since about 1850. His wife and children soon joined him in the locality, built to house the labourers in Victoria Docks, the coal wharves and the shipbuilding works on Bow Creek. Union work led to involvement in working-class political practice in both its forms as defined by Michael Savage – that is, '*formal* politics, the character of which is defined by the nature of the state and existing party structures' and '*practical* politics, which form the issues over which formal politics can operate but which are much more closely tied to the social structure'.[8] Forty years on, he still belonged to the community in which he spent most of his working life, both physically and by class identity. There he died among those he described as 'my people – dockers, labourers, casual workers in many queer and unpleasant trades. Our world is over-populated, our houses are small and poor, often a tightening of our belt strap takes the place of a meal. Towering factory chimneys are our sentinels, and the ships – tall ships, bright ships of many flags from far-off lands – our only inspiration'.[9]

Will joined the newly formed SDF about 1884 and fought successfully as a socialist in the 1891 election to the West Ham town council. The local press responded to the result with enthusiasm. 'Thorne', wrote the editor of the *West Ham Herald*, 'is one of the most earnest, straightforward, reliable common sense men, in the Labour movement ... a man whom the workers love and are proud of, a man who never backbites another, and a man who works solely for the movement and has absolutely no personal aims'.[10] As a trade union leader, Will combined loyalty to the SDF with conventional attitudes within the TUC. A member of the Parliamentary Committee of the Congress from 1894, he was its chair in the years 1896–97 and 1911–12. In 1900 he stood as parliamentary candidate for West Ham South but was defeated. Mary and her friend Daisy Warwick campaigned on his behalf in the 1906 general election, the Countess advising everybody that 'they had a man in Mr Will Thorne who was the envy of the constituency'.[11] They appear with him in a campaign photograph reproduced in his personal memoir, with Mary standing at his left shoulder. This time, the Liberals returned to power after ten years in the wilderness and Will entered the House of Commons as MP for West Ham with a majority of 5,225 votes.

In London, most organised elementary teachers belonged to the non-aligned National Union of Teachers (NUT) or the Metropolitan Board Teachers Association. Mary's involvement with the Gas Workers' Union points to her identification with the new political trade unionism. In 1933, trade unionist and Labour MP W.J. Brown (b. 1894) interviewed Mary for *The Millgate*. He asked her why she had joined the Gas Workers' Union. 'With that radiant outlook with which she won the hefty manual workers to take up the cause of the children she replied: "I was a gas worker on the platform and a general labourer at home"'.[12] She was not alone. In Bristol, the campaign for the Eight Hour Day attracted middle-class women workers for socialism, like schoolteachers Katherine Bruce Glasier and Enid Stacy.[13] Nonetheless, the perpetuation of traditional female roles, the political focus on male labour, the role of the unions and realpolitik at the centre of the trade union movement effectively displaced them from front-line action. One obstacle proved to be the change to TUC rules, such that from 1896 leading socialists who were neither active workers nor full-time union officials could not attend Congress as delegates.

Having drifted from job to job since he was 7, Will had no formal education beyond a short spell in a dame school. He was no bookworm and, unlike other major New Unionists, no autodidact. For example, Dockers' leaders Tom Mann and Ben Tillett (b. 1860) started their self-education in Sunday school. Tom used Henry George's enormously popular tract *Progress and Poverty* as a primer and Ben studied Greek and Latin while working as a sailor. Will, instead, gained his education with help from Eleanor Marx, who taught him to read. After his election as General Secretary of the Gas Workers in June 1889 Eleanor played a part as clerk, working alongside a male treasurer. Later Will relied on skilled office assistants and itinerant organisers like J.R. Clynes (b. 1869), whose self-education had already thrust him into a position of leadership. 'The Oldham men who wanted to form a local branch of this union were all of them older than I, but they needed a secretary who had "education" and my peculiar fondness for books was well known'.[14]

However, Will was deeply hurt when Philip Snowden (b. 1864), former insurance clerk and the first Labour Chancellor of the Exchequer, wrote sneeringly of his 'unfettered ignorance and unfitness for Parliament' in an article for the *Labour Leader*. In his memoirs, it was this which he singled out as the one thing 'which really threatened to affect my spirit'. Not surprisingly, his union also resented the attack. 'Instead of taunting Labour spokesmen with lack of an educated manner', the General Council complained, 'you ought to sympathise with and sustain men who as boys had to work at hard labour when for years they should have been at school. Anyhow, against the polish of whoever writes your paragraphs, we set the splendid pioneer work of Mr Thorne as an educationalist agitator to secure for every working lad the schooling advantages of which he was deprived'.[15]

The Gas Workers began campaigning around education and child welfare in the mid 1890s.[16] Mary claimed the credit for drafting policy resolutions, petitions, and the Education Bill which Will presented to Parliament in 1906. In December 1906 Will made the following note in his General Secretary's report:

> Educational policy making rapid headway in all parts of the country, and thousands of men who at one time thought our ideals were too revolutionary, beginning to embrace the same ideals. At the rate we are making converts, it will not be very long before the rank and file of the organised workers will declare in favour of state maintenance, secular education, periodical medical examinations for school children, and a complete change in the method of teaching children in the elementary schools, besides raising the ages of children to prevent them going into the factories and workshops at such tender ages … the Countess of Warwick and Mrs Bridges Adams rendering our union invaluable services in this direction.[17]

In an interview with Phillip McCann toward the end of his life, William Bridges-Adams said that his mother became the educational mentor of the TUC.[18] The key policy demands were for compulsory education, school meals and medical care at school, a secular curriculum, and for the extension of educational opportunities *within* the elementary school system.

New Unionism's reach was inclusive, but most workers of late Victorian Britain did not belong to a trade union. To combat this in the capital, socialist agitators sought to revitalise the LTC, the most important trades council in the country. With aspirations to be 'London's Labour Parliament',[19] it represented over a third of London's trade unionists and became a significant part of the pressure for independent labour politics. With this in mind, Fred Knee and other Social Democrats on the LTC offered practical support to Mary in various ways. They promoted her candidature for the LSB and tried to win her a seat on the governing body of

Woolwich Polytechnic and to secure her co-option to the LCC Education Committee. When it came to the debate about the abolition of the local school boards, the LTC backed the position upheld by the National Labour Education League, namely free school meals and medical inspection, workers' control of state schools and free, secular instruction for every child from elementary through to higher education.[20]

Of nonconformist descent, Fred Knee was the single most important working-class housing reformer of his generation. His parents were both weavers and he attended British schools in Frome, Somerset, until the age of 14, when he became an apprentice compositor. Known as the 'mighty atom', as a young diarist he claimed he was 'sixty and a half inches in height – out of boots – and thirty inches round the chest'.[21] The theme of conversion is evident in his life history. Congregationalism and temperance provided the chapels and clubs in which he learned to debate and organise. He served his political apprenticeship as a lay preacher and said he 'ceased to be respectable' in 1888, when he became a Socialist. Fred arrived in London in December 1890 and immediately joined the Regent Street Polytechnic. By July, he and his friends had formed a Social Democratic Party in the 'Poly Parliament'. At about this time he joined the Fabian Society. Besides the Fabians, he was also engaged in the activities of the Eleusis Club, one of the largest political working-men's clubs in the capital. By devoting his time and energy to 'making socialists in Chelsea', Knee found his satisfaction complete.[22] In 1898, Fred founded the Workmen's Housing Council to campaign for better housing for workers. He campaigned for Mary in the 1900 School Board elections and they co-wrote a pamphlet on housing for the Labour group on Woolwich Borough Council.

Like Mary, Fred was never afraid to give voice to his convictions. His public work included a spell as an alderman for Battersea Council. At the Council meeting of 25 January 1901 he moved a resolution condemning the British military conduct of the South African war and demanding the restoration of Boer independence and an immediate cessation of hostilities. Amid a good deal of personal abuse and general disruption, fellow councillors threw it out. Later that year, Fred and Mary attended an elected persons' conference that preceded the annual conference of the ILP. Emmeline Pankhurst (b. 1858), Labour member of Manchester School Board, also attended the pre-conference event with her daughter, Sylvia (b. 1882). When the meeting broke up the majority of delegates accepted an invitation to go to tea. Sylvia's account complicates our sense of Mary's disregard for what people think: 'Old Mrs Bridges Adams came to us afterwards in her knowing way: "I went for the experience, of course, but I was surprised at you taking your daughter!"[23] Emotional stresses and strains may have aged Mary, and activism took its toll. Overwork killed some, others had breakdowns, and a popular orator like Bruce Glasier (b. 1859) did not expect to reach the age of 40.[24]

Fred Knee promoted labour unity when he sat on the LTC Executive. He wanted to see independent labour representation in central and local government and he considered a strong party machine, like those of the other political parties, a crucial factor. Although he sought to reconcile support for his views, Harry Quelch as chair and James Macdonald (b. 1858) as secretary of the LTC impeded his efforts. Head of the West End branch of the Amalgamated Society of Tailors, James was one of four SDF representatives at the founding conference of the LRC (forerunner of the Labour Party), in February 1900, where he moved the unsuccessful resolution to base the new party upon recognition of the class war. He wanted to see militant trades councils become an alternative to the TUC and circumvent its Lib-Lab philosophy and leadership.[25] In the capital, unity talks did not get under way until after the death of Harry Quelch in 1913. James Macdonald resigned the secretary's post, which Fred Knee filled. A year later Knee became first secretary of the newly formed London Labour Party.

The full range and scope of her activities remain hidden, but it is clear that Mary spent a large part of her time on the platform between 1900 and 1912. Britain's first Marxist paper, *Justice*, for which Fred Knee worked, contains numerous references to her speaking at meetings in these years. In July 1908, for example, the Croydon district organiser of the SDF wrote to say 'our comrade Mary Bridges Adams spoke on Sunday to a record crowd who stood spellbound, and enthusiasm ran high. Her subject "the child" touched all present. A Tariff Reformer tried to hold a meeting a little higher up the street but after half-an-hour shouting to a group of children he gave it up.'[26] The local branch was happy: the audience gave more cash than at any previous meeting, and it enrolled more members. Mary spoke around the country on labour platforms, addressing branches of a divergent Left spanning the Fabians, the ILP, miners' lodges, the SDF, Socialist Sunday Schools, socialist adult education, working-men's clubs and the Brotherhood movement. The latter spawned a number of communities in the countryside where members lived together. Influenced by William Morris, its politics were Christian socialist and pacifist.[27]

While practical necessity bound her to Daisy Warwick, who employed her in the post of secretary and organiser, Mary established herself as itinerant propagandist. She campaigned consistently on education and welfare policy. After the 1906 general election she and the Countess were euphoric at the return of twenty-nine Labour MPs, seeing it as a stepping-stone to socialism. As in the case of other purists of the Left, however, Mary's euphoria was short-lived. Disappointed by the performance of the new Parliamentary Labour Party at Westminster, she was part of a circle of dissidents who gravitated toward the enigmatic Victor Grayson, who captured the enthusiasm of socialists across the country.[28] This irritated a politically shrewd leader like Ramsay MacDonald. His developmental model of socialism was rooted in a belief that the self-interest and free competition of advanced capitalism would disappear because its success would create new problems – like greater material inequalities – which only altruism and co-operation could solve. Therefore, Ramsay took the evolutionary rather than the revolutionary road.

Victor Grayson

Victor Grayson grew up in a working-class district of Liverpool. Mrs Grayson was a domestic servant before her marriage and Mr Grayson was a soldier-turned-carpenter. Mystery surrounds Victor's birth but there were strong rumours that he was the love child of one of the English aristocracy. If so, outside family assistance could be the answer to the question of how his parents paid for his elocution lessons, before which he was, quite literally, tongue tied. It may also explain how he was able to remain at elementary school until he was 14 and then finance himself through college in Manchester.

As a youth, Victor twice ran away from home. The second time, he persuaded a sailor friend to smuggle him on board a ship bound for South America. Discovered and put ashore in Tenby in South Wales, he never forgot the discomfort of the three hundred-mile walk home to Liverpool. After Victor left school he spent six years as an apprentice turner, and from the age of 18 he began attending services at local missions, where he gained his first experience in public speaking as a Sunday school teacher. In his early twenties he came under the influence of a local Unitarian minister and followed his mentor into the Unitarian Church. The autumn of 1904 saw him enrol as a theology student in Manchester at the Home Missionary College, which specialised in taking recruits from industrial areas for the Unitarian ministry in similar districts. Once there, he began to neglect his studies in favour of a politics of the street corner, and he seized the chance that fate offered by standing in for Will Thorne in the course of the general election campaign in Huddersfield in December 1905.

Victor emerged as a star speaker. The young student had already impressed his academic referees, as well as his friend and neighbour Percy Redfern (b. 1875), journalist and historian of the Co-operative movement, with his powers of oratory. Now it was the turn of the Colne Valley Labour League, whose members were among the audience in Huddersfield. Invitations to speak flooded in and the early months of 1906 saw Victor making frequent visits to the area and swiftly gaining a following, especially among the younger men and women in the Colne Valley villages. Here he found a well-oiled Labour Party machine, accompanied by a flourishing counter-culture organised around the social and recreational worlds of the Clarion Clubs. Buoyed by Labour's electoral success nationally, local activists were already looking to run a candidate for the next election and Victor's followers determined that his name should go forward. On 11 April 1906 the would-be politician wrote to Keir Hardie. 'I am invited to allow my name to be submitted as Labour candidate for the Colne Valley Division, and am inclined to do so. I finish my University course at the end of May and feel desirous of throwing myself into the movement. As I entertain infinite respect for your judgement in such matters, I should be pleased if you could favour me with your opinion.'[29]

We do not know the response, but the League was to encounter difficulties in respect of its nominee. Unaware of the maelstrom into which it was hurtling, its Secretary entered into correspondence with the Labour Party's national body, desirous of having Victor's name added to the approved list of suitable Parliamentary candidates. In Colne Valley rumours were rife that the sitting Liberal member was about to be elevated to the House of Lords. The League did not want to miss the opportunity to contest the seat and, in the face of the equivocation of the national leadership, activists took matters into their own hands. On 22 June 1907 they adopted Victor as their candidate. On 28 June, the day the formal announcement of the peerage appeared in the press, the Labour Party issued a statement opposing Victor's candidature because it contravened new regulations regarding the selection of Parliamentary candidates at national level. The decision outraged his supporters, and enthusiasts descended on the constituency, adding their weight to a tumultuous and passionate by-election campaign.

Once elected, the charismatic young politician was uncompromising: 'this epoch-making victory has been won for pure revolutionary

Socialism. We have not trimmed our sails to get a half-hearted vote. We have proclaimed our Socialism on every platform … We stand for equality, human equality, sexual equality – for the abolition of sex.'[30] Amid the euphoria, *Justice* noted Mary's reaction. Said to be 'highly gratified at the result', she 'was scarcely less delighted with the great meetings she held in the constituency during the election, and the enthusiasm of her audiences over the most pronounced and revolutionary Socialist utterances. Especially to be noted, was the reception accorded to all references to the "immediate" Socialist proposals (that is raising the school leaving age, free maintenance) on behalf of the children'.[31] 'Good old Red Flag,' shouted Will Thorne as Victor took his seat in the House of Commons.

To unravel the alignments, Mary's position and that of the SDF need clarifying. In 1900, the group had affiliated to the Labour Party, but disaffiliated in 1901. In 1907 it was renamed the Social Democratic Party (SDP), presumably to imply that the new organisation considered itself as a direct competitor to the Labour Party. Suspicious of the electoral strategy of the Labour Party leaders, Social Democrats gloated at the role they had played in Colne Valley, and the party contested three further by-elections in the coming year, in direct contravention of the 'Labour Alliance'. Lobbying continued and Mary was at the centre of a party-sponsored attempt to mobilise public opinion against child labour.

SDP agitation for the abolition of the 1893 Half-time Act, which allowed 10 and 11-year-olds to attend school as well as work, targeted Lancashire's textile industry and Mary formed a duo with former seaman and railwayman Dan Irving (b. 1854). Dan, who had lost his leg in a railway accident, was secretary of the Burnley branch of the SDP. This was the party's strongest provincial branch and the only provincial presence that came near to rivalling its London strength. In the winter of 1907/8 Dan and Mary addressed meetings in the mill towns of Briercliffe, Clitheroe, Colne, Nelson and Padiham. A sympathetic report in *Justice* recorded that Mary's 'capable and brilliant manner … could not fail' to build up support.[32] On 25 January 1908 she was speaking with Victor Grayson to an audience in London. 'Grayson got the blood of the meeting up and Mrs Bridges Adams kept it at boiling point', exclaimed an excited reporter for *Justice*.[33] Despite the optimism, the half-time system lasted until 1921, when it became illegal for 12-year-olds to work in factories for half a day every day.

In Parliament, the Labour Party leadership would lose patience with Victor's dramatic interventions in the House of Commons and flouting of parliamentary procedure. Time and circumstance would reinforce tensions between the organisational men in the ILP leadership and those who shared the SDP view that class struggle was the way to achieve socialism. A letter of 13 September 1899 from Ramsay MacDonald to Mary, as LCC candidate for Woolwich, illustrates this. 'My Dear Mrs Bridges Adams,' he wrote, 'I am told that I have a very good chance. If you can do anything I should therefore be obliged'.[34] Ten years on, he was the senior in the association. Whereas reformism frustrated Mary, Ramsay seethed at the 'Colne Valley crowd', whose hero was already showing his feet of clay. Increasingly unreliable and politically discredited, Victor failed to secure re-election in 1910. Seven years later, the erstwhile darling of the British Left took up arms. Perhaps the greatest mob orator of his time, Harry McShane considered him 'one of the greatest speakers in the socialist movement'.[35] The Valley communities kept his memory alive. 'No-one could draw the crowds like Grayson. Wherever he spoke they came in thousands to hear him, and having heard him they came again and again, and never quite forgot the things he said, the way he spoke, or the things inside themselves that responded.'[36]

Marxist education

Perhaps Ethel Carnie heard Mary speak at a mill town. Educated at a nonconformist elementary school, Ethel started part-time work, aged 11, at Delph Road Mill in Great Harwood, Lancashire. Both her parents were weavers and she was in full-time employment at another mill from 13. At school, she showed promise in composition and often had her essays read out to the rest of the class. Encouraged by her mother, she continued to write and met with considerable local acclaim. Further publicity followed the publication of Ethel's first book, *Rhymes from the Factory*, in 1907. In July 1908 Robert Blatchford visited Ethel at home for an interview with his paper, the *Woman Worker*. On his advice, she left the mill to earn her living through her writing. When she arrived in London to begin her pre-war journalism contemporaries described Blatchford's new recruit as 'five foot three inches tall, with dark hair, grey eyes, firm lips and an oval face'.[37]

Like Mary, Ethel moved from group to group, aligning herself with the ILP and the SDF at particular points in time. She was an associate of Dan Irving and probably first met Victor Grayson through Robert Blatchford. In February 1909 Robert offered Victor a job on his socialist weekly, the *Clarion*, and Victor virtually controlled the paper's political stance between 1909 and 1911. Victor also wrote a weekly column for its sister paper, *Woman Worker*, which Ethel edited from July to December 1909. Following a brief return to factory work in 1910, Ethel combined extensive travels in Germany, shop work with her mother, time attending Owens College, Manchester, and two years at Bebel House.

Ethel founded the Rebel Pen Club while living with Mary. The Club was dedicated to teaching working women how to write in the interests of socialism. Ethel's articles in the various socialist publications show that she trusted Mary's political perspective, and their writing style is equally direct. For example, Ethel wanted to see a united Socialist Party in Parliament and she was sick of waiting. 'Once I saw a picture of the crucified Christ. That wan brow, and anguished look – you need not go into a picture gallery to see it. Stand at the end of a summer's day, and see the operatives trail out. The little half-timer by the loom, straining to reach – with thin hands throwing the shuttle, you may see it there. But I forgot, it takes two thousand years to clear the mist from our eyes and see our crucified.'[38] Eddie and Ruth Frow suggest that Ethel's apprenticeship as a writer, as a woman and a socialist ended with her marriage to Alfred Holdsworth in April 1915. 'Shortly after the wedding, Ethel marched with Alfred to the railway station to see him off on his journey to his military call-up. She carried the Red Flag.'[39]

Ethel's action is a reminder of the realignments within the British Labour movement in the First World War. The trajectory of Mary's anti-war activities was a measure of the changes within her activism during the previous decade, changes which had turned her away from reformism and toward revolution. A firm believer in the need to construct a revolutionary leadership out of the common people, in 1909 Mary was one of the founding members of the Central Labour College. Through this organisation she had become involved with new forms of adult education and a new generation of educator activists, like Noah Ablett, who worked as a miner until he went to Ruskin College, Oxford on a miner's scholarship in 1907.

Noah Ablett was the tenth child in a family of eleven, born in Porth in the Rhondda. On returning to the valleys he set up Marxist educational classes and went on to become checkweigher at Mardy colliery, a pivotal figure in the union structure elected by the colliers to ensure that their trucks of coal were weighed correctly. He first became prominent when there was a strike, in the pits owned by the Cambrian Combine, to establish a guaranteed minimum wage. The strike lasted from October 1910 to September 1911, rioting broke out and additional police forces and a detachment of troops were sent into the valley. Mary took up the cause of the miners, speaking for them in Tonypandy, where she supported the relief fund appeal and urged the authorities to exercise their power to feed the children of strikers. Whereas Noah opposed accepting the terms of the owners, the trade union recommended their acceptance and he, along with others, formed an Unofficial Reform Committee that published *The Miners' Next Step* in the hopes of finding a wider audience. Drafted by Noah, it is notable for its mixture of Syndicalism and Marxism. It contains a plea for the formation of one vast industrial union and advocates workers' control and ownership of industry, trusting that involvement in disputes combined with independent working-class education would lead men naturally on to 'revolutionary consciousness'.[40]

Mary and Noah accepted the necessity for independent political action with an emphasis on the socialist construction underpinning William Morris's politics, and captured in the well-worn phrase 'making socialists'. For Mary, as for Morris, this was an urgent precondition of anything else. Never dominant, always residual or emergent, it was there in the practical politics of her friend John Maclean. When he received a sentence of three years' penal servitude for seditious behaviour Mary expressed her views in the columns of the *Cotton Factory Times*. She helped to publicise his case, mounting a vigorous campaign for the release of 'one of the best men' she had ever known.[41] Later, he returned the compliment, speaking of 'my revered friend, Mrs Bridges Adams'.[42]

John's parents moved to the Clyde region as young children, part of the mass emigration from the Scottish Highlands in the face of aggressive landlordism. John was 8 years old when his father, a potter, died of a lung disease common among workers in the pottery trade. His mother took over as the mainstay of the family and, by returning to work as a weaver, she ensured that John was able to stay on at school beyond the normal leaving age and enter higher education. John became a pupil teacher in 1896 and followed that with a teacher's certificate at the Free Church Teachers' Training College. From 1900 to 1915 he taught in five schools under the auspices of Govan School Board, but was often in conflict with the school authorities and was eventually dismissed in controversial circumstances. While a student teacher he began studying at Glasgow University and he obtained his MA in 1904, specialising in political economy from a Marxist standpoint. For many years he lectured widely for both the Social Democrats and the Co-operative movement, taking hugely popular classes in economics and industrial history.

John travelled to the Rhondda Valley during the Cambrian Combine Committee strike in the summer of 1911, where he met Noah Ablett.

From then on, he began to assume a more formal commitment to the systematic development and provision of Marxist education. On his return, he poured energy into the campaign to create a Scottish Labour College.[43] He and Mary both joined the newly formed BSP in 1911 and he became its leading figure in the West of Scotland. In the eyes of John McArthur (b. 1899), who retired in 1964 as Fife District Secretary of the National Union of Mineworkers (NUM), he was a hero. McArthur records the impression Maclean made on the leader of the Kirkcaldy branch of the BSP. '"With Maclean" he said, "you sit with your mouth open, you swallow everything, and when he finishes you close your mouth and have the revolution"'.[44] Harry McShane regarded his economics classes as 'the most attractive feature of the Glasgow movement before the first world war … It wasn't just his oratory that influenced people but the feeling that he was a man who could be trusted, a man of integrity. There was no show about John Maclean'.[45]

Born and brought up in Glasgow, Harry McShane was the eldest of eleven children of a Catholic builder's labourer who was an active trade unionist. The space he called home was a tenement 'with a ground floor and three storeys above that. Each separate entrance, or close as we called it, had several one-and-two room dwellings on each floor. The toilet at the stairhead of each close served the purposes of three or four families. In the back court of each tenement was a washhouse with a boiler and a place for a fire. The women did their washing in these boilers and it was hard, hard work'.[46] Unlike many of the other children, he did not go to school bare-footed because his father and grandfather worked very long hours to earn the equivalent of skilled men. During his youth, his father took him to hear the open-air speakers and debates on Glasgow Green; 1908, one of the worst years of unemployment the city had known, was his epiphany. The ILP and the SDP joined the propaganda for more poor relief and he began to read all the socialist literature he could get, including *Forward*, the paper of the Glasgow ILP. One Sunday night he heard Mary speak at Glasgow's eighteen hundred-seat Pavilion Theatre, a building with an imposing terra cotta façade and a domed ceiling surmounted by an electrically operated sliding roof.

Harry joined the ILP as an apprentice engineer. Mechanisation drastically altered the semi-handcraft basis of the metal trades with the result that, having previously been rather conservative, by the 1900s metalworkers were the characteristic leaders of militant labour movements. In Harry's words: 'It might have been due to the work they did – there was a logic in engineering; yet they were also more slaves to their machines than the other trades, particularly if they worked as machine-turners, hole-borers and shapers. The engineers' trade union was also very democratic'.[47]

The link between skill structure and working-class politics is crucial to Michael Savage's analysis of local political cultures, in which he differentiates between 'craft' and 'factory' skills,[48] the former acquired through apprenticeship, the latter based on promotion through an internal labour market whereby skill acquisition frequently took the form of patronage. Building on 'labour aristocracy' theories that stress the existence of a working-class elite earning more and with greater job security than most workers, Savage seeks to explain why some craft workers rejected employer-led initiatives. Their response was mediated by what he calls *capacities*, that is, cultural and organisational resources rooted in the local social structure, which facilitates some types of political mobilisation in the pursuance of practical politics, rather than others. Oases of socialist communities in Burnley, the Colne Valley, Glasgow, the Rhondda and Woolwich corroborate his thesis.

There was a striking lack of unanimity on the question of the Socialist response to the First World War among Mary's friends and allies. On the one hand, Ethel Carnie, Victor Grayson, Henry Hyndman, Will Thorne and Daisy Warwick responded to the calls for patriotism and supported the war effort. On the other, the ILP section of the Labour movement was overwhelmingly hostile to the war, which it regarded as a capitalist struggle in which the working class had no interest. Countrywide, the anti-war minority was tiny. To name but a few casualties, Ramsay MacDonald resigned his position as chair of the fledgling Labour Party, Victor Grayson enlisted and the pro-war Hyndman group left the BSP to form the National Socialist Party. Mary, with no conceivable hope of putting her policies into practice, sought to gain acceptance for them through writing, promulgating her views by means of articles for the *Cotton Factory Times* and its sister paper the *Yorkshire Factory Times*, virtually a house magazine of the wool-textile unions. As some old ties loosened, her path crossed that of another 'kindred spirit' in the shape of Georgii Vasilievich Chicherin, himself a friend and correspondent of Alexandra Kollontai (b. 1872).[49]

Russian revolutionaries and Lyulph Stanley

As newly weds, Mary and Walter lived in the same neighbourhood as Prince Peter Kropotkin, who first arrived in 1876, and lived permanently in England between 1886 and 1917. A Cossack officer, eminent geographer and the leader of European anarchism, he was profoundly affected by the defeat of the Paris Commune of 1871. What happened then triggered the following reaction. As he wrote:

> Science is a very important thing. I know and appreciate the joys it brings if only because many of them have been mine. But what right had I to all these higher joys when all around me I could see utter beggary and a heart-rending struggle for a stale crust of bread, and when all I spend in order to live in the world of high intellectual achievement must inevitably be at the expense of those who grow corn for others but have not enough bread for their own children?[50]

Alexandra, Georgii and Peter were all born into the Russian aristocracy and found themselves influenced by revolutionary ideas as adults. At different historical moments, they each began a double life of underground political activity, which in Peter's case culminated in imprisonment at St Peter and Paul's fortress on a small island on the Neva River at St Petersburg. Friends helped him to escape in June 1876 and thus begin his long exile until the February Revolution of 1917. In the 1900s, Kropotkin supported Mary's practical politics in the form of the National Labour Education League, turning out a pamphlet on its behalf.

Alexandra Kollontai first visited London in the summer of 1899 while she was attempting to educate herself in European working-class politics.[51] Her father was a general in the Tsar's army and she was educated at home but much influenced by her governess, who was a radical. In 1893 she married an engineer, against the wishes of her family, and the following year her son, Misha, was born. As her socialist convictions developed, family tensions increased. In 1898 she left her husband and son to study Marxist economics in Zurich, where she attended lectures at the university before travelling to Germany and England.

Following her return to Russia, Alexandra began underground political activity for the Russian Social Democrats and had to leave the country in 1908. In exile, she lived first in Berlin, where she joined the German Social Democratic Party. Her friends included Clara Zetkin, the leading theoretician of the socialist women's movement. She and Clara visited London in the spring of 1909 and Alexandra returned in 1912 to tackle the issue of maternity provision under the 1911 National Insurance Act. A six-month stay followed, between June and November 1913, to conduct research at the British Museum on her forthcoming book, *Society and Motherhood.* In this period, she and her friend Isa Persinnen, a Finnish socialist, attended some meetings on maternity insurance at Bebel House.[52] After the Bolsheviks seized power in November 1917,

Alexandra became People's Commissar for Social Welfare, making her the most prominent woman in the new Soviet administration.

Georgii Chicherin arrived in London some time after the German armies swept through Belgium. He received his education at a traditional classical gymnasium, thereafter graduating from St Petersburg University with a degree in history and languages. One of his closest school friends was Mikhail Kuzmin (b. 1872), Russia's first openly gay writer, on whom he had a major influence.[53] Their mutual interests included music, philosophy and the history of religion. Georgii spoke all the major European languages and a number of Asian ones. He entered the Foreign Office in 1895. Transferred to the Russian Embassy in Berlin in 1904, he joined the Menshevik faction of the Russian Social Democratic Party, resigned his post and renounced title to his estates. Forced to leave Germany, he was compelled to seek asylum in France. Here he went to Paris, where, under the pseudonym of Ornatsky, he devoted himself to party activities, working closely with the French socialists and the British Labour movement.

In London, Georgii became an active member of the Kentish Town branch of the BSP, as did fellow émigré Peter Petroff (b. 1884). In 1936 Petroff wrote Chicherin's obituary for *Labour*, in which he remembered 'an essentially human idealist, a man of high culture and many interests. Apart from politics, he took a great interest in literature and art, especially music. But in little matters of daily life he was unpractical and sometimes helpless as a child'.[54] After his conversion to socialism, Georgii rejected his past habitus, living a life of democratic manly comradeship as a vegetarian and teetotaller who dressed in tattered, worker's clothes. Whether by choice or design, he and Mary both lived in considerable squalor. His attic 'was damp and uncomfortable' and he lived amongst unmade beds, half-eaten food and piles of literature 'so high that they reached the window-ledge and so wide that you could barely pass between them and the table'.[55] His asceticism sometimes irritated Ivan Maisky, who could not see the need to relinquish fine clothes, food and wine for the sake of the cause.

For a long while, Mary had taught English to Russian political emigrants, and many refugees in difficulties had acquired the habit of turning to her for advice and assistance. When it came to his pacifist and relief activities, Georgii Chicherin was no exception. The Bebel House circle included political refugees and Ivan Maisky first met Mary in her role as Assistant Secretary of Georgii's committee for assisting political prisoners in Russia. The past and the present are interwoven in his memoirs through the juxtaposition of three London arrivals – in 1912, 1914 and 1932. In 1932, memory and imagination transport the newly appointed Soviet Ambassador to his youth. 'I wandered along through familiar scenes and places in the giant city and the people and happenings of days long gone by came to life again before my mind's eye.'

For Ivan, the British Museum Reading Room was 'library, study and mental laboratory' and Lyons Corner House the affordable space to which he escaped to eat his favourite meal of Welsh rarebit.[56] His characters include Alexandra Kollontai, 'a sort of bright, friendly flame which to some degree dispelled the gloom of our London life and to which we all went for a little warmth and encouragement'. He expresses a very low opinion of Mary, whom he remembers as a 'fervent suffragette who smashed shop windows and attacked Members of Parliament', suggesting that she was 'one of those English people who somehow fail to come to terms with life and so devote all their passion and determination to some "cause" which fires their imagination or touches their heart'.[57] This is the only evidence of Mary's using militant direct action, although Margaret Cole (b. 1893), historian of the Labour movement, journalist and author, told John Saville that she 'did just know Mrs Bridges Adams that suffrage termagant, but no more than that I'm afraid'.[58]

Ivan Maisky's assessment of Mary's character and contribution is a mixed bag of allegations and accusations, insults and implied criticism. Alexandra Kollontai was more generous. In August 1925 she wrote to Mary to explain why she had not come to visit when she was last in London:

> I was delaying the day, when I call on you and then left London more suddenly than I expected. I got your letter afterwards. You thought I was one of those, who forget old friendships and who do not know to value personal ties ... What could I answer? I felt I was wrong in not seeing you in London, and then – I know I could not have done it. So I just kept silent. But today I found your letter from the 24 May and I cannot help writing to you. You were always so good and kind to me. You were the real revolutionary comrade at the time, when many did not venture to know us. You went with us at the worst times ... and you have done great work. How can I forget all that? In the bottom of my heart I esteem you now, more than ever before and I feel the necessity of saying it to you frankly. But I feel you must have a bitter feeling against me. I understand it, but it hurts me. Dear, dear comrade! You have lived long enough to know people, one does not write such a letter – if one does not feel it![59]

Alexandra stresses how happy she would be to get a reply and how she hopes they will meet again. 'There is much that I would like to talk to you about. Farewell and believe me to be dear comrade, your old, old friend.'

In fact, Mary's longest political friendship was with someone from outside the 'family' of socialism. Driven by a fervent anti-clericalism, Lord Sheffield, as the Hon. Lyulph Stanley was styled after 1909, was educated at Eton College and a Fellow of Balliol College, Oxford. Although he helped his mother to raise funds for Girton College, Cambridge, until his late thirties he was only marginally involved in education.[60]

Mary and he first worked together as members of the LSB, where he was leader of the Progressive party. Elected for the Marylebone division in 1876, Lyulph held the seat until 1904, with one break (1885–88). A person renowned in local government circles for having a remarkable memory, his only lapse was to forget that a stove had already been placed in the corner of a particular school classroom that he suggested might be used for a 'museum cupboard'. Lyulph also had a phenomenal capacity for hard work. He would arrive at the school board offices at ten in the morning, having read 'masses of official papers and visited a couple of outlying schools' en route. Once there, he 'would sit continually on committee after committee, driving the business all the time, would go without his lunch and hastily swallow a cup of tea, and would still, even though he were in poor health, be toiling at seven or eight in the evening'.[61] Mary and Lyulph corresponded until his death. In defending her extreme political views in the House of Lords during the First World War, he described her as 'a keen politician. She takes great interest in English as well as foreign politics, in education questions, and in the extension of the system of public management as against private management of schools'.[62]

Mary engaged in socialist politics because she thought it possible to change the world. Her campaigns took her into the nooks and crannies of the Labour movement. If some thought she wasted her life supporting lost causes, others professed them 'the causes that make for a better future for the human race'.[63] In stark contrast to Ivan Maisky's sexist assessment of her contribution, Ron Grant suggests it was she, not Georgii Chicherin, who was the leading figure in their propagandist work that 'linked the causes of British and Russian workers in a way never seen before'. Neither one of them 'was a theoretician', nor was there a 'British equivalent of the Freikorps to provide a gory ending', but for him, 'Chicherin and Bridges Adams emerge as Britain's Liebknecht and Luxemburg'.[64] To achieve socialism, Mary saw the political way forward in terms of education, agitation and propaganda. The insights provided by group biography show the elements of another practice, a proletarian redefinition of formal politics that never happened but that remain in this spider's web of messy social positions and experiences.

Mary managed to make connections with Co-operation, New Unionism and Syndicalism, the ILP, the SDF, the SDP, the BSP and the Plebs League. She had links with radical Unitarian networks and Russian political emigrants. One enemy labelled Georgii Chicherin a 'graphomaniac', and Mary had the same capacity for hard work, always ready to unleash a polemic for the cause. In common with Mary also, the experience of Alexandra, Harry, John, Noah and Will indicates that their involvement in strikes was a turning point in their more active engagement with socialist politics. It shows also that there is no common pattern of politicisation. Mary's experience of organising around the relation between working-class culture and working-class politics in Woolwich influenced her distinctive propaganda style. Mary already identified herself with the cause of the working-class and was used to speaking in public as a qualified schoolteacher. In the autumn of 1894 she grasped the opportunity that the well-organised Woolwich Labour movement offered and stood unsuccessfully for the LSB. The next chapter will tell the Woolwich story.

Notes

1 J. Common, *Kiddar's Luck* (Newcastle: Bloodaxe Books, 1991), p. 136.
2 P.Y. Betts, *People Who Say Goodbye: memories of childhood* (London: Futura, 1991), p. 151.
3 W. Bridges Adams, *The Rights of Morality: state of society in England* (London: 1832), pp. 146–7.
4 W. Thorne, *My Life's Battles* (London: George Newnes, Ltd, 1926), p. 88.
5 Thorne, *My Life's Battles*, pp. 19–20.
6 W.S. Sanders, *Early Socialist Days* (London, 1927), p. 51.
7 Thorne, *My Life's Battles*, p. 35.
8 M. Savage, *The Dynamics of Working-Class Politics: the Labour movement in Preston, 1880–1940* (Cambridge: Cambridge University Press, 1987), p. 19.
9 Thorne, *My Life's Battles*, p. 13.
10 Quoted in E.A. Radice and G.H. Radice, *Will Thorne: constructive militant* (London: George Allen & Unwin Ltd, 1974), p. 50.
11 Quoted in Radice and Radice, *Will Thorne*, p. 59.
12 W.J. Brown, 'Open-air recovery schools', reprinted from *The Millgate*, in *Comradeship and the Wheatsheaf*, December 1933, p. xvi.
13 J. Hannam and K. Hunt, *Socialist Women Britain, 1880s to 1920s* (London: Routledge, 2002), p. 38.
14 J.R. Clynes, *Memoirs 1869–1924* (London: Hutchinson, 1937), p. 62.
15 Thorne, *My Life's Battles*, p. 219; Radice and Radice, *Will Thorne*, p. 73.

16 C. Griggs, *The Trades Union Congress and the Struggle for Education 1868–1925* (Lewes: Falmer Press, 1983), p. 16.

17 Gas Workers' and General Labourers' Union, Quarterly Balance Sheets, General Secretary's Report for quarter ending 29 December, 1906, p. 5.

18 W.P. McCann, 'Trade unionist, co-operative and socialist organisations in relation to popular education, 1870-1902', unpublished PhD thesis, University of Manchester, p. 423 citing private information from Mr William Bridges-Adams.

19 J. Jacobs, *London Trades Council 1860–1950* (London: Lawrence and Wishart, 1950), p. 71.

20 TUC Lib., London Trades Council Minute Books, 14 June 1894; 25 June 1896; 3 February 1898; 12 July 1900; 24 April 1902; 30 April 1903; 10 March 1904; 13 December 1906; 11 November 1907.

21 D. Englander, *The Diary of Fred Knee* (Warwick: Society for the Study of Labour History, 1977), pp. 12, 35.

22 Englander, *Diary of Fred Knee*, pp. 7–8.

23 S. Pankhurst, *The Suffragette Movement* (London: Virago, 1977 edition.), p. 158.

24 L. Thompson, *The Enthusiasts: a biography of John and Katherine Bruce Glasier* (Littlehampton: Littlehampton Book Service, 1971).

25 Macdonald, James (1857–1938), in J.M. Bellamy and J. Saville (eds), *Dictionary of Labour Biography* (Macmillan: Basingstoke, 1987), pp. 143–7.

26 *The Reformers' Year Book* (formerly the *Labour Annual*) (Manchester, Labour Press Society; London, The Clarion and the New Age Press, 1897–1910); 'The movement', *Justice*, 25 July 1908, p. 10.

27 Bridges Adams Papers, Bakhmeteff Materials: Folder 6, arranged correspondence A–W; Folder 9, Mary Bridges Adams appointment schedule, receipts.

28 Details taken from D. Clark, *Victor Grayson: Labour's lost leader* (London: Quartet Books, 1985); R. Groves, *The Strange Case of Victor Grayson* (London: Pluto Press, 1975) and D. Marquand, *Ramsay MacDonald* (London: Jonathan Cape, 1977), pp. 106–8, 111–12, 114.

29 Clark, *Victor Grayson*, p. 16.

30 Clark, *Victor Grayson*, p. 41.

31 'A victory for the children', *Justice*, 27 July 1907, p. 4.

32 'Campaign against child labour', *Justice*, 7 December 1907, p. 10; biographical details on Irving from M. Crick, *The History of the Social Democratic Federation* (Keele: Ryburn Publishing, 1994) p. 308.

33 'Feed the children, public meeting in Queen's Hall, Langham Place', *Justice*, 25 January 1908, p. 1.

34 J.R. MacDonald to Mrs Bridges Adams, 13 September 1899.

35 H. McShane and J. Smith, *Harry McShane No Mean Fighter* (London: Pluto Press, 1977), p. 37.

36 Groves, *Strange Case*, p. 90.

37 R. Smalley, 'The life and work of Ethel Carnie Holdsworth with particular

reference to the period 1907 to 1931' (University of Lancashire PhD, 2006), p. 47; P. Fox, *Class Fictions: shame and resistance in the British working class novel, 1890–1945* (Durham and London: Duke University Press, 1994), p. 153.
38 E. Carnie, 'The home life of factory workers', *Woman Worker*, 24 March 1909, p. 270.
39 E. and R. Frow, 'Ethel Carnie: writer, feminist and socialist', in H. Gustav Klaus (ed.), *The Rise of Socialist Fiction 1880–1914* (Sussex: Harvester Press, 1987), p. 264.
40 D. Smith, *Aneurin Bevan and the World of South Wales* (Cardiff: University of Wales Press, 1993), pp. 74, 75, 83, 201.
41 *Cotton Factory Times*, 30 June 1916.
42 *Cotton Factory Times*, 9 November 1917.
43 For biographical details on John Maclean, see B.J. Ripley and J. McHugh, *John Maclean* (Manchester: Manchester University Press, 1989).
44 I. MacDougall, *Militant Miners* (Edinburgh, Polygon: 1981), p. 11.
45 McShane and Smith, *Harry McShane*, p. 54.
46 McShane and Smith, *Harry McShane*, p. 7.
47 McShane and Smith, *Harry McShane*, p. 25.
48 M. Savage, *Dynamics of Working-Class Politics*, pp. 41–63.
49 R. Grant, 'G.V. Chicherin and the Russian revolutionary cause in Great Britain', in J. Slatter (ed.) *From the Other Shore: Russian political emigrants in Britain, 1880–1917* (London: Frank Cass, 1984), p. 119.
50 Cited in: I. Maisky, *Journey into the Past*, translated from the Russian by Felix Holt (London: Hutchinson, 1962), p. 113.
51 Details taken from C. Porter, *Alexandra Kollontai: a biography* (London: Virago, 1980).
52 Porter, *Alexandra Kollontai*, p. 192.
53 J.E. Malmstad and N. Bogomolov, *Mikhail Kuzmin: a life in art* (Harvard: Harvard University Press, 1999).
54 P. Petroff, 'George Tchitcherin', *Labour*, Vol. 3, No. 12, August 1936, p. 306.
55 Maisky, *Journey into the Past*, p. 73.
56 Maisky, *Journey into the Past*, pp. 29, 9, 10, 94.
57 Maisky, *Journey into the Past*, p. 75.
58 HUA, M. Cole to John Saville, 25 September 1976.
59 A. Kollontai to Mary Bridges Adams, 18 August 1925.
60 A.W. Jones, *Lyulph Stanley: a study in educational politics* (Waterloo, Ontario: Wilfred Laurier Press, 1979).
61 G. Wallas, *Men and Ideas* (London: George Allen and Unwin, 1940), p. 83.
62 Parliamentary Debates, House of Lords, Wednesday 7 March 1917, pp. 406–7.
63 *Yorkshire Factory Times*, 6 January 1916.
64 Grant, 'G.V. Chicherin', p. 134.

3

Labour politics in London

> The "Woolwich Pioneer" comes to utter the voice of the Labour Movement of Woolwich. To fulfill its end it must not be the utterance of a single editor, or of a group of journalists, earning their living by expressing their own thoughts or exploiting their own personality. It must be the voice of all in Woolwich who work, all who hope, all who care for the ideals which have given birth to labour movement after movement in the past and the Labour Representation movement of to-day. (*Woolwich Pioneer*, 1904)[1]

Socialist Woolwich

This is how the Woolwich Labour Party carried its propaganda to the locality as it launched its own journal in the autumn of 1904. The proclamation captures the great upsurge which sustained a strong political culture and provided the backdrop to Mary's entry in London politics. She lived in the district known as Westcombe, from which the ribbons of house building linked eastwards to Woolwich, still something of a market town located on the south bank of the river Thames. Mary flourished in such surroundings and quickly emerged as a significant figure. Active as a propagandist and eagerly putting forward her particular interpretations of events and issues, it was not long before she had the opportunity to put the ideas and arguments of social democracy before the electorate. A year after settling in the district, she took little persuading to stand for organised labour in the Greenwich division of the LSB, which included the parliamentary seats of Deptford, Greenwich, Lewisham and Woolwich.

This chapter is a companion piece to chapter 2 in that it takes up again the issue of networks. In this case, the emphasis is on a culture of progressive improvement, party politics and constituency organisation in late-Victorian Woolwich, which was peculiar in being a working-class community, dependent on the dockyard, Arsenal and military barracks. The separate studies of Paul Thompson and Paul Tyler have shown how these factors provided a basis for the emergence of independent working-class politics in the locality, while Kim Yoonak Stenberg suggests that they also encouraged the full, if not equal, participation of women, and political couples were the norm in Woolwich.[2] Not one of them mentions Mary, possibly because elections to the school boards receive less attention than those for municipal bodies and the boards of guardians. I argue that Mary's role, notably when she stood successfully for the LSB in 1897 and 1900, contributed to the building of the Woolwich Labour Party and, in the longer run, the London Labour Party. Therefore, her involvement in political life needs situating in this context.

In Woolwich, Mary found a powerful kind of political organisation, rooted in the local social structure. The major employers were the Royal Arsenal, the Dockyard, the cable works of Siemens Brothers and G.A. Harvey, engineers. In 1901, when the Arsenal had added importance thanks to the Boer War, the whole population, including soldiers in the barracks, was just under 131,000. Of this figure, twenty thousand were male Arsenal workers, mainly skilled artisans who reaped the benefit of relatively stable employment combined with higher and more regular earnings. As Charles Booth reported, they were 'such as save and buy their own houses in Plumstead, and live comfortably; a selection, and not the ruck; men with a trade, not labourers; men who earn good wages and spend them on their homes and wives and children'.[3] Like most military towns, Woolwich had a surfeit of public houses, but there was a relative absence of desperate poverty. Growing up in households with a higher standard of living than the generality of the working class enabled some children of Woolwich artisans to seize the social and educative opportunities available to them. An average of 5 per cent of the borough's elementary school population won scholarships, whereas in London as a whole the figure was less than 3 per cent.[4]

Railways came to the borough in 1849 and, since the Thames passenger steamboats had ceased, they were the only means of communication with the built-up London area. Yellow horse-drawn trams lit by oil lamps moved people between Greenwich and Plumstead, and the opening of the Blackwall Tunnel in May 1897 helped coordinate and mobilise activity across the Thames.[5] Many North Country and Scottish artisans migrated to work there and Woolwich became associated with a strong trade unionism, which was a rarity for London. The Amalgamated Society of Engineers (ASE) alone had eight Woolwich branches with two thousand members and socialist influence was evident among the Engineers, who had grown more militant in the wake of technical change, including the introduction of American methods of work timing.

Highly motivated individuals helped to found the Royal Arsenal Co-operative Society (RACS), which fostered a spirit of self-improvement and provided a forum for those socialists willing to participate in its activities. Engineers made up the core of the male membership. Their union encouraged thrift and mutual help, and a tradition of popular learning formed an essential part of the borough's social fabric.[6] Museums and exhibitions, choral and orchestral societies, amateur dramatics and a growing number of parks all provided opportunities for 'improving' recreation. Reading rooms and discussion groups flourished and a counter-culture to the materialism of Victorian capitalism evolved. Collective occupational and associational cultures in the wider community contributed to the development of class consciousness.

This, then, was the background against which the stalwarts of the *Woolwich Pioneer* were planning for success, and men and women alike played their part in this development. Woolwich Trades Council connected the industrial and political wings of the Labour movement, which became the leading labour political force in the borough. By the mid 1890s activists from near and far had settled in the borough, which proved fertile ground for the ILP, the SDF and the Socialist League. When Mary entered the scene, the community accepted and supported her activism, which often depended on the assistance of women friends and neighbours not themselves involved in active campaigning.

The Royal Arsenal Co-operative Society

The area had a long tradition of co-operation. As early as 1760, a co-operative corn mill was established which prospered for eighty years. From then on, there were numerous initiatives, the largest being the Woolwich Co-operative Provident Society founded by dockyard workers in 1851. The Royal Arsenal Supply Association, which became the RACS, emerged from a meeting of the Woolwich branch of the ASE, in 1868.[7] The man who proposed it was William Rose (b. 1843), a tool room worker in the shell foundry at the Arsenal. It attracted twenty people who each pledged to buy a £1 share. William became secretary and agreed to run a co-operative shop from a room in his house, gradually aiming to increase the range of goods for sale. When unemployment forced him to emigrate to Canada in 1869, the fledgling Society had taken on rented space and was operating extended opening hours. Another key figure was Alexander McLeod (b. 1832), a mechanical engineer from Fife in Scotland. Serving as the Society's first chair, he and his wife worked hard to promote its growth in the 1870s. After her sudden death in 1878, he left the Arsenal to become its first full-time secretary and paid member of staff. By 1900, the Society had six retail stores, one bakery, one bank, a boot and shoe works, a building department, two farms stabling seventy horses, a tailors' workshop and a fleet of sixty-five delivery vans.

Early Woolwich co-operators located themselves squarely within older working-class values of equity and solidarity. Typically, RACS members ranged across the spectrum in terms of why they became co-operators. For most, the level of the dividend was an important factor. A handful of activists seized upon ideas emanating from Christian Socialist and co-operator Edward Vansittart Neale (b. 1810) and/or from Edward Owen Greening (b. 1836), who lived in south London at the time and imported the outlook of Robert Owen (b. 1771). Owenite socialism nourished a radical agenda, advocating a new economic and social order which stressed co-operation and harmony rather than competition and discord. Owen thought the environment shaped personality and behaviour, and the classless, co-operative community represented the ideal circumstance for the development of happy and moral lives. Asserting ideals of self-reliance and independence, the co-operation of the RACS reflected attachment to the Owenite desire to change the world, alongside the preoccupations with the practical details of its trading operations.

Although the ideal of a communal society free of every inequality, including sexual inequality, found voice within the co-operative movement, men and women had different experiences. In theory, co-operative societies (retail shops) ran on democratic lines, allocating one vote to each member and distributing their trading surplus as a dividend proportional to purchases. In practice, generally mother shopped at the co-op stores and collected the 'divi', while father held the membership of the society. Female membership of the RACS stood at nearly 40 per cent, the stores were dependent on the loyalty of the working-class homemaker for their survival and growth, but conventional gender roles often shaped actually existing co-operation in the Society. Nonetheless, the female co-operators who figure in this chapter contested women's marginality in the movement. Like the 'typical guildswoman' sketched by Gill Scott, they were married, of the skilled working-class, in their middle age and not in paid employment.[8] Determined to ensure that co-operative claims of equality should not remain empty rhetoric, they mobilised the language of social motherhood to contest elections to school boards, boards of guardians and, once women were eligible (in 1907), to the local councils.

The best-known example of this was Mary Lawrenson (b. 1850), founder of the Woolwich WCG. Shaped by a culture and a politics of working-class association that stretched back through her father, a local printer active in the trade union and co-operative movements, she attempted to enlist public support for her ideas. A teacher prior to her marriage to a government clerk, with whom she had one son, she shared her father's faith in a fusion of Roman Catholicism and Christian Socialism. In February 1883 she responded to a request for 'co-operative mothers meetings' in the 'Women's Corner' section of the *Co-operative News*. The WCG emerged from this proposal. Lawrenson established the Woolwich guild with twenty-two members in December 1883, the second of three founded nationally during that year. Branches at Charlton, Erith and Plumstead swiftly followed, each with a base in the community served by the retail store. Two more started in the 1890s but the Plumstead Guild became the strongest. Occupying a position on the RACS Education Committee, in 1885 Lawrenson became Guild leader. Nonetheless, her avowal of philanthropic work and adherence to the co-operative movement's formal neutrality towards party politics was unpopular. Internal conflicts culminated in her resignation as Woolwich branch secretary in 1885 and from the Education Committee in 1888. She had only limited involvement with Woolwich guildswomen thereafter.[9]

Lawrenson's successor as Guild leader in 1889 was Margaret Llewellyn Davies (b. 1861). The niece of Emily Davies (b. 1830), one of the first women members of the LSB and co-founder of Girton College, Cambridge, she learned her political lessons at a young age. Margaret was a proponent of a larger role for women within the Co-operative movement, supporting their claims to undertake educational and political work. What struck Mrs Layton (b. 1855), a guildswoman who entered domestic service at the age of 10, was the contrast between the Mothers Meetings she attended 'where ladies came and lectured on the domestic affairs in the workers' homes' and those of the Guild. 'From a shy, nervous woman, the Guild made me a fighter. I was always willing to go on a Deputation if there was a wrong to be righted or for any good cause, local or national.'[10] Her view was similar to that of Marion Deans (b. about 1854). The daughter of a nurse who married a fellow co-operator, the mother of four had been an elementary schoolteacher prior to marriage. President of the Plumstead Guild, she combined involvement in co-operation with roles in the Midwives' Registration Association and the State Children's Association. Marion served on the RACS Education Committee between 1896 and 1902, subsequently becoming a Labour member of Plumstead Board of Guardians.[11]

Therefore, Mary's activities as a co-operator were not without precedent in the RACS. Given the presence of such formidable co-workers, the woman local co-operators referred to as 'Mrs Adams of Westcombe' must have been a dynamic force. She bursts onto the scene in the autumn of 1894, when the RACS asked her to chair one of a series of lectures organised in conjunction with the Co-operative Union for education and propaganda purposes.[12] Having joined the Woolwich Guild, she helped other branches to run meetings, contributing to the activities with lectures on adult education and the school board.[13]

In 1878 the RACS decided to use a proportion of its profits to finance educational work. This was usual in the larger societies and the amount allocated, 2.5 per cent of net trading surplus, was what the movement recommended. John Attfield's study, *With Light of Knowledge*, suggests that the setting up of the Education Department was an ambitious attempt to raise the status of the RACS.[14] It was a step that made the RACS one of the most advanced co-operative societies in England, one that Christian Socialists considered a shining example of one run in accordance with their belief that material conditions govern moral well-being.

Engineers dominated the early membership of the RACS Education Committee – men like Arsenal engineer John Arnold (b. 1837), its first chair, who spent several years on the executive committee of the ASE. John agreed with Robert Owen when he said the unequal distribution of property had as its foundation the unequal distribution of knowledge, and promoted co-operation as a vehicle for the emancipation of the working classes. Self-improvement came first, but he tapped into a language of moral regeneration, urging co-operators to link co-operation to collective change, with socialism. Building the collective via self-education could and did aid social mobility, of course. For example, Alexander McLeod and William Rose studied geography at evening classes together in the 1860s, when a degree of cultural 'tone' could smooth the path to promotion in the Arsenal. In 1879, the Education Committee opened its first public library. Members also devoted considerable energy to promoting adult education classes in conjunction with the Working Men's College and Toynbee Hall, the first men's university settlement house in London's East End, which became a centre for social investigation and a training place for public service.

In October 1897 the RACS Education Committee launched a local newspaper, *Comradeship*, under the editorship of Charles Grinling (b. 1860). He trained as a social worker at Toynbee Hall before working as a curate in Nottingham, where he attracted the wrath of the church hierarchy because he criticised the low wages and poor working conditions of Nottingham's women lace workers. In the aftermath, socialists sought him out, and he met Harry Snell (b. 1865), the son of agricultural workers, who was 8 years old when he started work in the fields and 12 when he left home and stood for hire in the marketplace at Newark-on-Trent. Charles's influence was such that the young man redoubled his efforts to acquire an education against the odds, espousing the belief that a person should prepare themself 'for political and social work with as much diligence and care as for any other of life's duties'.[15]

Charles moved to Woolwich in 1889 to become secretary of the Charity Organisation Society (COS). There he established important political relationships with reforming clergy who opposed the pure doctrine of the 1834 Poor Law to withhold relief that did not make the recipient self-supporting. The chairman of the Woolwich committee was a Christian Socialist and he brought a socialist curate, also connected with Toynbee Hall, with him. Charles was set on Harry Snell's joining him, and on Good Friday 1890 Snell set off for Woolwich on his bicycle. Nonetheless, their support and Charles's obvious ability could not prevent a clash with the COS leadership and his dismissal for his unorthodox approach to social reform. The interventions of Reverend Horsley, a vigorous campaigner for sanitary reform and Labour Poor Law Guardian probably helped Harry Snell avoid the same fate, but he left his post soon after, unable to tolerate the severe orthodoxy imposed after Charles Grinling's departure.

Charles Grinling believed in Woolwich 'as a laboratory of the Labour Movement' and the improving spirit was a keynote of his life.[16] The extent of his influence should not be underestimated. During the 1890s he would go on to organise University Extension Classes in the locality, as well as Sunday meetings in his rooms on Woolwich Common 'to read, at one period Browning, at another Walt Whitman'.[17] He gave credence to local co-operative education, helping to maintain the RACS libraries and reading rooms. The Society's magazine prospered, winning praise from Peter Kropotkin. Charles's first editorial propagated its objectives. *Comradeship* 'will proclaim the gospel of social equity and industrial peace', he wrote, encouraging all 'to enter in, to take part in the government, to enjoy equal share in the fruits of labour and the love of the pioneers of the past, and to earn the gratitude of the Woolwich of the future as its pioneers of the present'.[18] His successor as editor was Gilbert Slater (b. 1864), an economics lecturer at Woolwich Polytechnic. Like Charles, he was a past resident of Toynbee Hall and a cultural outsider. The son of a schoolteacher, he returned to teach in his home town of Plymouth after a

Cambridge education. There he maintained an association with socialism triggered by having heard Henry Hyndman and William Morris address the Cambridge Union. An energetic and effective advocate of the Gas Workers' struggle for the eight-hour day and a founder member of the local branch of the Fabian Society, he campaigned in local elections but failed to become a member of Plymouth School Board.[19]

I have paid attention to these personalities to suggest the vitality of a broader working-class culture that fed into the transition from co-operation to the primacy of independent labour representation at the turn of the nineteenth century. Making socialism a living reality was a way of life in Woolwich. It was necessary first, to make socialists, and the ILPers who came to enjoy prominent positions in a number of the important borough organisations used the activities of the RACS Education Committee to further raise workers' consciousness. Nearly every item on the Woolwich Labour movement's internal agenda attempted this task of cultural 'elevation': a collective bootstrap-pulling operation on a grand scale. Mary wanted to push the RACS in a socialist direction, but for her, political activity entailed no breach with the world of family and community. In common with other migrants to the area, she had a vision of Utopia and shared enthusiasm for the self-improving possibilities of her spatial location. At this stage in her political career she belonged to the ILP and the modes of socialist thought and feeling that were relevant to her are recognisable as being connected with the sentimental Walt Whitman–Edward Carpenter-ethical society tendency. As studies of her socialist contemporaries suggest, local factors were significant in shaping political affiliations.[20]

New Unionism

Craft unionism remained important, but New Unionism touched Woolwich. The organising principle was that of mass recruitment and Will Thorne's Gas Workers sought to attract as wide a membership as possible with a low subscription of 'tuppence' a week. According to Thorne, news of the foundation 'spread like wildfire; in the public houses, factories and works, in Canning Town, Barking, East and West Ham, everyone was talking about the union'.[21] At a co-operative conference addressed by Gertrude Tuckwell (b. 1861), secretary of the Women's Trade Union League and editor of its journal, the *Women's Trade Union Review*, much of the discussion turned on whether women should join mixed unions or form their own unions. Mary expressed an earnest desire to see women become members of the Gas Workers 'and then get others to join'.[22]

In the wider arena of London politics, party organisations steadily increased their grip. From the 1880s, two main groupings contested municipal elections. The Moderate Party, allied with the Anglican clergy and the Conservative associations, versus the Progressives, who included all shades of liberal opinion, later fortified by the socialist groups. As exemplified in Woolwich, the main centres for working-class politics were the recently established radical clubs. This changed with a lecture series on industrial history and socialist economics by Bernard Shaw. Former engineer William Barefoot (b. 1872) appeared to believe that the working-class politics he describes in the 'official' history to commemorate twenty-five years of the Woolwich Labour Party originated at this point.[23]

Incoming activists opened up the party's development. Scotsman Robert Banner (b. 1855) provides an illustrative example. A teetotal bookbinder from Edinburgh, Robert was inducted into the socialist movement by Andreas Scheu (b. 1844), an Austrian furniture designer. Robert joined the Democratic Federation when it only had around two hundred members and followed Andreas to London. One of the few socialists to have read the writing of Karl Marx, Robert was renowned for his library and occupied a post as one of the original governors of Woolwich Polytechnic. In 1884 he was on the SDF executive, but resigned together with Walter Bridges Adams, Eleanor Marx and William Morris (among others) to found the Socialist League. He found it hard to attend meetings, due to unemployment, but became a respected figure in the Woolwich Radical Club, where Shaw took classes and was making the Club a focus for his propaganda.[24] Looking back, Harry Snell remembered 'a widely read man, a Marxian in economics and in politics an out-and-out social democrat'. Robert's knowledge of Marx led Henry Hyndman to describe him as the 'workman economist'. Edward Thompson asserted that he was 'exceptionally gifted'.[25] Robert involved himself in the struggle for independent labour representation through the formation of Woolwich Trades Council in 1893, which quickly came to occupy an important place in the neighbourhood with three thousand affiliated members, including two of the radical clubs.

Within the RACS, Marion Deans and Charles Grinling were among the would-be leaders, believing that co-operation must link up with the wider socialist movement. To this end, in 1897 the Society carried the resolution, put by trade unionist activist James Turnbull (b. 1835), 'That in the opinion of this meeting, the time has arrived when the RACS in conjunction with the various working men's organisations and the Trades

Council of the district, should take a more active part in municipal affairs, and the Society hereby invites the co-operation of its members in supporting any action in this direction.'[26] Turnbull helped build up the Plumstead Progressive Association, serving as a Progressive vestryman and later as Labour councillor.[27]

Meanwhile, the Woolwich branch of the ILP began publishing monthly *Labour Notes*, edited by William Barefoot, secretary of Woolwich Trades Council. Three thousand free copies were distributed and William presented the argument for unity. 'Although occasionally one meets the enthusiast who dogmatically affirms that by adopting his particular method would be found the panacea for all ills, a growing majority are realising that only by combined action can we hope to successfully combat the terrible evils with which we are today confronted.'[28] Within the year Robert Banner was secretary of a newly formed Progressive Association, succeeded by a Labour Representation Association with Charles Grinling as its chair, and finally by Woolwich Labour Party. In 1903 William Barefoot resigned from his engineering post to become its first full-time secretary.[29]

The presence of working-class politics and organisation in the district provided a cadre of local activists who could orchestrate protest. During this period, the regular Sunday morning meetings at the Arsenal Gates in Beresford Square were vital in the battle to secure Labour's breakthrough.

2 Beresford Gate, Woolwich

The main speakers were Robert Banner and Harry Snell, who captured the tremendous political optimism.

> Our enthusiasm was intense, and our faith in Socialism was untouched by knowledge of the administrative and other difficulties in the path of its speedy realisation. Sufficient unto the day was the faith and our devotion to it. The campaign was more like a religious revival than a political agitation, and the singing of labour hymns at every meeting contributed to the feeling that we were the pioneers of a new faith.[30]

The object of outdoor meetings was to transmit ideas more broadly at the community level. Most important was the desire to build the collective, as opinion leaders lashed their opponents from the huge platform in front of the monumental Victorian gateway to the Royal Arsenal. Of tremendous symbolism to their audience, on weekdays the space thronged with shoppers at the daily market, which ran from 5 a.m. to 9 p.m. and, unlike less busy thoroughfares, enjoyed the benefit of gas lighting.

School Board candidate

Mary's candidature was the product of this crusading atmosphere. Representatives of the Labour movement asked her to contest the 1894 triennial election to the LSB and she accepted their nomination. She also enjoyed the backing of the London Nonconformist Council. Her election address went beyond the standard labour education programme of the period, with its support for the provision of universal education and free school meals. Consequently, the editor of the *Blackheath Gazette*, an arch-opponent of socialism, raised doubts about her suitability and questioned her 'special claims' on the electorate. One of her supporters, a letter writer named 'Justitia', responded to the criticisms. 'Justitia' stressed Mary's support base among local parents and ended with the heartfelt plea, 'I sincerely hope all your readers will vote, not for the man who promised to keep down the rates, but for the woman who pledges herself to see that we get our money's worth in the shape of a well-fed, well-taught, enlightened and healthy population'.[31]

Speaking at mass demonstrations and public meetings, Mary used her oratorical powers to whip up people's emotions. For example, she tried to make political capital out of public money being spent on 'extravagances', like a gold key for the royal opening of a new elementary school, when Board members refused to buy heating apparatus for a truant school bath. In reply to questions, she urged the appointment of more workers as school managers, and greater use of school buildings as community spaces. Using the words, meanings and ideas of the respectable working class, she expressed disapproval 'of young mothers being School Board teachers, believing that home was the best place for them'.[32]

From press accounts, Mary appears to have communicated her ideas from mass platforms using a self-selective language of acceptability. However, it ought to be emphasised that her endorsement of state maintenance for children set her apart from the ILP on one point. This was the question of who was responsible for bearing the cost. She believed that the state should bear the full cost of feeding all children whose parents wanted them fed. This was the SDF position and Greenwich Progressives were showing signs of worry, as an incident at a campaign meeting for wealthy nonconformist solicitor and father of seven Henry Gover (b. about 1835) and John Wilson (b. 1854), pastor at the Woolwich Baptist Tabernacle, shows.[33] One interrupter shouted out in Mary's favour, saying 'free meals for school children were more important than taking part in theological discussions'. John Wilson, who regularly preached to over eighteen hundred people, responded with a condemnation of the interruptions, which, he claimed, broke a promise to 'leave himself and Mr Gover alone'.[34] When Mary's youthful supporters resorted to heckling at a Moderate meeting, the hapless chair told people to give their names during question time, at which point the audience 'convulsed' with laughter as a 'Mr Orange Blossom' gave way to a 'Mr Key' (with a question about the aforementioned gold key) and to another who quipped 'Young's the name I rejoice in'.[35] Mary addressed outdoor meetings at Deptford, Greenwich, Woolwich and Penge. One of the Dockers' organisers, Irish-born Tom McCarthy, spoke on her behalf, as did Mary Lawrenson and Enid Stacy. Although narrowly defeated, she secured strong labour support and a highly respectable poll. This was in stark contrast to the performance of the socialist men in the county council elections the following month.[36]

Within the year, Henry Gover was dead. The longest serving member of the LSB, with a 'deep interest in the teachers', he had been a Greenwich representative for twenty-two years.[37] Mary's supporters moved swiftly, determined to see her inherit the seat. The correspondence pages of the School Board Minutes show that branches of the Engineers, the Gas Workers, the ILP and the Labour Protection League all pressed her claim, as did the educational council of Plumstead Radical Club and Woolwich Trades Council. Undoubtedly the letter from the South Woolwich branch of the Gas Workers was heartfelt. In its opinion, 'Mrs Bridges Adams, from her learning, great scholastic experience, lucidity of thought and expression, aptness of resource and charm of presence would add distinction to the Board. She had the full support, during the last Election of all the Labour Bodies, and polled the largest number of votes of any defeated candidate'.[38]

Board members refused to bow to external pressure, however. In contravention of established protocol, Greenwich representatives proposed the co-option of Progressive lawyer George Warmington (b. about 1845), who had recently suffered defeat at the polls in Lewisham.[39] Members voted for him by thirty-four to one (the dissentient explained his error) and the *Labour Leader* commented angrily on how the established parties closed ranks.

> On the question of keeping a socialist out they troop solidly into the same lobby, with the exception of the misapprehension. Where was Mr Stewart Headlam? And where, oh where, was Graham Wallas, the wild-eyed Fabian revolutionist? The first public meeting that the Rev. John Wilson attends in Greenwich School Board division will be attended by a few Independent Labour Party members and they will put it to him in a plain manner and he will be invited to explain.[40]

Months previous, Mary had been a topic for discussion at a Fabian dinner party. Having concluded that she and Graham Wallas (b. 1858) should meet, Bernard Shaw rather patronisingly offered his services as an intermediary. 'He will tell you and me what he thinks he thinks, and then I can tell you what *I* think he thinks.'[41] Her response may have been unprintable, but the Woolwich Labour movement had the organisation and the political conviction to answer back.

Sponsored by a Progressive Election Committee, Mary again contested the Greenwich seat. James Turnbull and Progressive Poor Law Guardian Dr Albert Lindow (b. about 1864) were among those who signed her nomination papers, while she also received financial support from the RACS.[42] The general secretary of the Labour Protection League, formed among stevedores in the London docks, was among those who endorsed her campaign. He contended 'that Mrs Adams, because of her past experience as a teacher in the schools and her knowledge of the labour movement and of educational work, was one of the most suitable Candidates to represent the division and he trusted everyone on the side of progress would register four votes for her'. Social Democrats were prominent in the campaign, notably Eleanor Marx and the internationalist Joseph Frederick Green (b. 1855), treasurer of the SDF and editor of *Free Russia*. He asked electors to vote for her because she was a woman and 'they had too few women on the Board'. He also stressed her educational credentials, saying 'few Candidates had had so great an experience as a teacher and that she was a long friend of the cause of labour'.[43] The momentum was high and Mary won cheers when she maintained that 'it was the theological explanations and the theological explainer and not the Bible that she would abolish', further commenting that 'she did not believe in the cheap and nasty in the education of the children'.[44]

These months were deeply troubled, with the Engineers in the midst of a desperate struggle to win the eight-hour day, following the national lockout of July 1897[45] William Barefoot took on a leadership role as treasurer of a local strike committee and Mary was quick to offer the strikers her support. On one occasion she addressed a crowd of around two thousand people in Beresford Square following a street parade involving the fife and drum bands of two local schools.[46] Shortly afterwards, she and Will Thorne spoke at a mass rally in Siemens' Field. Moving a resolution of sympathy with the men:

> She said this was largely a woman's question and if it was true that the men had been brave, it was also true that the women had not been cowards. She urged the men to be patient with their wives in a time of terrible struggle, for though it might be hard for men to stand about the streets with no work to do, it was ten thousand times harder to women to have to make ends meet ... Let them stand shoulder to shoulder and show sympathy with their wives and children.[47]

Ultimately, the tactics of the lockout, the use of ex-policemen as counter-pickets and blackleg labour from the provinces helped the employers to crush the strongest of the craft societies. In January 1898 the Engineers accepted defeat.

Mary, on the other hand, scored a notable victory. There had been strong opposition to her candidature, but her supporters made full use of the method of voting, a cumulative vote, which was different from that used in local council elections. This method allowed voters in a multi-member constituency to plump for just one candidate and had the effect of increasing the chances of election of Labour movement candidates. The figures show that over 77 per cent of those who voted for Mary gave her all four of their votes. Therefore, she was able to oust a Moderate to become the first Labour woman to represent Greenwich.[48] By her own account she 'was successfully returned upon a purely educational programme as the only Labour member of the present Board, when at the time she was quite unknown in the district to any but workers and possessed neither influence nor money'.[49]

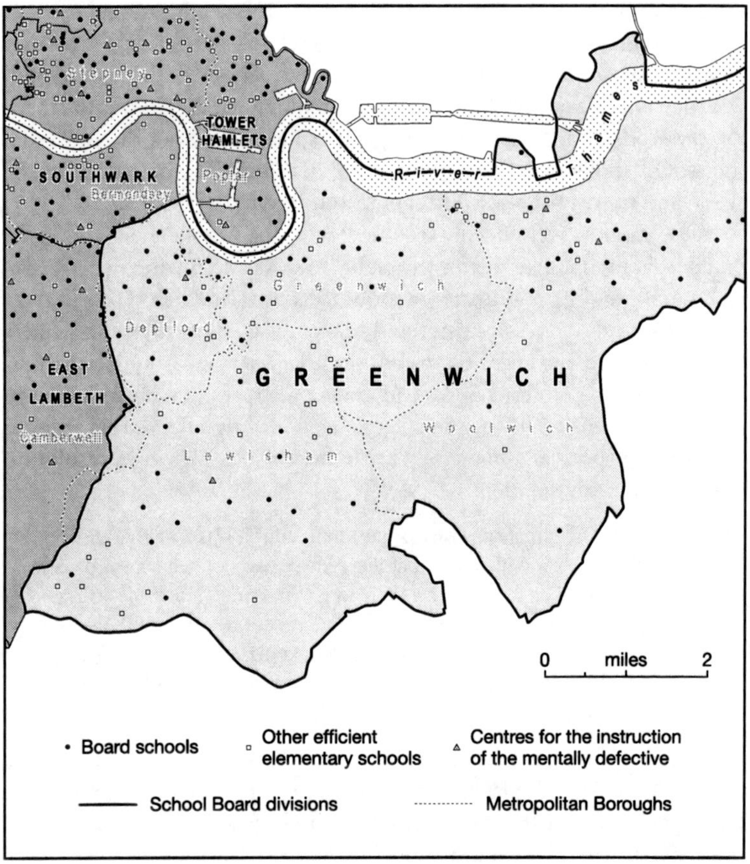

3 School Board for London map

Socialist campaigner

Having proved in practice that working-class people were interested in education, Mary took the battle for radical ideas to middle-class philanthropists. Invited to give a talk at the Women's Institute attached to the newly opened Grosvenor Club for Women in London's Hyde Park, she elaborated proposals to alleviate the class hatred that she claimed existed among working-class Londoners. The basic idea was for 'well-to-do women' to become residents 'in these poor districts and make themselves comrades and friends of their less fortunate fellows'.[50] Subsequently she used the pages of the feminist periodical, *Shafts*, to launch an appeal for funds to enable her to develop a non-denominational women's philanthropic settlement house among the 'labouring population' of Greenwich. Sunday lectures and concerts, baths and art exhibitions were among the planned activities and she called for 'cultivated women' to put themselves forward as managers of the ten local board schools in her charge. Perhaps she had the example of Marion Deans, already a school manager in Plumstead, in mind here. Emanating from and responsive to community networks, the object was to expand educational opportunities for women.[51]

Mary also set about organising an exhibition, concert series and art classes to provide 'Art for the Workers', with help from Jewish artist Felix Moscheles (b. 1833). An approving Trades Council noted her achievement 'in securing the help and sympathy of a number of well known people' in the art world. Walter Crane (b. 1845), then Britain's leading socialist artist, opened the event, also attended by Royal Academician Val Prinsep (b. 1838) and sculptor Hamo Thorneycroft (b. 1850), at Woolwich Polytechnic on Saturday 22 July 1899.[52] Mary and Moscheles coordinated a consultative committee that included Daisy Warwick and her sister, Millicent, Duchess of Sutherland (b. 1867). Like her elder sibling, Millicent was a society beauty and social reformer. For example, the previous year she had set up the Potteries and Newcastle Cripples Guild to provide medical treatment to children and to instruct children in a trade or craft.[53] Several RACS members were involved, notably Plumstead engineer and father of five James Steer (b. about 1858) of Woolwich Trades Council.[54]

Housing was another area of concern that Mary shared with RACS educational activists like John Arnold, who were optimistic of what the Co-operative movement might achieve. Speaking in the run-up to the 1900 election for the School Board, she told her audience 'to take a lively interest at all times, and to see that their elected representatives, who are public servants do carry out their pledges – another state of affairs that will obtain *when the people wake up*'.[55] She played a part in developing policy through an Investigation Committee into Woolwich housing conditions, set up by local labour organisations involving Fred Knee, besides Woolwich co-operators and ILPers. In the autumn, Mary co-wrote a twelve-page pamphlet calling on the borough council 'to build cottages on a large scale'.[56]

In her third contest, fought under an independent socialist label, Mary concentrated on equality of opportunity, trade union rates of pay for all the Board's employees and equal pay for men and women. Again, she vigorously defended her position that 'a starving or underfed child should be fed – and fed not as a little pauper but as a future citizen'.[57] Daisy Warwick spoke on her behalf, as well as Engineers' leader George Barnes (b. 1859), local Labour leader Will Crooks (b. 1852), Edward Greening, Fred Knee and Will Thorne. Still in the wilderness as far as the other members for Greenwich were concerned, all her female colleagues supported her candidacy, as did Stewart Headlam (b. 1847), Lyulph Stanley and Dr T.J. Macnamara (b. 1861), President of the National Union of Teachers (NUT) and editor of the union's journal, the *Schoolmaster*.[58] Labour Parliamentarians and naval architect Sir Nathaniel Barnaby (b. 1829), who began his working life as a draughtsman in Woolwich dockyard, offered moral support also.[59] In a letter to the editor of the *Woolwich and Deptford Observer*, James Steer insisted that 'plumpers and plumpers only' would secure her return. He wrote of her special claim 'on behalf of the thousands of female children and teachers' whose 'special requirements of teaching and treatment can best be dealt with by one of their own sex'. An advocate of 'Progress with Prudence' urged Progressives not to vote for her, while another anonymous writer advised electors to spread their votes, 'allowing the Labour candidate fifty per cent more votes than the others and returning two candidates who will support the Labour candidate instead of two who will oppose Labour'.[60]

In the event, Mary won with an increased majority. To appreciate the result, the circumstances of the Second Boer War of 1899–1902 and her opposition to it should be emphasised. The crowd smashed her windows during the Mafeking celebrations, a memory still vivid in the late 1990s when her grandson retold the tale to me. Tensions and conflict did not disturb Mary, however. By now, she was moving toward the more difficult path of social democracy rather than the more orthodox political route for aspiring socialists offered by the ILP.

Elsewhere in the inner London region another former pupil teacher, Ramsay MacDonald, was busily climbing the political ladder. His wife had a private income of £460 a year and they gave regular 'at homes' for radicals and socialists in their roomy flat at Lincoln's Inn Fields.[61] In June 1905, he received a venomous letter from Arthur Field, secretary of the south-east federation of Trades Councils, complaining that the Countess had broken a speaking engagement.

> I knew she would sell us, for her guardian and pet hypnotist Mrs Bridges Adams thinks us too little committed body and soul to the S.D.F., and what Mrs Adams says the dear Countess believes ... We have heard by a side wind that Mrs Adams has said that she don't care if it incommodes us or

even kills the Conference as she had no room for anything but the Simon Pure R-r-r-revolution.[62]

The manoeuvres of Field, a founding member of the ILP, occasionally come into view in the notes and news section of the *Labour Leader*. An earlier breach surfaced at a national labour conference on state maintenance. Mary spoke for the SDF and MacDonald grumbled away. 'The object of the conference is to take the wind out of our sails and is part of the declared policy of the London Trades Council and the S.D.F. to temporarily capture the Political Committee (of the T.U.C.) to our damage.'[63] Suspicions ran deep on both sides. The Trades Council's institutional history rather ruefully reflected that many delegates at the foundation conference of the LRC believed MacDonald 'an ambitious but almost unknown political aspirant' who owed his election as secretary to confusion with their secretary James Macdonald, 'a veteran and highly respected figure in the trade union world'.[64]

In 1909 the Deptford branch of the SDP adopted Mary as their candidate in the forthcoming elections for the LCC. However, her intense commitment to Internationalism led her to take a stand against those Social Democrats who supported a strong policy of national defence. Having spoken alongside Victor Grayson at a right to work rally on behalf of the unemployed, she tried to challenge the views of Henry Hyndman and his associates on international issues. For example, on Christmas Day she expressed disappointment at the failure of *Justice* to criticise Robert Blatchford's anti-German letter recently published in the *Daily Mail*. Her disquiet began to reach a climax at a public meeting when the Countess of Warwick refused to disassociate the Party from Robert Blatchford's war crusade.

Mary supported the Russian and Jewish political refugees, like Peter Petroff, who decisively challenged the Hyndmanite policy, and eventually withdrew her candidature. The fact that she left it until four weeks before the election caused sparks to fly. The Deptford branch of the SDP was staggered and bitter. In April it published a resolution 'protesting against the manner in which Mrs Bridges Adams treated them'. Two weeks later *Justice* printed her response, in which she expressed 'surprise' and explained her decision to withdraw 'as I felt that complications, fatal to success, would inevitably have resulted from the fact that I was no longer a member of the Social Democratic Party'. The dispute ended in impasse. Perhaps the most vitriolic comment came from the pen of a social democratic rank-and-filer. It transpired that she had been contesting the seat under a Labour and socialist alliance and had received an assurance from branch officials 'that, in view of the fact that she declared herself to be as sound and unwavering as ever in her Socialism, she could still count upon the loyal and undivided support of its members'. The debacle damaged her reputation. Activists were angry because they failed to contest the election, which meant money wasted on a lost opportunity.[65]

Disqualified by her sex as both a voter and a candidate until 1907, had Mary won Deptford for Labour she would have joined a mere handful of women elected as local councillors in a city where local politics and women's suffrage had long gone hand in hand. Deptford, like Woolwich, was on the outskirts of London. They were both geographical locations in which trade union or Labour candidates could win elections. Independent working-class politics could result in relatively homogeneous areas such as these, where trade unionism tended to occupy a commanding place in working-class culture. Collective occupational and associational cultures meant that the association of mother with home did not necessarily mean that the homes of workers in skilled trades became depoliticised havens.[66] It was unusual if not abnormal for women elementary schoolteachers to be involved in London socialism, and Mary had married a comrade who supported her local government work. With such closeness between public and private life, what rendered her different from other women was her articulacy and public visibility. As time went by her rhetoric increasingly reflected class combativity and her radicalism found expression in a fresh demand for independent working-class education, following some years of experience of the new state education system.

Notes

1 'What we stand for', *Woolwich Pioneer*, 14 October 1904, p. 5.

2 P. Thompson, *Socialists, Liberals and Labour: the struggle for London 1885–1914* (London: Routledge and Kegan Paul, 1967); P. Tyler, *Labour's Lost Leader: the life and politics of Will Crooks* (London: Tauris Academic Studies, 2007); K. Yoonak Stenberg, 'Working-class women in London local politics, 1894–1914', *Twentieth Century British History*, 9:3 (1998), pp. 323–49.

3 Cited in M. Williams, *John Wilson of Woolwich* (London: Marshall, Morgan and Scott Ltd, 1937), p. 67.

4 S. Maclure, *A History of Education in London 1870–1990* (London: Allen Lane, 1990), pp. 124–5.

5 E.F. Jefferson, *The Woolwich Story 1890–1969* (Woolwich: Woolwich and District Antiquarian Society, 1970), pp. 59, 75.

6 See, for example, T. Woodin, 'Working-class education and social change in nineteenth and twentieth-century Britain', *History of Education*, 38:4–5 (2007),

pp. 483–96.

7 The discussion that follows draws on R. Rhodes, *An Arsenal for Labour* (Manchester: Holyoake Books, 1998), pp. 1–15.

8 G. Scott, *Feminism and the Politics of Working Women* (London: UCL Press, 1998), p. 21.

9 J. Gaffin and D. Thoms, *Caring and Sharing: the centenary history of the Co-operative Women's Guild* (Manchester: Co-operative Union Ltd., 1983), pp. 2–4, 10–12, 22–3, 31–3.

10 M.L. Davies (ed.), *Life As We Have Known It By Co-operative Working Women* (London: Virago, 1984), pp. 41, 49.

11 1891 Census; 'Our Reformers' Gallery: Marion Angela Deans', *Woolwich Labour Journal*, January 1903, pp. 1–2.

12 RACSP, Royal Arsenal Co-operative Society Education Committee, Minutes, 1 February 1894.

13 'Women's Co-operative Guild Diary', *Comradeship*, April, July 1898; April 1899.

14 J. Attfield, *With Light of Knowledge: a hundred years of education in the Royal Arsenal Co-operative Society, 1877–1977* (London: The Journeyman Press, 1981), pp. 6–10.

15 Lord Snell, *Men, Movements and Myself* (London: J.M. Dent & Sons Ltd, 1936), p. 67.

16 'Borough Council Election: the Labour candidates', *Woolwich Pioneer*, 12 October 1906, p. 4.

17 F.H. Spencer, *An Inspector's Testament* (London: English Universities Press, 1938) p. 174.

18 C.H. Grinling, 'Editorial', *Comradeship*, No. 1, October 1897, p. 1.

19 'The Mayor-elect of Woolwich', *Woolwich Pioneer*, 3 November 1905, p. 5.

20 See, for example, J. Hannam K. and Hunt, *Socialist Women Britain, 1880s to 1920s* (London: Routledge, 2002); D. Howell, *British Workers and the Independent Labour Party 1888–1906* (Manchester: Manchester University Press, 1983), pp. 209–12.

21 J. Jacobs, *London Trades Council 1860–1950* (London: Lawrence and Wishart, 1950), pp. 68–9.

22 'Why women should join trade unions', *Comradeship*, December 1902, p. 5.

23 W. Barefoot, *Twenty-five Years of the Woolwich Labour Party, 1903–1928* (Woolwich: Woolwich Labour Party, 1928), p. 9.

24 Attfield, *With Light of Knowledge*, pp. 8–9.

25 E.P. Thompson, *William Morris: from romantic to revolutionary* (London: Merlin Press, 1977), p. 298.

26 RACSP, Royal Arsenal Co-Operative Society Half-yearly Report, July 1897.

27 'Pen Portraits of Woolwich Worthies – Mr. James Turnbull', *Woolwich Pioneer*, 23 April 1909, p. 3.

28 *Woolwich Labour Notes*, February 1899, p. 1.

29 Thompson, *Socialists, Liberals and Labour*, pp. 162–3, 252 and 257.

30 Snell, *Men, Movements and Myself*, p. 108.
31 *Blackheath Gazette*, 19 October 1894, p. 5.
32 *Blackheath Gazette*, 26 October 1894, p. 7.
33 1881 England Census, Dulwich, Camberwell; 1901 England Census, Dulwich, Camberwell.
34 'The School Board: Messrs Gover and Wilson's meetings at Lewisham High Road', *Kentish Mercury*, 9 November 1894, p. 3.
35 'Some humours of the School Board contest', *Kentish Mercury*, 28 December 1894, p. 3.
36 'The Candidature of Mrs Bridges Adams', *Kentish Mercury*, 16 November 1894, p. 3; Thompson *Socialists, Liberals and Labour*, pp. 164.
37 'London School Board', *Kentish Mercury*, 29 March 1895, p. 3.
38 LMA, London School Board, Minutes, 2 May 1895, p. 1128.
39 1901 England Census, Lee, London.
40 *Labour Leader*, 18 May 1895, p. 8.
41 G. Bernard Shaw to Mrs Adams, 24 January 1894.
42 *1901 England Census Record* [www.1901censusonline.com]; *Kentish Mercury*, 5 November 1897; 'Pen Pictures of Woolwich Worthies – Dr Albert Lindow', *Woolwich Pioneer*, 4 June 1909, p. 3.
43 *Kentish Mail and Deptford and Greenwich Observer*, 19 November 1897, p. 2.
44 *Kentish Mail and Deptford and Greenwich Observer*, 19 November 1897, p. 2.
45 Snell, *Men, Movements and Myself*, p. 151.
46 *Kentish Independent*, 30 October 1897, p. 5.
47 *Kentish Mail and Deptford and Greenwich Observer*, 19 November 1897, p. 2.
48 *Kentish Mercury*, 3 December 1897, p. 5.
49 'Club Records', *Shafts*, February–March 1898, p. 22.
50 'Club Records', *Shafts*, February–March 1898, p. 22.
51 'Proposed settlement for Greenwich', *Shafts*, May–June 1898, p. 89.
52 *Woolwich Gazette and Kentish Advertiser*, 21 July 1899, press cuttings file, Woolwich Polytechnic Archive, University of Greenwich.
53 D. Stuart, *Dear Duchess: Millicent, Duchess of Sutherland* (Littlehampton: Littlehampton Book Services, 1982).
54 *1901 England Census Record* [www.1901censusonline.com].
55 *Woolwich and District Labour Notes*, September 1899, p. 6.
56 *Comradeship*, August and September 1900.
57 *Greenwich and Deptford Observer, Woolwich Gazette and Kentish Advertiser*, 16 and 23 November 1900.
58 R. Betts, *Dr Macnamara 1861–1931* (Liverpool: Liverpool University Press, 1999).
59 P. Watts, 'Barnaby, Sir Nathaniel (1829–1915)', *Oxford Dictionary of National Biography* (Oxford: Oxford University Press, 2004; online edn, October 2006) [www.oxforddnb.com/index/10103599 accessed 23 September 2009].
60 *Greenwich and Deptford Observer, Woolwich Gazette and Kentish Advertiser*, 16 November 1900, p. 2.

61 D. Marquand, *Ramsay MacDonald: a biography* (London: Jonathan Cape, 1977); J. Martin, 'Gender, the city and the politics of schooling: towards a collective biography of women "doing good" as public moralists in Victorian London', *Gender and Education*, 17:2 (2005), pp. 143–63.

62 Arthur Field to J.R. MacDonald, 2 June 1905, Labour Party correspondence.

63 J.R. MacDonald to J. Sexton, 6 December 1904, Labour Party correspondence.

64 Jacobs, *London Trades Council*, pp. 70, 71, 89; obituary, 'Mr James Macdonald', *The Times*, 4 June 1938, p. 14.

65 *Justice*, 11 September, 27 November, 25 December 1909; 23 April, 7 May, 14 May 1910.

66 G. Stedman Jones, *Languages of Class: studies in English working class history 1832–1982* (Cambridge: Cambridge University Press, 1996 edition), pp. 218–20.

4

Rethinking socialism and education

> Education towards Revolution seems to me to express in three words what our policy should be; towards that New Birth of Society which we know must come, and which, therefore, we must strive to help forward so that it may come with as little confusion and suffering as may be. (William Morris 1886)[1]

Radical struggles over education

These are the words of William Morris, British writer, designer, artist and socialist. He joined the newly formed Democratic Federation in 1883, though an early split resulted in the foundation of the Socialist League, which tended to emphasise education. Morris argued that socialism would be won by 'educating the people into desiring it' and 'organizing them into claiming it effectually'.[2] Mary never back-tracked from the vision of socialism defined as 'a cause, a new order of society to be set up'.[3] She dedicated her life to this political propaganda and presented her ideas using language informed by Marxist understandings of the relation between knowledge and power.

This chapter will consider the dissonance between the construction of her son's educational trajectory and the way in which Mary approached questions of class as a campaigner for state schools. Her route map was oppositional but she used a range of strategies according to particular issues, which could change over time. The intention is to look at the constituent parts of her agitation and propaganda from the mid 1880s to the 1920s – not to present them as representative, but to situate her activism within broader political narratives. Her propaganda provides a prime example of a radical education tradition, one which owes something to the popular educational politics of which her struggle was a part.

Here I use Italian Marxist Antonio Gramsci's suggestions relating to hegemony and the role of civil society. Gramsci argued that education provides much of the terrain wherein political struggles for hegemony around the interests of the dominant class take place.[4] He believed that the attainment of cultural dominance and, where necessary, brute force, was what enabled the ruling class to secure and maintain power. In his view, educational activities and institutions constitute the very core of hegemony, since they reinforce the ability of the dominant class to instil its conception of the world and its values into every capillary of society. In examining struggles over meaning, Gramsci argued that hegemony also works to produce forms of complicity and dissent. Marginalised social and cultural groups retain the capacity to produce a counter-hegemony or world view that might modify, negotiate, resist or even overthrow the dominant culture. Hence the importance of 'organic' intellectuals, who emerge with the formation of new economic classes 'as functioning to elaborate ideologies, to educate the people, to unify social forces, and to secure hegemony' for the social class to which they are linked.[5]

Gramsci's ideas on the political function of 'organic' intellectuals, who make interventions of various sorts, provide a heuristic map on which to plot Mary's engagement with socialist politics. This is not to deny, as Jane Miller notes, his failure to think of women as 'potential agents (except inadvertently) in the processes of change and renewal'[6] or to address the politics of gender that made the fully educated working woman still more 'an accidental being' than the fully educated working man. Of particular relevance to the analysis of Mary's political propaganda is the distinction between what the Education Group at the Centre for Contemporary Cultural Studies, Birmingham call 'substitutional' and 'statist' approaches to educational change:

> Substitutional strategies concentrate on building an independent popular educational provision more or less in contestation with philanthropic or state agencies. The solution is to do it ourselves, drawing on resources that already exist within communities, but improvising new, more flexible forms … Statist strategies, on the other hand, have centred on agitation over the public provision of educational facilities and the state's regulation of adjacent spheres (for example, the length of the working day, children's employment, child health). The strategy here has been to adopt the state system or a part of it as 'the people's schools' and work to improve its quality and accessibility.[7]

The competing values embodied in these choices were in a real state of tension towards the end of the nineteenth century. Mary expressed a strong alternative cultural tradition in her political propaganda and it is possible to identify links with the spirit underpinning popular struggles of the past.

From the 1790s onwards, radical minorities conducted a running critique of all forms of 'provided' education.[8] At its heart was a vision of an alternative educational future, in contrast to the governing-class tradition epitomised by the expectations which Anglicans brought to the provision of elementary education that placed the higher priority on social control. Early radical practices rejected the imposition of schooling and allied cultural forms. They refused the distinction between 'truth' and 'usefulness' and insisted that '*really* useful knowledge' was what it was really important to know. This was a satire on the Society for the Diffusion of Useful Knowledge, a liberal, middle-class educational association founded in 1826 as an antidote to the output of the radical presses. It also expressed radicals' desire for knowledge that was relevant and suited to their needs. An education that would be useful *and* cultural, calculated to foster understandings of the realities of life, instead of the moral precepts enshrined in religion and the Classics.

In the 1830s and 1840s, Chartists and other reformers developed a vigorous and varied educational practice which included formal provision in secular schools, as well as informal schooling through the mechanism of radical culture. Substitutional activities involving alternative media, alternative forms of schooling and alternative practices were organised on a large scale. Ideas discussed in workplaces, pubs and meetings, often from items read out from the radical working-class press, contributed to an important internal debate about education as a political strategy. However, with the loss of confidence in the immediate political prospects of the People's Charter and the spread of proletarian conditions of existence, the 1850s marked a transition. Under these circumstances, priorities shifted. The 1850s saw the growth of a strategy that put greater stress on state educational provision, with local democratic control of schools.[9]

Hence, the 1870 Education Act reflected the balance of power between two education pressure groups. One was the National Education League, supported by a broad coalition based upon the Liberal Party, nonconformists, radicals, trade unionists and the newly enfranchised middle classes. Lined up against them and opposing further state intervention was the National Education Union, comprising the Church of England and the Tory Party. Ultimately, the agitation produced a legislative compromise. Church schools benefited from additional public revenue but, if voluntary effort failed to meet the need, new schools would be organised under the aegis of locally elected school boards, financed by a central grant and local rates. While the Church schools remained the front-runners in the provision of education for the working classes, the Act provided the catalyst for the rapid development of a new network of secular elementary or board schools.

All male, as well as single and widowed female, rate-payers could vote in school board elections, and in London each elector could cast as many votes as there were seats in his or her division. In the event, a system of voting that was designed to assuage the fears of religious minorities that the new local educational authorities would be dominated by the Anglican clergy favoured the representation of electoral minorities, especially the working classes and women. Time, money and social status were facilitative of public careers, but school board politics seem to have combined just the right degree of adversity and hope to encourage supporters of independent labour representation and of the women's suffrage movement to make it a part of their work.

A thoroughgoing recognition of the social value of work and of those who worked in society shaped socialist understanding of educational questions. The Woolwich ILP phrased it thus: 'We have been subjected ourselves to the crushing and degrading forces of competition and commercial ideals which regard human lives merely as the raw material for making profits; therefore we see that we must win for our children the joy of life'.[10] Attempts to change the experience of class in education melded the desire to protect child life with recognition of the need for material improvement. As Will Thorne put it in his autobiography: 'Socialism proposes to abolish the system of wage slavery, and establish instead governmental, municipal co-operation, securing to every honest worker the full value of his labour, partly in personal remuneration, and partly in social and public benefits, such as education and recreation, sustenance and care in old age'.[11] There is, in this analysis, a self-evident emphasis on the toppling of capitalism.

Nonetheless, socialists faced a recurrent dilemma. On the one hand, they valued the acquisition of knowledge very highly indeed. On the other, they were aware of the poverty of the educational resources at hand. This is evident in Mary's struggles in and around education fields. In public life, Mary opposed the elitist orthodoxy that monopolised the means of learning, preserving discussions of content and control that tended to perpetuate the structural, class-based division. As a widowed mother, she accepted financial assistance from her in-laws and her aristocratic patron to enable her son to take advantage of elite education.

Mary's views on education

In the summer of 1899, Mary attended the Education Section of the International Congress of Women held in London. She raised the question of elementary education and told delegates: 'For herself, she was a Socialist, but she would not, for all that, send her child to a board school, because she felt that the system of education was bad'.[12] She claimed that the object of the 1870 Act was 'simply to instruct the working classes, to place them in a position to compete with the foreign trade; it was purely a commercial system, not a system to train boys and girls to be good citizens'. Next, she castigated 'the pernicious, the wicked, the damnable system of payment by results' and said it 'would have to be abolished'.[13]

Introduced in 1862 and virtually abandoned in 1895, payment by results emphasised the need to ensure value for money. It linked government finance to attendance and to the examination results of each pupil in the 3Rs, plus needlework for girls. This had the effect of narrowing the curriculum, since teaching concentrated upon grant-earning subjects, with undue pressure on learners and resulting demoralisation of teachers. In these circumstances, rote learning became firmly entrenched and the educational positions of 'progressives', including the Froebelian, child-centred approaches that Mary advocated, did not penetrate infant education in elementary schools. When combined with reductions in education spending, teacher training and teacher status, this administrative principle made it inevitable that teachers would try to cram their pupils for the examinations upon which their own livelihoods were crucially dependent. 'Could it really be abolished', she asked, 'if the teachers had been trained into it?'[14]

In a subsequent discussion of the actual structure of provision, Mary expanded her criticism of the denominational training colleges, based on a class reading of the elementary–secondary divide. She noted what might have been the hard lesson of personal experience and concluded:

> High educational qualifications were considered almost a disadvantage if one went into an elementary school. The elementary schools said they would not have the secondary school teachers because they could not teach; while the governing authorities of the secondary schools said they would not have the elementary school teachers because they were not ladies. She agreed cordially with the suggestion that education should come first and training afterwards, for she saw the evil of the opposite cause every time she went into an elementary school.[15]

In particular, Mary advocated the need to equip teachers to realise their full potential as human beings and not send them to specialist elementary training colleges. 'They were denied the liberalising influences of contact with those who were entering other professions, and in that narrow, cramping atmosphere they were trained to teach the children of the people. They wanted more humanity, more breadth. She would have equality in the teaching system of the day.'[16]

Mary's proposals for education are the particular focus here, explored through the connections between personal and political worlds. As already discussed in chapter 1, William Bridges-Adams attended a succession of private co-educational boarding schools, culminating in Bedales. The relationship of families to class structures is complex, and the Adamses response to the education market involved considerable expenditure in order to plan a particular future for their son. Their deployment of the family's material capital suggests that political principles may have given way to private pragmatics. Others from middle-class backgrounds who joined the newly formed socialist groups did not use middle-class strategies to secure privilege and advance, however.

For example, Alfred Salter (b. 1873) was a founder member of the Bermondsey branch of the ILP. He came from a middle-class family of limited means and became a doctor with the help of a scholarship from his old school. Alfred turned his back on a promising research career to work among the Bermondsey poor and he met his wife, Ada Brown (b. 1868), as a social worker at the Bermondsey Settlement. For the Salters, socialism was a moral vocation as well as a political practice. In the words of Alfred's biographer: 'They were concerned to save human beings from the horrors of the poverty they knew in Bermondsey, to create social conditions which would allow the children to grow in physical, mental and spiritual health, and to spread among the people the spirit of fellowship, service and equality.'[17] The Salters lived in the locality, brought up their daughter, Joyce (b. 1902), there and sent her to the local elementary school. In contrast to the Adamses, they did not suspend their principles in relation to an educational ideal until circumstances changed. Tragically, Joyce Salter died of scarlet fever when she was 8 years old, having survived two previous bouts of the highly contagious childhood disease – even though, unlike her school friends, she had access to the very best the medical profession could offer, including her father's past colleagues at Guy's Hospital, London.

In the recent past, the issue of school selection has proved contentious for several New Labour politicians – Tony Blair, as new leader of the parliamentary opposition in 1994, followed by Harriet Harman in 1996 and Ruth Kelly in 2007. Both the media and the party faithful pilloried Harman when she confirmed that she was sending her son to a grammar school, and Kelly faced accusations of hypocrisy over her decision to purchase educational provision from the private sector for her son, who had special educational needs.[18] However, there is no evidence that Mary attracted a similar opprobrium. Ramsay MacDonald sent his sons to Bedales when he was chair of the LRC, and in July 1903 Mary declared her own attitude at a meeting of the Women's National Liberal Association. Having asserted that her son attended an 'ideal school', she anticipated a time when all children would share his experience of schooling. 'On the grounds of justice and expediency', she said, 'I claim for every child in this country the same education as I ask for my own.'[19] Her vision was of a common school system that would provide equal opportunities for all.

Bedales started life in 1893 as a boys' boarding school founded by John Haden Badley (b. 1865), the only son of a prosperous Midlands doctor, who had previously been a teacher at Abbotsholme in Staffordshire. Educated at Rugby, where he felt confined by a narrow curriculum devoted almost entirely to the classics and highly critical of the absence of care for individual boys, Badley became convinced of the need for reform while an undergraduate at Trinity College, Cambridge. The Fellowship of the New Life, a group that would gradually progress to Utopia by individual change of heart or by voluntary co-operation, influenced him greatly, as did the poetry of Walt Whitman. Abbotsholme, founded in 1889, launched what supporters called the 'New School' movement in England. The teaching strategies of a 'New School' emanated from what Badley and others saw as the drawbacks of the 'Old Schools'. For example, traditional, single-sex public schools like Rugby were criticised for their authoritarian, strict, preordained knowledge approach. The mantra of the 'new' conception of education, as opposed to the 'old', was 'learning by doing'. There was demand for hands-on learning, coupled with the desire to create whole, well-rounded individuals.

At Bedales, situated in the countryside, the new head would impart his vision of the school as a miniature commonwealth, a self-supporting secular community. The self-conscious rural life was romanticised and an ideology imposed on it. Spatial location was an important aspect of the education philosophy on offer, since fresh air and beneficial exercise had a vital role to play in the development of a healthy mind and body. The aim was 'to give a real training, of body, mind and character that is not confined to one class or sex or portion of school-life'. Values, lifestyle and educational philosophy merged with a concern for diet and clothing – which should be homespun, giving warmth and freedom. Badley preferred to wear sandals rather than shoes, and when William was a pupil there his favoured dress code was a Norfolk jacket and knee breeches.[20]

Bedales moved to its present site at Petersfield, Hampshire in 1900, having introduced co-educational boarding in 1898. Badley drew up a broad curriculum designed to combat the drift toward specialisation and the traditional emphasis on a thorough classical schooling.[21] As an alternative, Bedales imparted a common basic education which combined manual and mental labour and learning to use one's hands in craft activities. Free-time work was encouraged, as was participation in school societies such as the Classical, the Literary, the Musical and the Scientific, as well as the variety entertainment in which William Bridges-Adams shone. Occurring once a term, these social occasions (called Merry Evenings) gave opportunity 'to all ages for acting, dancing, singing, reciting and "grinning through a horse collar"; especially the tendency to comic pillory and friendly burlesque, whether of the annual Shakespeare play, of some boring lecturer or some educational crank'. Badley felt that they 'saved the School from taking too seriously the fact that it was an "Experiment" and a school that people talked and wrote about'.[22]

The aims of education that Badley put into action sought to unify moral and material means and ends. He identified three things which a school had to do. These were training for a working life, training for an inner life and training for a communal life as a citizen. As a champion of poorer children on the LSB, Mary believed this kind of education should be a right for all, to promote the collective advance of working-class communities. Her critique of the status quo involved an attack on the values of a culture that was elevated by a two-tier education system which condemned the bulk of the population, who worked with their hands, to a life of, at best, second-class citizenship. Against this, she recommended the education principles set out in John Richardson's book entitled *How It Can Be Done; or Constructive Socialism*. In her opinion, this 'would form a good basis for a constructive London Education programme, which, if it were adopted as the programme of the Socialist, Trade Unionist, and Co-operative Congresses, could not fail to have an influence on education legislation in the future'.[23]

Described by Kevin Manton as 'a vision of the future that was statist in the extreme',[24] Richardson's utopian description of life under socialism includes a blueprint for a State Education Act setting out proposals for co-educational schools organised in age-defined stages. Formal education would begin at Infant or Junior School for those aged 4 to 7, followed by Second Grade schools for 7- to 14-year-olds and residential Continuation Schools for those aged 15 to 18. These older students would live in the schools for eight to nine months a year, while those growing up in 'unsuitable homes' would stay there or in some other school during the holidays. Additional proposals included the suggestion that the Second Grade Schools include some sleeping accommodation to protect the vulnerable from 'dangerous moral surroundings'.[25] Also attached to these institutions would be infirmaries for children with mental and physical disabilities. Between the ages of 19 and 21 every young person would attend a single-sex residential college, of which there would be eight types: agricultural, artistic, classical, legal, mechanical, medical, musical and scientific.

The strategic vision of work encapsulated both in the socialist discourse of the period and in J.H. Badley's vision of the 'New School' transcended the issue of the academic–vocational divide. It went further than this, however, through the advocacy of co-education and curricula which did seriously challenge the gendered organisation of labour into men's work and women's work. For example, Richardson's curriculum for 7- to 14-year-olds included teaching carpentry, knitting and sewing to both sexes, and greatly extended the existing elementary syllabus to include French, German, Italian, Spanish and music. His ambitious plans for the Continuation School involved the building of classrooms, lecture halls, laboratories, workshops, and museums of 'representative fossils, minerals, physiological and anatomical specimens'. There were also reading rooms, drawing rooms and parlours, gymnasia and swimming pools. Senior pupils could choose to study what they liked from a curriculum which would include 'ancient and modern history and languages, geology, chemistry, metallurgy, anatomy, physiology, astronomy, maths, physics and electricity; music, solo and part singing, the playing of all kinds of musical instruments, drawing, painting in oil and water colours, gymnastics, dancing, drilling, fencing, shooting, horse riding'.[26] All children would spend four hours per day in the workshop to learn skills and handicrafts, although gender segregation crept in with female exclusion from building lessons and male exclusion from dressmaking and fan-painting lessons. Richardson advocated a maximum class size of twenty, each class having its own garden where the students would raise fruit and vegetables.

Architecture and design also feature. School buildings 'shall be artistically and substantially built, and shall be fitted with the most perfect sanitary, mechanical and scientific appliances for economising labour and facilitating work'. So does the SDF position on state maintenance. To counter the suggestion that such provision would erode parental responsibility, Richardson notes that food and clothing are 'already given in England to Princes, prisoners and paupers'. Developing the theme of the infants' school uniform, donned after an early-morning dip in a plunge bath, he continues:

> This is a matter of more importance than seems at first sight. Instead of the common, and often very ugly, uniform now used in many charity schools, which causes the children to be objects of scorn and derision, the costumes worn should be of very good quality material, and be as prettily and tastefully made as is compatible with their use as school uniforms. Coming, as the children would do, from homes with various standards of comfort, from extreme poverty to affluence, it is essential that they should be all placed upon the same level at once; and that level must be the highest.[27]

Above all, clothing should be warm, light and porous, to allow freedom of movement. Richardson's guidelines also contain a message about the importance of hygiene, preventative health care and outdoor exercise. Again, the emphasis on a healthy mind in a healthy body resembles the educational positions of the 'progressives' like J.H. Badley. At Bedales, the school day began with a morning run, followed by breakfast, making beds and class work, with regular breaks and summer bathing at 12.30 followed by lunch, after which the boys changed into 'flannels' and girls into 'gymnastic dress' to spend the afternoon on hand work.[28]

Political participation was encouraged, if not expected, in Richardson's education programme. At the centre he placed a State Council made up of the Presidents of the sixteen directly elected Educational Boards, each responsible for local educational provision within a specific geographical area. After the age of 21, 'each student will be expected and required to devote eight hours each working day to productive service of the State, under the direction of the local authorities, and shall continue to do so for four years'.[29] Forged out of political commitment, these principles put education first, educational administration second. Mary shared this view. 'Let us make up our minds as to what we want to do with the machinery when we have constructed it', she said.[30]

The National Labour Education League

In the winter of 1901/2 Mary's convictions, allied to growing concern about retrogressive moves in educational terms, prompted her to set up the National Labour Education League. The closest thing to a Labour education policy at this period, the League had three main aims:

> 1. The strengthening and developing of the Educational side of the Labour movement.
> 2. The freeing of Popular Education from the Control of the great obstacles to Educational Reform – (*a*) Sectarians (*b*) Political Wirepullers (*c*) 'Interests.'
> 3. The securing by legislation of a System of Education which will bring the highest Educational advantages *absolutely* within the reach of every worker's child.[31]

The antipathy to 'wirepullers' had a popular base. It referred to the technique of feeding facts to people in the hope that they might use them and was a dig at the Fabians, notably Sidney Webb (b. 1859), a strong proponent of the 1902 Education Act. Mary became the League's honorary secretary, pledged to a national public speaking tour to mobilise support, which meant working with broader working-class organisations.

By appealing for support via the local and socialist press, Mary hoped to unite working-class aspirations. Her intentions were to counter 'the efforts of the privileged classes to curtail even the very meagre educational advantages within the reach of the children of the workers'. This required a collective response. In advocating this approach, Mary called for 'equally determined and *combined* efforts on the part of the organised workers who should be ready, not merely with a *negative* policy of opposition to a bad bill, but with a *constructive* programme'.[32] An alliance of 'Lib-Lab' MPs and councillors, co-operators and leading trade unionists endorsed the Appeal, notably Will Thorne and Alexander Wilkie (b. 1850) of Newcastle School Board, past chair of the TUC Parliamentary Committee.[33] The Countess of Warwick also came out as a supporter. In another sideswipe at Sidney Webb, Mary hoped it would plant a bomb among 'a certain select party of diners at a well known Liberal Club' and thus save the country from 'dinner table legislation'.[34]

Within two weeks, forty-five trade unions had affiliated to the League and Mary was busy organising demonstrations, deputations and meetings, distributing pamphlets and speaking all over the country. In December she briefed the *Labour Leader* that the League was making 'good headway', and weeks later, that the League would shortly hold an inaugural conference in London.[35] This did not mean, however, that she won the co-operation of the entire trade union leadership. Will Thorne was active in promoting the League's development, but the TUC Parliamentary Committee moved warily when it met in December 1901. Thorne was overruled, and Committee members turned down Mary's request to use their office as a covering address for the League. Further to that, the committee decided to organise a rival education conference and effectively excluded trades council delegates, who probably took a more radical stance, from attending.[36]

The National Labour Education League remained active until the abolition of the LSB. Daisy Warwick's salon at Carlisle Mansions became the League's headquarters, and Daisy and Mary had high expectations of what it might achieve. As an organisation, it disappears from view after 1904, vanquished in the battle to save the school board arrangement. For W.P. McCann, the collapse probably reflected its reliance on Mary's 'personality and driving force' to exert pressure for change, with trade union and co-operative leaders 'willing to lend their name but little more'.[37] McCann also comments on the lack of differentiation between the League's function and policy and those of the TUC. Hardly surprising, if we accept the analysis of William Bridges-Adams, that his mother became the education mentor of the trade union movement at that time.

In much of her political propaganda, Mary chose to focus on the need to counter the forces at work within the Establishment and the state. For example, she returned to her theme at the 1903 conference of the volunteer, civic-minded organisation the National Union of Women Workers. The delegates had moved from Cheltenham to Gloucester and the subject under discussion was the Conservative government's Education Act of 1902. Mary savaged the idea of a ladder for the few at a time when the retention of fees in grammar schools ensured that the social bias of secondary education became more entrenched. 'Free education had never been regarded as pauperising the distinguished men who had been educated on the foundations of the old public schools', she said. 'She held that the Elementary Schools were of the first importance, and that the pay for teaching in these schools should be equal to the pay of secondary schools.'[38] This was a powerful novelty, and it is possible to discern the response. Lady Louisa Knightley of Fawsley (b. 1842), leading official of the Primrose League, staunch churchwoman and imperialist, recorded in her diary: 'One awful woman, Mrs Bridges Adams of the LSB, ranted away – but she was the exception which proved the rule: the tone and the conduct of the Conference on the whole was most admirable'.[39] Here was a censure redolent of the class feeling reviled by Mary in both its form and its content.

Mary's reference to the public school foundations is crucial here. The restoration of the misappropriated educational endowments was a key aspect of the popular politics of education in these years. It was a goal that provided the organised labour movement with the means by which it said it would fund its education policies. Will Thorne called Mary the Gas Workers' expert on educational endowments, and delegates frequently raised the issue during the annual education debate at the Congress of the TUC. In 1906, for instance, Ben Tillett called for an endowments enquiry. 'The poor have been robbed. If these bequests were looked into, we should take away from the middle and upper classes some of the schooling that really belongs to the poor.'[40] The elite purloining that Tillett had in mind was the work of the Endowed Schools Commission, set up to apply the Endowed Schools Act which a Parliament largely composed of former public school boys passed in 1869. The Schools Inquiry Commission, which sat from 1864 to 1868, examined endowed secondary schools and proprietary schools and found that provision was woefully inadequate. For example, there were only thirteen secondary schools for girls countrywide. Otherwise, the distribution was uneven and the endowments were misused. The Commissioners' remit was to ensure that these categories of schools had enough money and were spending it in 'appropriate' ways.

This involved the adaptation of ancient foundations, old statutes and trust deeds that had begun as endowments for the education of poor and indigent scholars. In practice, this meant abolishing the *free* education willed by benefactors in the past, as well as the removal of restrictions on curricula. The Commissioners also confiscated funds from charities providing food and cash for poor families that they regarded as outmoded, and handed them over to the secondary schools. To adapt endowments to the needs of their own day, as they saw them, the Commissioners effectively made admission to the public schools dependent on winning a scholarship through 'merit', which usually meant proficiency in Latin or Greek, subjects to which the ordinary child was unlikely to be exposed.

The 'restoration of the educational endowments which have been stolen from the poor' was crucial to the realisation of the education programme of the trade union movement and Mary was tireless in her campaigning on the issue. Will Thorne gave her a great deal of the credit, writing of her 'splendid work in this direction.'[41] The issue quickly became a sticking point between Mary and her supporters, and Albert Mansbridge (b. 1876), founder of the Workers' Educational Association (WEA) in 1903. Albert's father was a carpenter, and scholarships dispatched him from board to grammar school, but he left at 14 because his father refused to allow his fourth son the privilege of an education denied to his three elder brothers. It was as editor of the magazine of the Junior Civil Service Prayer Union that Albert came to the attention of Charles Gore (b. 1853), then canon of Westminster Abbey, later Bishop of Birmingham. The patronage of men like Gore provided a link with Canon Samuel Barnett (b.1844) of Toynbee Hall.

Albert attended classes at the East End's famous university settlement and sought Barnett's advice on what it might cost to launch an 'Association to Promote the Higher Education of Working Men', the chief function of which would be to forge an alliance between the Co-operative movement and university extension lectures, pioneered by Cambridge in 1813. Barnett estimated £50,000 and Albert took the news back to his wife. 'That very evening', he averred, 'in a completely democratic meeting attended by both of us and no one else, she appointed me honorary secretary, *pro tem.*, contributed half a crown out of her housekeeping funds, and the movement was on foot'.[42] As Lawrence Goldman expressed it, 'Here was an almost classic example of one sort of man who had frequented university extension and would be attracted to university tutorial classes after 1908; intelligent, but educationally frustrated, and locked into low-grade white-collar employment'.[43] Mary and Albert both wanted working people to take their education further, but whereas she was interested in an alternative cultural/educational tradition, he held firmly to the dominant liberal-romantic tradition in the hands of England's elite.[44]

The WEA and education endowments

In the fight for financial backing from the trade union movement, Albert faced a problem of credibility. It was important to present the WEA as a working-class organisation, independent of capitalist bodies. This was difficult when opponents immediately pointed to the middle-class bias of its governing body and prominent aristocratic supporters. In the attempt to appease those who opposed the notion of neutral education, especially vocal critics in the railway unions, he often raised the endowment issue. For instance, he exposed the financial footings of Eton College that outstripped the 'endowments of all secondary schools in Scotland' and had recently benefited additionally from the sale of land whose value had escalated massively since the initial bequest. 'As everyone knows, no poor scholar can look inside the gate at Eton. Perhaps someone will ask a question in Parliament. This is it in brief. Land for poor scholars, plus the unearned increment, becomes £151,000 for the aggrandisement of an aristocratic foundation.'[45]

Mary's convictions ran counter to those of Albert Mansbridge. Mary wanted the endowments restored to the people and campaigned for popular control over them. From 1907, the WEA was successful in attracting state money to provide workers' education and she saw this as dealing a potentially fatal blow to the Labour movement case regarding the restoration of the educational endowments. Albert's call for a Royal Commission on University Education only exacerbated her fears. In response, she earnestly tried to dissuade trade unionists from wasting time on this diversion. To this end, she spoke in the capital and the provinces, including making an appearance, at a fringe meeting to establish a Socialist Teachers' Association, at the NUT annual conference.[46] Acrimonious debates underpin the following comment from Albert, made in response to Robert Morant's oft-quoted assurance that the Board of Education would 'pour a stream of gold into the WEA':

> Now, anyone, who knows anything abut education, knows that any class promoted by anybody which conforms to the Board of Education regulations, can receive of this 'golden stream'. If Mr Will Thorne's own union promoted a class it would have just the same chance of recognition as the WEA classes have. The railwaymen who know WEA meetings, and there are many, will smile at what Mr Will Thorne thinks to be the sting in the tail of his letter.[47]

Carrying the disagreement to the learning spaces of the *Labour Leader*, Mary asked Margaret McMillan, a member of the WEA executive, where she might 'find the restoration of the Educational Endowments included in the objects of the Association'.[48]

In the autumn of 1910, Mary appealed to socialists to keep themselves firmly on the side of the Gas Workers' long-running agitation for the restoration of the university and public school endowments. The WEA, having won the support of the Co-operative movement for a Royal Commission on University Education, was now targeting the official leaders of the Labour movement, she wrote. She specifically drew attention to the silence on the question of local democratic control when making demands, 'in the name of work people', for large Treasury grants for Oxford University, as the WEA's ally, to fund academic salaries and research. Through it all, Mary denounced the WEA for its refusal to endorse the trade union education programme: 'The Gas Workers Union claims that time has now come for these endowments to be restored to the people. Popular education is starved, the children are not yet fed adequately, they do not get the medical treatment they need, and we have not secured the maintenance of the children necessary for raising the school age'.[49]

Mary's vision

Mary set up the National Labour Education League to create a workers' education alliance that would focus on the role of elementary education under capitalism. This could have been enormously fruitful and she did not lose sight of her goal. As she wrote in 1916:

> My work in education … has been on the lines of the education programme, which for so many successive years was endorsed at the Trades Union Congresses. This was not strange, seeing that the programme was wholly of my drafting, and that the introduction of the most far-reaching and fundamental of the proposals contained in it was due to my initiative. Further, the circular on education, which the Parliamentary Committee reproduced in their official report for 1903–4, was also of my drafting. I paid for the 100,000 reprints referred to in the report and I organised the distribution, without any assistance from the Parliamentary Committee. Not only so, the Education Bill, introduced into the House of Commons by many members of the Labour Party soon after the 1906 election, was of my drafting, and, as I did this without the aid of a lawyer, the Bill means what it says, and says what it means: so much so, indeed, that its appearance caused no small alarm in high circles, as may be seen from the criticisms at that time in the Tory Press.[50]

Called 'Education, Trades Unions and the London County Council Elections', the circular to which she refers was produced for the first election after the abolition of the LSB, and hence of immense strategic significance. The measure which she says she drafted was the Labour Party's Education (Provision of Meals) Bill, which Will Thorne promoted in Parliament in the spring of 1906 as Labour MP for West Ham. The Bill sought full public control of all state schools; free, secular state education from primary school to university; and a generous system of non-competitive maintenance scholarships funded by the granting of public money and the restoration of misappropriated educational endowments.[51]

This radical educator-activist built her vision of the people's schools on these tenets. The restoration of the misappropriated educational endowments would fund the right to free and compulsory education provided by means of a common school system under popular control, with state maintenance accompanied by medical inspection and treatment. Inspired by the child-centred arguments espoused by the New Education movement, she defined a radical education in terms of Bedales, the school she chose for her son.

For Mary, a common school with a wide and generous syllabus was the only rational response to the existing capitalist society and the influence held by religious denominations. She placed herself firmly at the head of campaigns for secular education and opposed the granting of special privileges to religion in state schools. Writing as a member of the BSP in 1912, she warned of the strength and danger of clericalism as a political force because it was symptomatic of the undemocratic nature of the state – part of the 'forces of reaction', as she called them, now controlling the schools supported out of public funds.[52] She did not swerve from the position she articulated at the Queen's Hall, London in January 1904, when she spoke alongside Keir Hardie, H.M. Hyndman and leaders of the secularist movement to advocate 'popular control of all State-supported schools, with secular education'.[53]

In 1927 Mary returned to the pursuit of educational goals in a political article for the *Cotton Factory Times*. Writing in the wake of hard-fought working-class defeats, the lesson she had learned from the 1926 General Strike was that the conflict-based model of industrial relations must end. The full egalitarian spirit of wartime, the hope that men 'fighting together in the trenches would promote unity between the classes', had not been realised and the country was still deeply conservative in its distribution of educational resources. 'It would be interesting to see what would be the result of "Duke's child and cook's child" being taught together in the People's Schools,' she wrote. For her, this meant 'schools in which the needs of "cook's child" were recognised as being identical with those of "Duke's child", even in such matters as adequate floor and air space within the schools, and playing fields without'.[54] The people were now educated just as mainstream socialism had wanted in the 1880s and 1890s, but she regretted the failure to undo the intertwining of social class and educational opportunity.

Newcastle writer Jack Common (b. 1903) expressed a popular sort of insult when describing his educational experiences in the years leading down to the First World War. In his fictionalised autobiography, *Kiddar's Luck*, he wrote:

> Always the pride that prevailed in this working-class school was that it succeeded in turning out less recruits for the working-class than any other of its kind in the district. That less was still the majority, mind you, a great crowd that stayed on for two or three years after the scholarship culling was over and were then worked upon and encouraged to flash out what talents they had. But the school's official boast was not of them. The names in blue and red displayed on a whole row of rolls-of-honour hanging in the hall were those of educable small fry that had taken kindly to a scholastic bunk-up and been duly dispatched to the sphere of Higher Education.[55]

This was not what Mary meant by equal opportunity. She defined educational purpose in terms of the advancement of the class as a whole and sought to establish a radical alternative in the name of socialist objectives.

In practice, Mary's politics meant balancing reformist and revolutionary demands. Her strategy was to advance and unite working-class aspirations by working with the working-class movement. On the one hand, she embraced statist strategies for educational and welfare policies. On the other, she remained fundamentally opposed to the concept of neutral education as espoused by the WEA, which she saw as capitulating to capitalism. Even so, she did not rewrite the cultural script of the Adams family when it came to the question of private schooling for her son. Mary made sense of her actions in contradictory vein. That is to say, her existing concerns on the nature of provision made state schooling too great a risk for her child.

Notes

1 Cited in: J.W. Mackail, *The Life of William Morris* (New York, London: Benjamin Bloom, 1968 edition), p. 154.

2 E.P. Thompson, *William Morris: from romantic to revolutionary* (London: Merlin Press, 1977 edition), p. 378.

3 J. Clayton, *The Rise and Fall of Socialism in Britain 1884–1924* (London: Fale & Guryer, 1926), Preface, pp. vii–viii.

4 D. Müller, F. Ringer and B. Simon (eds), *The Rise of the Modern Educational System: social change and cultural reproduction, 1870–1920* (Cambridge: Cambridge University Press, 1989). The term 'hegemony' was used by Antonio Gramsci (b. 1891), founder and briefly leader of the Italian Communist Party. Gramsci was imprisoned by Mussolini and his writings in captivity were later published as *The Prison Notebooks*. Gramsci defines hegemony as the organising principle or world view diffused through agencies of ideological control and socialisation into every area of social life. In this context the key conceptual tool is what Gramsci calls cultural hegemony. Central to this idea is the notion that the dominant class lays down the terms and parameters of discussion in society; it tries to define and contain all taste, morality and customs, religious and political principles. However, hegemonic control has to be won and maintained. Subordinate classes can always produce a counter-hegemony in an attempt to modify, negotiate, resist or even overthrow the dominant culture. In humanist Marxism as articulated by Gramsci, humankind and the question of agency becomes the central focus.

5 A. Gramsci, *Selections from Prison Notebooks*, edited/translated by Q. Hoare and G. Nowell-Smith (London: Lawrence and Wishart, 1971), p. 334.

6 J. Miller, *School for Women* (London: Virago, 1996), p. 128.
7 Centre for Contemporary Cultural Studies Education Group, *Unpopular Education: schooling and social democracy in England since 1944* (London: Hutchinson, 1981), p. 36.
8 See R. Johnson, '"Really useful knowledge": radical education and working-class culture', in J. Clarke, C. Critcher and R. Johnson (eds), *Working Class Culture* (London: Hutchinson, 2nd edn, 1980); Centre for Contemporary Cultural Studies, *Unpopular Education: schooling and social democracy in England since 1944* (London: Hutchinson, 1981), pp. 34–46.
9 K. Flett, *Chartism after 1848* (Monmouth: The Merlin Press, 2006).
10 *The Pioneer*, 6 March 1908, p. 3.
11 W. Thorne, *My Life's Battles* (London: George Newnes, Ltd, 1926), p. 63.
12 I. Aberdeen (ed.), *Women in Education. Transactions of the Educational Section of the International Congress of Women* (London: T. Fisher Unwin, 1899), pp. 49–50.
13 Aberdeen (ed.), *Women in Education*, pp. 49–50.
14 Aberdeen (ed.), *Women in Education*, p. 48. Mary also attended the 1901 conference of the Froebel Society, though her contribution to debate went unrecorded. See *The Journal of Education*, February 1901, p. 164.
15 Aberdeen (ed.), *Women in Education*, p. 48.
16 Aberdeen (ed.), *Women in Education*, p. 48.
17 F. Brockway, *Bermondsey Story: the life of Alfred Salter* (London: Stephen Humphrey, 1995), p. 35.
18 'It's the incompetence, stupid', *The Spectator*, 10 January 2007.
19 Mrs Bridges Adams on equality of opportunity for all children, Questionnaire Leaflet, Women's National Liberal Association, No. 32, July 1903, pp. 4–5.
20 R. Wake and P. Denton, *Bedales School 1893–1993* (London: Haggerston Press, 1993), pp. 22–36.
21 J.H. Badley, *Bedales School: outlook of its aims and system* (Cambridge: Cambridge University Press, 1900).
22 J.H. Badley, *Bedales: a pioneer school* (London: Methuen & Co. Ltd, 1923), pp. 75–6.
23 J. Richardson, *How It Can Be Done; or constructive socialism* (London: Twentieth Century Press, 1898 edition).
24 K. Manton, *Socialism and Education* (London: Woburn Press, 2001), p. 40.
25 J. Richardson, *The Education Problem and Its Solution. Being seven chapters from "How It Can Be Done"* (London: The Twentieth Century Press, 1898 edition), p. 11.
26 Richardson, *The Education Problem*, p. 12.
27 Richardson, *The Education Problem*, p. 5.
28 J.H. Badley, *Bedales School: outlook of its aims and system*, p. 7.
29 Richardson, *The Education Problem*, pp. 172, 175.
30 Mrs Bridges Adams MLSB, 'The Education Crisis', *Labour Leader*, 20 July 1901, p. 237.

31 *Co-operative News*, 28 November 1901, p. 1396.
32 *Co-operative News*, 28 November 1901, p. 1396.
33 J. Jamieson, 'Alexander Wilkie', in *Northumberland at the Opening of the Twentieth Century* (London: W.T. Pike and Co, 1905).
34 *Clarion*, 23 November 1901.
35 *Labour Leader*, 21 December 1901, p. 407; 11 January 1902, p. 15.
36 C. Griggs, *The Trades Union Congress and the Struggle for Education 1868–1925* (Lewes: Falmer Press, 1983), p. 169.
37 W.P. McCann, 'Trade unionist, co-operative and socialist organisations in relation to popular education 1870–1902' (University of Manchester PhD, 1960), p. 425.
38 National Union of Women Workers, Conference 1903–4, pp. 100–1.
39 NRO, K2916, Diary of Lady Louisa Knightley of Fawsley, 5 November 1903.
40 'The Education Debate', Trades Union Congress, *Report*, 1906, p. 175.
41 *Justice*, 9 April 1910, p. 6.
42 A. Mansbridge, *The Trodden Road* (London: J.M. Dent and Sons, 1940), p. 60.
43 L. Goldman, *Dons and Workers: Oxford and adult education since 1850* (Oxford: Clarendon Press, 1995), p. 105.
44 See the discussion in M. Vlaeminke, *The English Higher Grade Schools* (London: Woburn Press, 2000), pp. 214–27.
45 *Railway Review*, 20 May 1910.
46 *Justice*, 13 April, 16 November 1907; *Nelson Leader*, 8 January 1908.
47 *Railway Review*, 20 May 1910.
48 *Labour Leader*, 20 May 1910.
49 *Justice*, 15 October 1910, p. 10.
50 *Cotton Factory Times*, 25 February 1916, p. 4.
51 See S. Bryher, *An Account of the Labour and Socialism Movement in Bristol Part Three* (Bristol: Bristol Labour Weekly, 1931), p. 4; 'Our Education Agitation', *Justice*, 10 March, 14 April, 28 July 1906; *The Pioneer*, 23 May 1906.
52 *Justice*, 29 June 1912, p. 6.
53 See *Justice*, 23 January 1904, p. 1; 27 February 1904, p. 8.
54 M. Bridges Adams, 'Obstacle to peace in industry', *Cotton Factory Times*, 11 November 1927, p. 5.
55 J. Common, *Kiddar's Luck* (Newcastle-Upon-Tyne: Bloodaxe Books, 1978), p. 84.

5

Education and class struggle

> She advocated for those she represented, the popular control of all schools, non-provided as well as provided; and urged that the schools – elementary, secondary and technical – should be free to all; and that no child should receive education that was in need of food first. As to secular education, she pleaded for this in the interest of justice and expediency. There should be no favour to any one Church in this matter. As to the Bible itself, she would retain that in the schools, side by side with other standard works of literature, but she would not give a special half hour to the reading of it, any more than to the reading of any other of the books in the school. She believed that the settlement of the controversy of the past thirty years would strengthen the position of the Churches in their proper sphere. She pointed out that the Nonconformist Progressives of the School Board party had declared they would 'never submit' to the Education Acts of 1902–3, while the Nonconformist Progressives of the County Council were declaring that they would work the Act 'impartially and fairly'. But there would be no peace until the religious question was buried once and for all. (Mary Bridges Adams, 1904)[1]

The London School Board

This was fighting talk. Stimulated to passion in the face of Conservative government education policy, Mary's plea to fellow members in the dying months of the LSB brings out the contemporary relevance of these events of a hundred and more years ago. An accomplished platform orator, after her speech on 30 January 1904 she moved and Stewart Headlam seconded the following resolution: 'The School Board for London declares that, in the interests of education it is essential that – 1. All state supported schools should be under full public control. 2. The education in all state-supported schools should be secular, and that the religious denominations be left free to impart, in their own way, at their own cost, and out of school hours, such instruction as parents may desire for their children'. Not unexpectedly, the motion was defeated by thirty-nine votes to five. What is interesting and important is that Mary kept alive the issue of control. Throughout this period and beyond she articulated a distinctively socialist voice, hinged on the promise of an education that would be secular and free. This chapter contains a detailed study of her contribution to education in London, in terms of campaigning to improve the quantity and quality of what was available for the vast majority of city children.

London was the centre and symbol of imperial and national power, and struggles over education provided a testing-ground for socialist and feminist politics from the earliest stage. The conspicuous strength of women was a feature both before and after Mary's election to the LSB. For example, Emily Davies and pioneering physician Elizabeth Garrett (b. 1836), the first woman in England to pass a recognised course of medical training, were both successful in the first elections.[2] From their foothold in 1870 women extended their presence so that they represented 18 per cent of the elected members in 1879. Not until the Labour party introduced all-women shortlists for the 1997 general election did parliamentary representation match this. All but three of the women members represented London Progressivism, a broadly based alliance comprised of Liberal Association members, trade unionists, nonconformists, social reformers and the rank and file of the working men's clubs. All but Mary Bridges Adams were from middle-class backgrounds, although their financial circumstances could vary considerably. Florence Fenwick Miller (b. 1854) was the youngest woman member, just 22 years old when she took her seat in 1876. Like Garrett before her, she married while serving, but was exceptional in continuing as an elected representative through pregnancy and childbirth. Annie Besant (b. 1847) was the only divorcee. Sixteen of the remaining twenty-eight were single women, eight were wives and mothers, two were widows at the time of their first election and another two were childless married women. In 1888 Besant topped the poll in Tower Hamlets in 1888, with a majority of nearly three thousand. A supporter captures her campaign's appeal: 'She was facing a hostile world on behalf of liberty and truth; and we young men, who had the passion of these things in our souls, responded readily to the passion with which she pleaded for them. We were carried away'.[3]

Not yet into her forties at the time of her first candidacy in 1894, Mary was just as dynamic as Annie. Her victory was the product of a socialist and union alliance and, once elected, she tried to act in a delegate-like manner, never forgetting where real power lay in the voter–member relationship. In office, she chose not to participate in women's work. Men's authority was based upon technical expertise, while the combination of education and maternal care was what provided educated middle-class women with an authoritative voice. Rejecting the stereotypes, Mary joined two male-dominated committees, Works and General Purposes, as well as the Evening Continuation Schools Committee and sub-committees responsible for Brentwood Industrial School and Contracts for Coal, Gas and Water. In 1900 she was placed on further sub-committees – Requisitions and Teaching Staff. Excluded from the national political field, she *had* gained access to what Felicity Hunt terms organisational policy: 'a middle level of decision-making which intervenes between government policy and actual school practice'.[4]

Held in public, weekly Board meetings were organised like a mini-parliament, beginning at 3 p.m. and usually continuing until 6.30 p.m., although it was often much later. Their main purpose was to hear the recommendations set out in reports from the various committees and to make policy decisions based on these recommendations. Members had a right to propose motions of policy, and debate them, before an open vote was taken, with each individual answering 'yes' or 'no' at the division. Besides participating in the Thursday debates which took place throughout the year with breaks at Christmas, Easter and in the summer, members were expected to serve on various committees and sub-committees as well as managing local schools in their division. Through this extra time devoted to constituency work they kept themselves informed about institutions, staff and students, developing a uniquely close working relationship with London's teachers and children.

Stewart Headlam recalled Lyulph Stanley saying that 'the member might belong to any party he pleased, but if he was once brought into contact with the schools he could not help developing interest, and as soon as he saw with his own eyes the need for apparatus and school books and staffs and premises, however pledged to economy he might be in the abstract, he would be the first to call out for money for his own schools'.[5] Both men combined School Board membership with active philanthropy. In Stanley's case this extended to a private fund to help pay the training college fees of poor pupil teachers and to help other protégées. On occasion this provided scope for embarrassment, like the time he befriended the school keeper's daughter at a North London school of which he was a manager and asked her parents if she might 'stay at his country house during school holidays'.[6]

Under Stanley's leadership the Board put strenuous efforts into the extension of the higher elementary schools, ably supported by Headlam, who represented Tower Hamlets from 1888, as chair of the Evening Continuation Schools Committee. Mary co-operated strongly with these men on common education policies. She also offered support for the line that the Liberal Dr T.J. Macnamara, a one-time pupil teacher who spent ten years as a board school teacher before he became a union official, was taking on staffing and teacher training.[7] Where they differed was on the question of the 1902 Education Act and supporting the voluntary schools from the rates. Macnamara put a contrary view to Adams, Headlam and Stanley, who opposed publicly funded faith schools.

Stanley's nephew, Bertrand Russell, said he 'spent his time fighting the Church on the London School Board'.[8] Headlam maintained that it was 'not the business of Board schools to teach religion', that 'parents should choose the parsons they prefer to teach their children religion, and the State should take no part in the matter'. 'The clerical and chapel elements' were 'equally obnoxious and equally mischievous' to Mary, commented the *Board Teacher*, a monthly newspaper for London teachers. As a consequence, she opposed the Greenwich practice of balancing church and chapel on board school governing bodies. Instead, she wanted 'to set the clergy free to look after their own "very bad schools"'.[9]

School Board politics

Mary based her claim to political power on the novel aspect of her contribution as the representative of organised labour. Re-elected for a second term, she defended her status with eloquence when others accused her of adopting the Progressive Party badge. As she explained: 'She stood here exactly as she did at the first meeting of the last Board – as a Labour representative and not as a member of the Progressive party'. Speaking on behalf of a fourth party, herself (as opposed to the Independent, the Moderate and the Progressive parties), she said she wished to support the motion to re-elect Lord Reay (b. 1861) as chairman of the Board because of the 'great sympathy he had shown to her as a representative of Labour'.[10]

On the LSB, Mary fought against under-funding and under-staffing of schools. She had strong ideas about curriculum, the use of corporal punishment, social distinctions in secondary education, initial teacher training and the abolition of the scholarship ladder. In May 1903, for example, with the Board already a condemned institution, she intervened in a debate on the raising of the school leaving age and unsuccessfully proposed the familiar socialist package that the Board should petition parliament for powers to make maintenance grants available to every 14-year-old able to reach a certain standard of achievement. 'She felt the proposal would then have the support of the organised trade unions of the country.'[11] She also supported efforts to make the system more democratic in its institutional structures and ultimately denounced the empowerment of bureaucratic experts like Sidney Webb on the Technical Education Board (TEB) and Robert Morant at the Board of Education.

Sometimes Mary's political position was close to that of teacher trade unionism in this period. Her maiden speech was on economic affairs and she made it in support of T.J. Macnamara's attempt to secure a better deal from a local taxation system that discriminated heavily in favour of boards outside London. Challenging the familiar accusation, she said 'their education, far from being expensive, was cheap, and cheap and nasty. Their teachers were not sufficiently educated for their work, their classes were too large, and many of their children were underfed.'[12] Subsequently she joined with Macnamara and others who disparaged the Board's failure to take steps to explore whether the law would allow it to establish a central day or residential training college. In her opinion, Lyulph Stanley's suggestion that they make more effective use of the existing, largely denominational training colleges was 'a thoroughly bad one with best intentions.' Mary 'expressed her pleasure at hearing the outspokenness of Mr Macnamara, as a practising teacher, attacking this scheme of Mr Stanley's for training the teachers. This was but an outcome of the return of the Progressives on the No Popery cry – it was an expression of anti-church feeling.' In response, Stanley 'expressed some hope of Mrs Bridges-Adams, and said he would rather deal with a fanatic than with a person utterly without enthusiasm for education.'[13]

Two weeks later Mary raised the question of teachers' pay. Here she used personal experience to support her argument for some kind of London weighting to help the capital's teachers afford the books and lectures she wanted them to have access to. 'She had lived in Birmingham as well as London, and had to manage on a small income, and she knew that one could secure a higher degree of comfort for £170 in Birmingham than could be secured in London for £200.'[14] On another occasion she implied the existence of corruption by making the allegation 'that those teachers who were active at election time secured promotion, with the result that there was dissatisfaction among Assistant Teachers.'[15] Another time it was the organised Labour movement that she sought to defend. In 1898 she and another new member, Frank Costelloe (one of the leaders of the Progressive Party on the LCC), were frustrated in their attempt to get the Board to appoint a special committee to investigate the effects and workings of the fair wage condition in Board contracts. The payment of trade union wage rates was a touchstone of Progressive achievements, but she and Costelloe drew a lurid picture of sweated labour, sub-contracting and a lack of transparency in its application by the various Committees of the Board.[16]

Questions of content were continuously present through the issue of religion, but Mary also favoured the introduction of peace studies. Her appeal failed. No one seconded the proposal and it was dropped.[17] However, her vote was always against militarism and imperialism, as a further example during the Siege of Ladysmith demonstrates. She opposed moves to make an exception of the Transvaal War Fund and lift the ban on school collections, and used her contribution to the debate to reflect a more consciously political ideology. 'Let the capitalists interested pay; or let the Board memorialize the Government to see the wives and children of our soldiers were properly supported and protected.'[18] She passionately opposed the Second Boer War and believed Marx's pronouncement that 'any nation that oppresses another forges its own chains'.[19] Her critics 'regretted that one effect of the proposition was the making of such a speech as that from Mrs Bridges Adams'. Popular at the Board for his slow speech and what the teacher politician Thomas Gautrey described as '"pawky humour"', John Sinclair, Scottish Congregationalist, journalist and minister, introduced himself as 'one of the sane few against this war'. However, though he distanced himself from Mary's position, Sinclair delivered a strong anti-militarist message. Needy soldiers were no more a special case than their counterparts who served their country in other ways, he said, and he 'objected to inciting the sympathies of children on the side of the brutal methods of warfare'.[20] In the event, the motion was defeated.

Mary also gave the reform of deterrent institutions a high priority. Then, as now, pupil absenteeism was a persistent problem. The ultimate sanction was committal to one of two types of corrective institutions. The first was a single-sex residential truant or industrial school. The second was a co-educational day industrial school provided for under the 1876 Education Act. In the spring of 1898 Mary aligned herself squarely with the Liberal Ruth Homan (b. 1850), who fought moves to re-instate the ritual of flogging male truants as an additional punishment for being sent back to industrial school. The *School Board Chronicle* offers a blow-by-blow account of debate within the School Board and Ruth is reported as saying 'that it was generally those who had been birched who wished to birch others'. Instead, she proposed that boys returning more than twice should attend classes for the whole day instead of being treated as half-timers.[21] Ruth's point was lost and things reached a climax a year later, when Mary joined forces with the feminist writer and lecturer Honnor Morten (b. 1861) to outlaw this treatment. Holding the besom broom used by staff at Highbury Truant School, she admitted that she would

Mrs. Bridges Adams: "This is a bloodthirsty instrument."

4 Mary Bridges Adams, cartoon from the *Board Teacher*

go further than her colleague who accused the Board of being 'birch-thirsty'. She would 'call it "blood-thirsty", for her instrument would draw blood'.[22]

Oral testimony from working-class inmates of these institutions suggests that she was right. 'That birch was like a besom broom … real birch. At the apex it'd be twelve to fourteen inches wide and tapered down. And this is what they birched you with. Drew blood – oh, it cut you.'[23] Reg Chubb was made to hold down his 7-year-old brother while he was publicly birched for absconding. 'They birched him six times. Four of us children held him down, two at hands an' two at legs, and a person in authority to give him the birch.'[24] In the event, the 1897 Board reinstated the additional punishment but gave instructions that it be carried out in private, as opposed to the gruesome gala Chubb described.

Mary also demonstrated her capacity to make a distinctive stand over women's interests. In March 1898 she supported Ruth Homan's demands for female representation on committees appointed to investigate charges against women teachers. Crucially, the vice chair of the School Management Committee flatly refused to serve with a lady manager in 'every case' and a majority of the men voted against the motion, which was unsuccessful.[25] When the question of a female appointment to the Inspectorate was raised in the Board, Mary joined with others in supporting it. The proposal was comfortably defeated, despite a tactical appeal from suffragist Emma Maitland (b. 1844) to allow for further discussion at Committee level.[26] Supporters may have suffered from an over-confidence, since the Education Department had recently appointed a number of women inspectors.

Emma and Mary were also unsuccessful in their attempt to increase the level of female representation on the TEB (set up by the LCC in 1891).[27] The TEB included twenty councillors and there were fifteen places for nominees of other organisations. Under the leadership of Sidney Webb, the TEB concentrated on building bridges between elementary and secondary education through scholarships and free places. Webb resigned in 1898, and it is conspicuous that Maitland's and Mary's action coincided with his absence on a world tour.[28] Nothing happened, since the matter was referred to the School Management Committee, a regular stalling mechanism. Lyulph Stanley and Graham Wallas, who served on both local authorities, advised School Board colleagues to use greater diplomacy, whereas Stewart Headlam broke ranks. He thought the School Board should have more places on the TEB, including a minimum of four women, grumbling that the TEB had 'discovered seven new deadly sins' since their rules forbade dancing, drinking, gambling, indecent language, profane language, smoking and drama in their polytechnic classes.[29]

Together with Labour representatives on the LCC, Mary was an outspoken critic of the work of the TEB.[30] They were most concerned about the failure to promote the education of the poorest children. As chairman of the Board, Webb secured the services of Hubert Llewellyn Smith, who had served as a research assistant to Charles Booth in his survey of *London Life and Labour*, to prepare a report on the state of technical education in London. Llewellyn Smith was inclined to see secondary education in relation to the needs of the middle class, while acknowledging a need to accommodate the hopes and ambitions of the brightest working-class children. His reports recommended the setting up of a system of junior and senior scholarships to help elementary school pupils to attend more advanced courses, and a programme of grants to support work in the secondary and technical schools and polytechnics. Since the available resources were limited, Webb thought it more efficient to restrict secondary education to fee-paying children from the middle classes, buttressed by 10 per cent of the elementary school population. Therefore he supported the idea of a 'ladder', designed to allow access to secondary education on a selective basis. The report he took to council was carefully researched and well informed and he was successful with a resolution allowing the London TEB to provide scholarships. As a start, it was decided to award five hundred junior county scholarships amounting to fees plus a maintenance grant of £10 a year, to help 13-year olds from elementary schools to go on to more advanced courses.

Scholarships were available for less than five in every hundred children and Mary considered the practice of setting working-class children a more rigorous examination than the routine admission test, taken by those whose parents could afford to pay for secondary schooling, an unfair one. In February 1898 she called for instant action on the extended opportunities for working-class children, wanting the Board to debate the question before the forthcoming Council elections. 'She severely criticised the methods of the Technical Board, and maintained that their funds were wasted. She looked forward to free education, elementary and secondary for all, but until that time came she wanted these funds made available to the children of the workers who used their schools'.[31] A year later she introduced a proposal that the School Board ask the TEB to allocate more money to the scholarship scheme and reserve half the awards for London pupils living in households where the income was less than two guineas a week. She felt their rival, the TEB, was too solicitous of those who 'could very well look after themselves'.[32]

The *Board Teacher* could not suppress a gasp at her approach. 'She does not mince matters. "Of all the frauds of the nineteenth century, the so-called Scholarships which are supposed to furnish the ladder from the slums to the universities" is one, and that the Scholarship lads are described as "horrid little Board School cads" in the secondary schools is the second of her ober dicta'.[33] But reports of speeches are second hand, and the journalist with an eye to good copy was always likely to remember best the exciting phrase, perhaps in the process giving it a prominence which it did not deserve. However, this conjuring up of her rhetoric in the Board chamber may throw additional light on Mary's political speaking.

Mary's language shows a pragmatic view of the need to import 'pithy paragraphs' into socialist propaganda to suit mass politics. While the comments escaped coverage in the *School Board Chronicle*, the sense of them was reflected in those of others. Anglican teacher the Rev. Richard Hoskyn said he 'sympathised with Mrs Adams's object, and, therefore, thought it a pity that she should spoil a good case by statements of that kind'. Lyulph Stanley thought 'Mrs Adams's references to "slum" children unfortunate, as coming from so good a democrat. There were poor children, but they were not necessarily "slum" children, and some of these poor children had earned scholarships'. Replying, she said 'that in referring to "slum children," she was quoting a phrase and not using it herself. The working classes were now almost educated enough to see how great was their ignorance, and they were very anxious that their children should have better educational advantages than they themselves had had'.[34] However, the successful motion was one proposing that the question be referred back to the School Management Committee for consideration and report. Fellow member for Greenwich, the Rev. John Wilson of Woolwich Baptist Tabernacle, refused to let it rest there, using due process in the Board chamber to carp at her. He hotly denied that the children of wealthier parents who paid for private tutors were unfairly advantaged. Citing the example of one teacher who gave free lessons to help five boys prepare for a scholarship examination, he concluded that the poorer children were 'not neglected to the extent Mrs Adams would have them think'. The educational press reported that he 'withdrew the "Previous Question" to laughter'.[35]

Mary endorsed the attempt to extend opportunities within the elementary system in her 1900 election manifesto. Recent years had seen a shift away from the provision of a largely 'elementary' curriculum aimed at the consolidation of a basic education for the students. Instead, a Progressive majority used the Board's relative autonomy from central government to finance education for students over the age of 15. Under Stewart Headlam's leadership, the numbers attending evening classes in advanced, post-elementary subjects increased, especially after the introduction of new regulations in 1898, when restrictions which had required a preliminary test in the 3Rs were relaxed and fees (up to then averaging 3d a week) were ended. In 1894 there were 80 institutes with 9,000 students, but ten years later the figures had soared to 395 and 147,000 respectively.[36] Trades Councils supported the initiatives, as did the Co-operative movement.

Anxious to spread the knowledge, Mary was largely instrumental in organising meetings at which she noted 'the people of London, working through their educational representatives, have in their Evening Schools a powerful means of checking the growth of "Hooliganism"'.[37] The phenomenon (with its capital 'H') hit the headlines in the wake of rowdy bank holiday celebrations in the hot summer of 1898. This opened the door for John Lobb (b. 1840), publisher of the *Christian Age* and Moderate member for Hackney, to make the charge that 'hooligans are bred in night classes'.[38] Thomas Gautrey, Progressive member for East Lambeth, remembered Lobb as 'an unblushing notoriety seeker who succeeded in making himself something of a public character in London'.[39] However, the *Daily Mail* published his attacks, including the allegation that 'pandemonium' reigned in several schools at a cost of £100,000 a year. An irate Headlam denounced Lobb at the Board, hitting back by referring to his miserable attendance record (he was at under half the meetings of the Evening Continuation Schools Committee), which showed how ill-informed he was.[40] Quite reasonably, Mary's sympathies were with Headlam.

Elementary education

In August 1901, the radical liberal Charles Masterman (b. 1873) described the School Board for London as 'probably the best hated body in England'.[41] Its Progressive policies antagonised powerful groups within British society, but the push to extend the scope of elementary education was especially controversial. Despite official support from Sir George Kekewich, who became head of the Education Department in the late 1890s, the tide was running in favour of those who wanted to sweep away all ad hoc bodies, that is to say single-purpose authorities for each public service, on the grounds that they led to duplication of effort and wasteful rivalries. The political prospects held out little hope from 1895 onwards, with Conservative governments returned in that year and again in 1900, and the Liberal Party in disarray. This was extremely fortuitous for the poorer endowed secondary schools and the voluntary church schools. The latter tended to be much inferior in scholastic achievement and saw themselves as the victims of unfair competition from the higher elementary board schools, financed with public money.

The tactic favoured by Sir John Gorst and Robert Morant was to check the growth of the more advanced work of the school boards, both in day schools and in evening classes. In May 1897 a Committee of Inquiry appointed under Gorst advised that grants to science and art schools might be distributed by competent local authorities, with an organisation for the promotion of secondary education. The recommendation found its way into a new Directory issued by the Science and Art Department at South Kensington. A new Moderate chair of the TEB, Edward Bond (b. 1844), soon raised the matter. Bond overrode the objections of the School Board representatives, so, as anticipated, the two controlling bodies both applied to become the sole London recipient of grants from the Science and Art Department. It was at this point that Robert Morant intervened. On 26 December 1898 he supplied evidence of a series of cases which threw doubt on the legality of the higher elementary work that the School Board had been developing in its higher grade schools and evening classes. After the Science and Art Department ruled in favour of its rival, Gorst took steps to have the School Board's position tested at the next local government audit.

Ruling cliques, led by the Cecil family, blessed the conspiracy and in June 1899 Camden School of Art duly made a complaint. In the House of Commons, the Church Party of Conservative MPs, now led by Lord Cranborne (b. 1861), the Prime Minister Lord Salisbury's eldest son, was still active as the traditional defender of Anglican interests. Cranborne and his brother Hugh Cecil (b. 1869) asserted themselves at Westminster, as did their cousins Arthur Balfour (b. 1848) and Evelyn Cecil (b. 1865). Recently resigned from the School Board, Evelyn was MP for Aston Manor and Parliamentary Private Secretary to the Prime Minister.

Within the wider Labour movement, Mary was at odds with those like the Fabian Sidney Webb who were beating the drum of national efficiency. Critically, the opposition was divided, and if the silence in the pages of *Justice* is taken as evidence, the SDF was unwilling or unable to associate with other groups with whom it shared a desire to save the school board system. Mary was well aware of the need to shape a popular educational politics to maximise opportunities for working-class involvement.

To defend the chances of election of Labour movement candidates, she made common cause with the women's movement and the classic popular Liberal Alliance represented in the National Education Association founded by Lyulph Stanley. With characteristic wit and ferocity, she explained that the alteration of the electoral basis in respect of the local council structures 'would place a hindrance in the way of the representation of women on educational questions. She was not a member of the Anti Man Brigade; she stood as a citizen, claiming a fair field and no favour. Corruption could only be fought by direct representation'.[42]

Fabians Stewart Headlam and Graham Wallas, chair of the School Management Committee, third-most important position in the Board's hierarchy, maintained their opposition also. Wallas explained the position to the Board in terms they could all understand and from which it was difficult for them to dissent. First of all, he complained of 'ungenerous attempts at delimitation from the authorities at Whitehall and South Kensington'. As a corrective, he believed it essential that they pay attention to 'what is meant by elementary education; what its objects are, and how far the methods we have chosen or inherited are sufficient to secure these objects'.[43] Meanwhile, Stanley produced a series of articles to present the case for direct democratic control of education under the administration of local bodies relating to the elementary educational needs of a specific geographical area.[44] Eventually the courts declared that the School Board was not entitled to run the technical and 'advanced' departments which it had opened.

Together with Sir John Gorst and Robert Morant, Bernard Shaw and Sidney Webb were prominently identified with the cult of national efficiency. Across the barrier of party they advocated a national minimum of nourishment, health and education to advance the cause of national security and social harmony. The 'ladders' of the efficiency group fitted in well enough with the object of national survival, and Webb, the expert administrator who climbed his own 'educational ladder', exploited the craze for imperialism to bring it into the service of social reform. Like Morant and Shaw, he distrusted popular control. Morant's views were set out in a special report that he prepared for the Education Department. This called for a new central authority which should be 'an aristocracy of brains, of picked men of educational (as well as of administrative) knowledge, wisdom and experience, chosen as such by the democracy for this express purpose, and invested accordingly with the supreme power over public education'.[45] Shaw and Webb wanted to increase the power of experts, with real responsibility confined to a political-administrative elite.[46] Opportunistically, the Conservative government managed to tie up the issue of county council control with the support of Church schools from the rates.

Working through the National Labour Education League, Mary launched a frontal attack on this Conservative reform, which she viewed with distrust. For her, the will of the people was preferable 'to the cupidity of the party wire-pullers in the country'.[47] Mary's object was to strengthen the opposition by supporting the activities of other groups who shared a desire to defend school boards – co-operators, feminists, Liberals and nonconformists. In the spring of 1901, the RACS helped to organise a protest meeting at which she, Stewart Headlam, Lyulph Stanley and Daisy Warwick were the main speakers. The Countess, while admitting she was labelled 'a harmless lunatic in educational matters' also said, somewhat illogically, that her secret ambition was to become a member of the LSB.[48] As events moved on, the Liberals received a deputation of co-operators at the House of Commons. In speeches at another protest meeting, Mary Bridges Adams, Keir Hardie and Stewart Headlam all bitterly contested attempts to undermine the school board system. Speaking at the Board a few weeks later Mary condemned Conservative proposals for neglecting 'the great defects of our education system. There was nothing in it to improve the educational position of the pupil-teachers for example'. Having 'given up all hopes of Sir John Gorst' she blamed 'the mischievous influence of the Fabian Society' for the situation in which they found themselves.[49] In the event, Gorst would resign from the government early in 1902 when he found he would not be given charge of the legislation.

Meanwhile Mary tried to energise the organised labour movement, urging the need to go beyond defence of the status quo. Labour might come to the rescue of nonconformity and Liberal Party radicals, she said, if it were to develop a constructive education policy. In a letter to the *Co-operative News* she dubbed the political situation an 'educational crisis'. 'As a labour representative on the London School Board for nearly four years', she wrote, 'I have been able to realise, as I never realised before, how tremendous are the obstacles in the way of securing a really adequate educational equipment for the children of the democracy'.[50] At about the same time she wrote another appeal for the *Labour Leader*, calling on socialists 'to bestir themselves on behalf of the nation's children'. She caught the atmosphere as she wrote, 'speaking as one who has had opportunities of seeing behind the scenes, I believe that there is at present a deliberate and determined attempt to curtail even the meagre educational opportunities at present within reach of the children of the industrial classes. The reason is not far to seek. Privilege must inevitably succumb before an educated democracy'.[51]

In March 1902, Lord Salisbury's nephew, Arthur Balfour, introduced the Education Bill in the House of Commons. It was intended to dissolve the school boards and transfer their powers to a committee of the county or county borough council which would co-ordinate all public services, an education committee having responsibility for education, and subsidise the voluntary schools (most of which were run by the Church of England) out of public funds.

Within the Board, Mary accused some colleagues of playing into Conservative hands. Contrasting the benign attitude of the leadership of the biggest teaching union, the NUT, with that of the rank and file, 'she said she believed the organisation was better than its leaders, and she appealed to it to give a strong lead, when she thought it possible that they might get a good Bill'.[52] Mary wrote a pamphlet for an external audience calling for popularly constituted school boards and absolute equality of opportunity. She also forecast that most of the revenue raised by the general rating authority would be spent on secondary education for middle-class children.[53]

In May 1902, she addressed a protest meeting organised by the National Labour Education League. She opposed the Bill on the grounds that it 'was not an Education Bill, and destroyed that which was democratic in the educational system'. She warned that 'sectarian jealousy would be increased' and again called for 'absolute equality of opportunity for all'. That same month she shared a platform with Lyulph Stanley at a Co-operative conference. 'In judging the system proposed', Stanley said, 'they must bear in mind that on an educational authority interest in the education of the people was more important than "culture"; that scarcely by any possibility could a working man get a seat on the County Council, of a county proper'. Mary invoked the principle no representation, no taxation. 'Parents were invited to entrust their children to people who did not dare to face them at an election. None but gentry or well-to-do tradesmen could attend County Council meetings, except in County Boroughs, and the chief landowner could always decide who should be made the public representative among the managers of his local school. It was sheer lunacy to call this popular control.'[54] People were asked to join the League, and two hundred leaflets were available for distribution.

Nonetheless, the government Bill was passed on 18 December 1902. All the school boards outside London were abolished and their responsibilities were transferred to a single education authority in each locality.

However, the School Board for London secured a stay of execution on the grounds that the metropolis and its educational administration constituted a special case. In addition to which, unlike the majority of English county councils, the metropolitan authority was not in Conservative hands. Some Conservative politicians, notably London Conservative MPs, undoubtedly viewed the LCC as the *bête noir* of the local government world, and this influenced their thinking.

Battle for the LSB

For different reasons, friends and foes were anxious to promote Sidney Webb as the architect of the Education Acts of 1902 and 1903. Fabian social engineers wanted to demonstrate the efficacy of politico-philosophic ginger groups. Marxist opponents in *Justice* gave him column inches, since they were keen to expose the nature of Fabianism to Labour supporters. Typically, *Fabian News* took the line that Fabian Tract 106, *The Education Muddle and the Way Out*, published in January 1901, was the fruit of Sidney's thinking and that this tract and the lobbying pressures brought to bear by Sidney greatly influenced the policy-making process.

What has been overlooked is that Tract 106 did not recommend the abolition of all school boards outside London, although it favoured a great reduction in their number. Therefore, Royden Harrison concludes that the case for Webb's influence is far stronger with respect to the London Education Act of 1903. Whilst Sidney probably did contribute to Arthur Balfour's ideas, his attempts at permeation, meaning the infiltration of the existing world of formal politics, were crucial to overcoming Conservative antipathy toward the LCC as the education authority.[55] For his part, Morant offered little constructive help. This was a signal for Beatrice Webb (b. 1858) to note in her diary: 'Morant gives strange glimpses into the workings of one department of English government. The Duke of Devonshire, the nominal education minister, failing through inertia and stupidity to grasp any complicated detail half an hour after he has listened to the clearest exposition of it, preoccupied with Newmarket [horse-racing] and in bed till 12 o'clock.'[56]

In contrast, Mary fought hard to secure the survival of the metropolitan authority on which she served. Three times she made the journey to meet Lord Londonderry, the titular head of the Education Department. In response, Lord Londonderry did not shrink from giving a clear intimation of the direction the wind was blowing. He wanted to guarantee the representative character of local democracy but argued the School Board for London did not fit that criterion, since it was elected by a cumulative vote.[57] In January 1903 Mary attended as a representative of the LSB, in March as part of the executive of the National Labour Education League and in April as a member of the London-based Women's Local Government Society.[58]

Avoiding party labels, the Society mounted a campaign to protect women's rights to elected office, since they were not then allowed to seek election to borough and county councils. Londonderry was absent on this occasion, so she met his deputy, Sir William Anson. Lord Reay mounted a passionate defence of the institution he served. 'If the same care, the same discrimination, were to be contributed as had hitherto been devoted to the organisation of a harmonious system of elementary education by representative citizens', he said, 'the contention of the School Board seemed rational that a process of selection which experience had proved to be effective should not be abandoned'. Lyulph Stanley put forward the woman's point of view, saying 'it would be a great loss to the educational interests of the community if women who had so much to do with the subject were not able to speak for their desires and convictions on the body which framed the policy'.[59]

The London Education Bill was presented to Parliament in June 1903 – on the very day the 1902 Act came into effect. In this circumstance, Mary advised Ramsay MacDonald, secretary of the LRC, to remember the ideological commitment to equality in education and to attack what she saw 'as a betrayal of the organised workers and the children of the Democracy into the hands of wire-pulling politicians and sectarians'.[60] In July she and Graham Wallas addressed the Women's National Liberal Association, where she told her audience that:

> She asked for absolute equality of opportunity for all children, no matter what their poverty, to be helped by education to develop their fullest powers. In the matter of education the democracy of England had been abominably betrayed by the privileged classes. The School Board should not be made the battle ground of creeds. 'On the grounds of justice and expediency,' she said, 'I claim for every child in this country the same education as I ask for my own'.[61]

With the School Board haemorrhaging members, whether through death from over-work, as in the case of Frank Costelloe, or the steady drip of resignations, opinion moved against her. Still Mary held out the prospect of popular control of all schools, public and private, the abolition of fees and a programme of free school meals. To stand aside from this struggle was at best to show oneself blind to its implications, at worst to conspire with the Anglican–Tory alliance. 'The true voice of the people was not heard through the party organs, owned by plutocrats, but through congresses such as those of the trade unions. The reform she now advocated did not entirely satisfy her as a "Revolutionary Social Democrat" but she should regard it as a "very good instalment" of the reforms necessary in our educational system.'[62]

However, most of her colleagues had begun to look ahead, and those who disagreed with her interpretation of events could hardly have been more ungracious, irritated by her eleventh-hour interventions. In February 1904, for example, she asked Bernard Shaw to address a socialist demonstration timed to precede the forthcoming elections for the LCC. Shaw expostulated, 'I am astonished to be asked by you, of all people, to take part in such maddening experiments in suicide. If you speak, back up the Education Act for all you are worth, and use it as a lever to lift the fainting cause of the right of women to sit on L.C.C.'[63] Mary *did* speak, sharing the platform with Keir Hardie, Henry Hyndman, Harry Quelch and Will Thorne.[64] Perhaps Shaw should have accepted her invitation, for he was soundly beaten in the contest for St Pancras.

More than ordinary political feelings had been aroused. For Sidney Webb, his victory came at a high price. His wife and political partner, Beatrice, outlined the problem from their opponent's point of view. '1) He is "in" with the government; 2) He might sacrifice the interests of primary to secondary and university education; 3) He ignores the "religious" difficulty and is willing to be impartial between Anglican and "undenominational" Christianity.'[65] Besides the negative effects on his friendship with Graham Wallas, who resigned from the Fabian Society in January 1904, having charged him with double dealing, there were others who viewed with distaste Webb's collaboration with Tory leaders. As a consequence, Ramsay MacDonald intrigued energetically on the LCC, managing the political force which ousted Webb from the chair of the TEB.

Mary's contribution

Attention to Mary's career on the LSB reveals something of her philosophy of education. It shows also her passion for social justice, her idealism and her enthusiasm. Her achievement in turning a thin majority into a safe seat in 1900 was impressive, and all the more remarkable given the showing against anti-war candidates in parliamentary elections at this time. The excellence of her organisation, her own hold on Woolwich's working class and her ability to capitalise on collective occupational and associational cultures in the locality had something to do with this success.

When the County Council took over, the new Education Committee was composed of thirty-eight men and five co-opted women (disqualified by sex from election to the new multipurpose local authorities), but these five did not include the only acknowledged representative of organised labour to serve on the LSB. As secretary of the LTC, Fred Knee tried to persuade Liberal-Labour councillors to join with them in supporting Mary's co-option, but without success.[66] The final meeting of the Board took place on 28 April 1904 and *Justice* issued a warning: 'we regret to see that in the selection of co-opted members, well-known friends of education and of the interests of the children, like Stewart Headlam and Mrs Bridges Adams, have been passed over.'[67] Headlam's biographer denounced the 'treachery' of London Progressives who cold-shouldered appeals to make Lyulph Stanley an alderman.[68] While Mary also protested Stanley's exclusion, guilty men anxious to commemorate his lifelong commitment to education proposed to name a new council school after him, but he resisted.[69] Instead, he asked that the school with which he had been most closely associated might become a site of commemoration. Among the old boys of the Lyulph Stanley School was the comedian and actor Kenneth Williams (b. 1926).

For six years Mary Bridges Adams articulated doggedly the concerns of organised labour, even though she was politically isolated and unsuccessful in most of her initiatives. It is arguable that she was prescient and ahead of her time. W.P. McCann sees her as one of the few who 'fully comprehended the fact that British educational development stood at the crossroads at the turn of the century, and saw the directions in which the two roads led.'[70] Certainly she was correct in her assessment of the operation and organisation of education as epitomised by the 1902 Education Act. There was no question that the alteration of the electoral basis would diminish the possibility of the election of working-class and socialist candidates. Additionally, the underlying theme of differentiation in education became more firmly defined. London's secondary schools continued to exclude working-class children and the inequalities of the fee-paying system were maintained.

As a root and branch opponent of the abolition of the School Boards and the transfer of their functions to ordinary local government, she deprecated the politics of permeation and backstage intrigue in which Sidney Webb played a considerable part. Instead, she brought the National Labour Education League into being and pursued the tactic of mass pressure from without. But there was a direction to their struggles that was his; 'The world is going your way at present, Webb, but it is not the right way in the end,' William Morris told Sidney in 1895.[71]

Notes

1 *School Board Chronicle*, 30 January 1904, p. 103.
2 For more detail on the London School Board women see J. Martin, *Women and the Politics of Schooling in Victorian and Edwardian England* (London: Leicester University Press, 1999).
3 M. Quin, *Memoirs of a Positivist* (London: George Allen & Unwin, 1924), p. 53.
4 F. Hunt, *Gender and Policy in English Education 1902–1944* (London: Harvester Wheatsheaf, 1991), p. 11.
5 F.G. Bettany, *Stewart Headlam: a biography* (London: John Murray, 1926), p. 148.
6 S. Maclure, *A History of Education in London 1870–1990* (London: Allen Lane, 1990), p. 22.
7 R. Betts, *Dr Macnamara 1861–1931* (Liverpool: Liverpool University Press, 1999).
8 Bertrand Russell quoted in: Maclure, *A History of Education in London*, p. 22.
9 *Board Teacher*, 1 November 1899, p. 259.
10 *School Board Chronicle*, 8 December 1900, p. 626.
11 *School Board Chronicle*, 9 May 1903, p. 397.
12 *School Board Chronicle*, 11 December 1897, p. 650.
13 *School Board Chronicle*, 2 July 1898, p. 7.
14 *School Board Chronicle*, 16 July 1898, p. 55.
15 *School Board Chronicle*, 2 November 1901, p. 438.
16 *School Board Chronicle*, 5 February 1898, p. 134.
17 *School Board Chronicle*, 22 April 1899, p. 426.
18 *School Board Chronicle*, 11 November 1899, pp. 501–2.
19 *Documents of the First International*, Volume 111 quoted in: Y. Kapp, *Eleanor Marx Family Life 1855–1883* (London: Virago, 1979), p. 119.
20 T. Gautrey, *Lux Mihi Laus: School Board memories* (London: Link House, n.d.), p. 66; *School Board Chronicle*, 11 November 1899, pp. 501–2.
21 *School Board Chronicle*, 5 March 1898, p. 243.
22 *Board Teacher*, 1 March 1899.
23 P. Thompson, *The Edwardians* (London: Routledge, 1975), p. 170.
24 S. Humphries, *Hooligans or Rebels?* (Oxford: Basil Blackwell, 1981), pp. 221–2.
25 *Board Teacher*, 1 November 1899, p. 259.
26 *School Board Chronicle*, 7 May 1898, pp. 477–8.
27 *School Board Chronicle*, 19 March 1898, p. 291.
28 N. MacKenzie and J. MacKenzie (eds), *The Diary of Beatrice Webb, Volume Two 1892–1905* (London: Virago, 1986), pp. 132–3.

29 *School Board Chronicle*, 19 March 1898, p. 291.
30 John Burns (b. 1858), Will Crooks, Keir Hardie and Ben Tillett.
31 *School Board Chronicle*, 12 February 1898, p. 164.
32 *School Board Chronicle*, 14 March 1899, p. 225.
33 *Board Teacher*, 1 March 1899, pp. 92–3.
34 *Board Teacher*, 1 March 1899, pp. 92–3.
35 *Board Teacher*, 1 March 1899, pp. 92–3; *School Board Chronicle*, 4 March 1899, p. 266.
36 Bettany, *Stewart Headlam*, p. 157.
37 *Greenwich and Deptford Observer, Woolwich Gazette and Kentish Advertiser*, 16 November 1900, p. 2.
38 G. Pearson, *Hooligan: a history of respectable fears* (London and Basingstoke: Macmillan, 1983), pp. 74–6.
39 Gautrey, *Lux Mihi Laus*, p. 64.
40 *School Board Chronicle*, 17 November 1900, p. 533.
41 *Commonwealth*, August 1901, p. 234.
42 Mrs Bridges Adams on equality of opportunity for all children, *Questionnaire Leaflet*, Women's National Liberal Association, No. 32, July 1903, pp. 4–5.
43 *School Board Chronicle*, 20 October 1900, pp. 317–18.
44 A.W. Jones, *Lyulph Stanley: a study in educational politics* (Waterloo, Ontario: Wilfred Laurier University Press, 1979), pp. 115–18.
45 R.L. Morant, 'The National Organisation of Education of all grades as practised in Switzerland', Education Department Special Reports on Educational Subjects, Vol. III, *Parliamentary Papers*, XXV (1898) [C.8988], p. 24.
46 G.B. Shaw, *Man and Superman* (1903, Penguin edition 1946), p. 268 quoted in: G. Searle, *The Quest for National Efficiency* (London: Basil Blackwell, 1990), p. 95.
47 *School Board Chronicle*, 25 May 1901, p. 557.
48 'National Education Conference at Leman Street', *Comradeship and Wheatsheaf*, April 1901, pp. 153–4.
49 *School Board Chronicle*, 25 May 1901, p. 557.
50 M. Bridges Adams, 'The educational crisis' (letter), *Co-operative News*, 6 July 1901, pp. 830–1.
51 Mrs Bridges Adams MLSB, 'The education crisis', *Labour Leader*, 20 July 1901, p. 237.
52 *School Board Chronicle*, 15 March 1902, p. 249.
53 *Manchester Guardian*, 17 April 1902.
54 *Comradeship*, June 1902, pp. 10–11.
55 R.J. Harrison, *The Life and Times of Sidney and Beatrice Webb 1858–1905: the formative years* (Basingstoke: Palgrave, 2001).
56 MacKenzie and MacKenzie, *The Diary of Beatrice Webb*, p. 247.
57 *School Board Chronicle*, 21 March 1903, pp. 238–9.
58 *School Board Chronicle*, 31 January 1903, pp. 99–100; *School Board Chronicle*, 21 March 1903, pp. 238–9; *School Board Chronicle*, 4 April 1903, p. 297.

59 *School Board Chronicle*, 31 January 1903, pp. 99–100.
60 M. Bridges Adams to J.R. MacDonald, 12 May 1903, Labour Party Archives, National Museum of Labour History, Manchester.
61 Mrs Bridges Adams on equality of opportunity for all children, *Questionnaire Leaflet*, Women's National Liberal Association, No. 32, July 1903, pp. 4–5.
62 *School Board Chronicle*, 21 March 1904, pp. 102–4.
63 G.B. Shaw to Mrs Bridges Adams, 10 February 1904.
64 *Justice*, 27 February 1904.
65 Mackenzie and Mackenzie, *The Diary of Beatrice Webb*, p. 273.
66 Minutes of Delegate Meeting, 10 March 1904, London Trades Council.
67 *Justice*, 26 March 1904.
68 Bettany, *Stewart Headlam*, p. 156.
69 *School Board Chronicle*, 30 April 1904, p. 423.
70 W.P. McCann, 'Trade unionist, co-operative and socialist organisations in relation to popular education 1870–1902', unpublished PhD thesis, Manchester University, 1960, p. 478.
71 R. Page Arnot, *William Morris: the man and the myth* (London: Lawrence and Wishart, 1964), p. 108.

6

The disinherited child and the politics of voice

> The 'disinherited' child is one of the best pegs on which to hang the teaching calculated to produce the divine discontent which lies at the back of the 'labour unrest'. When the 'unrest' appears we know that there is hope that the workers are realising that there is class war – a war which must be fought to a finish and we want our soldiers in that war to be well equipped. Therefore it is that I, for one, fight my best in the field of education. (Mary Bridges Adams, 1915)[1]

> We must learn, as no generation before ever learned, to succour the young children of all classes; but above all to help and uplift the poorest, the most neglected and the most helpless. These, let us note, are not the unfit or the backward. In the wild torrent of past industrial life, the fit and the unfit were engulfed in one hidden tragedy. It is given to you, in the morning of life, to come to the help of these; and to spare no pains in winning power to do it well. Your principal and myself greet you as you prepare to 'succour the helpless'. (Margaret McMillan, 1927)[2]

Margaret McMillan and children's welfare

The metaphor of the 'disinherited' child owed much to the human carnage of the First World War. In one register, this is the journalistic voice of Mary Bridges Adams urging cotton textile workers to campaign for the social needs of working-class children in April 1915. Mary's written voice did nothing to assuage the anxieties of her enemies, but this was nothing new. In December 1897, her spoken voice brushed aside objections to a proposal that the School Board for London should assume powers to provide meals for hungry children. With the courage of her convictions she said that most School Board members 'were able to gratify every wish' so they could not begin to understand what it meant to be inadequately fed. 'Poverty was an ambiguous term', she observed and 'there was the poverty of the poor as well as of the rich' – members pitied the poor relatives 'who had to manage on £400 a year'.[3] Her lost struggles helped to shape the wider culture of social reform, but in pursuing them the traces of another woman become part of the narrative.

Margaret McMillan also campaigned in the name of the child, and there is a sense in which she is the 'insider' in the archive, positioning Mary as the 'outsider'. In another, more pedagogical tone, Margaret was to act as teacher and guide to mothers in slum areas and her reported speech shows how she went about it in the late 1920s. It is taken from her 1927 Christmas message to the enthusiastic young women she recruited to work in the homes and streets around the garden in the slum that was the Deptford Centre. Firmly convinced that working-class mothers could not be trusted, McMillan assumed that the transmission of knowledge that she successfully established in her open-air treatment centre and school would reopen the linkages between the developing child and the physical, emotional and moral world which surrounded him/her.

This chapter takes memoir, along with administrative and socio-political history, to disentangle what Carolyn Steedman describes as the 'fictions of engagement'[4] that populate the mythic histories woven around popular understandings of Labour's past. By piecing together the forgotten aspects and interweaving Mary's efforts with those of Margaret McMillan, it becomes possible to trace a different, less tidy story. Steedman gives expression to the need to unpack, historically, the question of 'voice giving' to the hitherto unheard or rarely heard-of individuals and groups in history. Here 'voice' means the identity the subject chose to present, and a fabric of assumptions, values, ideas and associations. To map this terrain is to investigate the subtle interplay between the forces of the 'tutelary complex',[5] families, politics, socio-economic conditions and culture. The effect is to challenge prevailing orthodoxy about social welfare campaigns within the tradition of reform by offering alternative perspectives on the words and actions of two socialist women in the imaginative reconstruction of policy as text and action.

Margaret McMillan constructed a restorative programme for the education of working-class children that stressed the training of the muscular system and stimulation of the senses before the development of the mind. Essentially, it reflected 'an understanding of neurological function whereby sensation was deadened by dirt'.[6] In *The Camp School* (first published in 1917), she writes most memorably of slum children she taught, using metaphors of cleanliness and empire to connect her education practice with the lives of the very poor. Washed, changed and ready for bed, the elder girls reminded her of tall lilies as they passed the sleeping bodies of the babies. 'On rainy evenings they looked particularly fresh and well, as if the rain loved them. The cool flush of the *real* English-woman was on every face. Their *range of sensation* appeared to be greater after a time.'[7]

Water was part of a process of cure for a particular class of children with bodies and brain centres half deadened by an industrial system she condemned. She uses the sentimental rhetoric to convey the potential for regeneration of the individual child, a class and a nation. Monica, a 'wonderful little sensitive', spent one glorious June toddling in the baby camp before she died. 'Her first impressions must have been wonderful. We lifted her on the low terrace so that she was on a level with the geraniums and the hybrid roses all in leaf … A thrush sang loudly in the old plane-tree'. Seven-year-old Marigold was another pioneer camper who emerges as a tragic figure: a child undone by the immorality of her mother. In the camp, she had 'the manner and voice and look of a fairy princess', but her father died in a street accident and her mother 'moved', Margaret wrote, euphemistically. The next time they met, Marigold's 'lovely face had coarsened so as to be almost unrecognizable … Why dwell on one tragedy among so many thousands?'[8] Ted received lessons on voice production to correct a lisp. His unemployed father and inefficient mother (to use the hygienist language of the time) sent him to school unfed. Bowls of roses in the classroom served to ameliorate any feelings of weakness and dizziness in the hungry and malnourished children. So, when the teacher asked how his voice lesson went: 'His eyes filled, but his lips did not tremble. And he spoke out clearly, slowly, proclaiming his hard-won victory, "I am a strong man".'[9]

Posterity has been kinder to Margaret McMillan than it has to Mary. She was not (and is not) confined to the margins of socialist histories, despite the apostasy of her appearance on Conservative platforms campaigning for Nancy Astor (b. 1879) at Plymouth in 1929. She is one of the 'Famous Four' socialist women whose names crop up repeatedly in histories of the ILP.[10] In her landmark 350-page biography, Steedman depicts how McMillan secured her historical voice, virtually canonised as the rescuer of the utterly helpless, the visionary saviour of working-class childhood. One of the ways through which this was established was through McMillan's manipulation and use of genres in writing the life of her sister Rachel (published in 1927).[11] It is noticeable that this recasting of form is present in Albert Mansbridge's 1932 biography of Margaret McMillan, which is concerned mainly to chronicle her active part in public life, especially her contribution as an educational thinker.

The tone deployed is hagiographical and the reminiscences include those of Robert Blatchford, who supported her work as an elected member of the Bradford School Board in the 1890s.

According to Blatchford, she embodied a 'blend of Joan of Arc and Florence Nightingale, tempered by the humour of Jane Austen'.[12] From this starting point, Mansbridge composes a eulogy to those mystic and spiritual qualities that gave her knowledge of God and put her in touch with the saints. Hence, she took advantage of her ability to commune with philanthropists like the early Victorian reformer Lord Shaftesbury and her sister Rachel, both of whom became as living counsellors. 'My Rachel is so gay and sweet', she wrote in a letter to Blatchford in 1929, twelve years after Rachel's death. 'She laughs a great deal, and it is the laughter of an *angel.* She is here mostly all the time … She makes the climate, once she said to me "Snow!" So they' (the nursery school children) '*see* our atmosphere and weather' (original emphases).[13] A letter from Robert Blatchford to Albert written after Margaret's death recalls an early encounter between the Blatchfords and McMillan. A tired, sad, middle-aged woman when she arrived (she was then about 34), as she talked she grew younger. Later, Robert asked his wife if she noticed anything strange about her. 'I should think I did,' she replied. 'She frightened me … She kept getting younger and prettier. She turned into a beautiful girl.' It seems this was something she shared with her older sister, Rachel, and others noted the attribute – including a friend of Blatchford's, a matter-of-fact Yorkshire grocer.[14]

The emotional circumstances in which George Lowndes collated the written memories found in *Margaret McMillan 'The Children's Champion'* make it another site of commemoration, this time initiated by the Nursery School Association to mark the centenary of its founder and first President.[15] Here Lowndes likens McMillan to the German philosopher and humanitarian Dr Albert Schweitzer (b. 1875) – who was awarded the Nobel Peace Prize in 1952. By contrast, the streets of Bradford and Deptford are the setting for Elizabeth Bradburn's 1976 practitioner-oriented account of the educator activist as change agent.[16] The particular focus of Steedman's biography is the argument that in her lifetime McMillan rewrote the 'common senses' of working-class childhood in British social and political culture. Abetted by late-nineteenth-century developments in the sciences of neurology and physiology, McMillan stressed the importance of overt political intervention to remove barriers to the natural and organic development of the minds and bodies of working-class children. She believed it possible to refashion the slum child from deprived circumstances and make them completely well and strong. Her family motto, 'succour the helpless', became the watchword of the several private-sector health and educational schemes that she ran with the assistance of women trained in the emerging area of child welfare.

Steedman makes a convincing case for the scope of McMillan's influence and achievements. Combined, her social action on behalf of actual children and the child figure (both invented and real) as subject of her journalistic fiction helped to define the Labour party's vision of maternal and child welfare. Nonetheless, her political progress from committed socialist as an elected member of the Bradford School Board to voluntary social-welfare activities in London eased the way for shifts in political perception. By the 1920s, she reasoned 'Party is not enough', as she wrote of the 'good old Tories' who had made personal donations to help fund her ambitious ventures.[17] Analyses of her written work suggest the concern with national efficiency which permeated the worlds of politics and political ideas in the early 1900s.

Geoffrey Searle shows how the rhetoric of efficiency, which adopted a militaristic and technocratic political language, appealed to people from very different social backgrounds.[18] McMillan's *Labour and Education*, published in 1907, appropriates some of the arguments and metaphors underpinning the theme of Britain's loss of competitiveness, allied to fears about the possibility of the physical stock of the nation degenerating. 'It is disease and the fear of infection and racial decline that (more than anything else, perhaps) makes us now turn to the school doctor' she wrote.[19] Deficit thinking and the promotion of personal hygiene may be detected in McMillan's accounts of the physical unfitness of the slum denizens of the big cities. Home visits were not deemed necessary. 'There was ample opportunity to judge of the home from the open street door, and the appearance of the home-keepers in the street, as well as the state of the neglected child in school.'[20] This resonates with what Seth Koven describes as the 'politics of dirt' underpinning the cultural practice of 'slumming' which provided some middle-class men and women (like McMillan) with a position of authority in poor urban neighbourhoods.[21] The remedial approach that she promoted is amply reflected in a letter she wrote Blatchford in February 1929. 'This morning my wee children came in crying. They're not crying now. Jolly as sandboys. Hundreds of 'em. No poor mother can do that in their wretched homes.'[22]

The iconography of McMillan as heroine of childhood is embedded in the histories of school welfare services. Mansbridge shaped his telling of her life in this particular way and many discussions have built on this foundation. The familiar account begins with her pioneering work in this field, followed by the evidence of the Royal Commission on Physical Training (Scotland) (1903), and the Interdepartmental Committees on Physical Deterioration (1904) and Medical Inspection and Feeding of Children Attending Public Elementary Schools (1905). Many of the policy studies reproduce the views of historian Bentley Gilbert and it seems probable that he was influenced by the views of Mansbridge.

Both men see Margaret McMillan and Robert Morant as the principal actors. Gilbert conceives Morant as the far-sighted bureaucrat, making planned advances through a political-administrative 'trick' in which lay the origins of the school medical service. What is beyond question is the importance of Margaret McMillan, 'in whom the cause of better physical care for schoolchildren found a persistent champion'.[23] As Mansbridge describes it, having the ear of Morant as permanent secretary of the Board of Education from 1903 was one of the 'happiest pages' in McMillan's life.[24] Gilbert reproduced the views of Mansbridge to show how McMillan benefited from the relationship because Morant went along with her political action on behalf of underprivileged children. Cognisant of the need to win over his many enemies, Morant recognised that McMillan offered an indirect link to the Labour Party. Here is how he put it in a letter written after they first met: '*between us* we shall do something I am sure; if we can avoid raising public hubbub *against* our efforts'.[25] This takes us beyond the sphere of party politics, narrowly conceived. His concerns may be rooted in those of national fitness; the point of his intervention was to get things done to improve the efficiency of the population and the machinery of government. Is such attention to the political manoeuvres of Morant justified? In suggesting not, recent scholars make it hard to accept the conventional interpretation of McMillan's contribution, namely, that she gained access to power within the official central state by securing the trust of and imposing her views on the saviour of Gilbert's story, Robert Morant.[26]

In his specialist study of parliamentary debate on the educational legislation of 1906 and 1907, Neil Daglish undermines the case for Morant; as does Bernard Harris in his more general contribution to the history of British social policy, *The Health of the Schoolchild*. Crucially, they both undermine Gilbert's suggestion that the foundation of the school medical service was a part of Morant's 'hidden' agenda.[27] As they see it, these ideas were very much a feature of the wider culture of social reform at a time when populations, hygiene and welfare became a target for philanthropy in almost every European country.

In Britain the question of racial deterioration was taken seriously by various social groups, including government. Shaken by the poor state of health of recruits to the army for the South African war, it was in such circumstances that many leading minds focused on the attempt to implement a programme of efficiency. Against the background of warnings that the average level of public health was deteriorating, most medical experts agreed that urban, industrialised conditions were having a deleterious effect. However, some argued that particular characteristics could be inherited, so that the constitution of the parents (which might be strong or weak) could be passed down to their offspring. It was in response to concern about the cumulative consequences of hereditary transmission across generations that the Conservative government set up the Interdepartmental Committee on Physical Deterioration, whose report on the physical condition of the British population was published in 1904. Its recommendations on schoolchildren were threefold: 'schools should be established for children whose health made them temporarily unsuited to normal schools; every school authority should have the duty to make medical inspections of schoolchildren; authorities should be compelled to provide school meals for underfed children'.[28] Within this context – a growing body of evidence to support a medicalising strategy, one of preventive medical scrutiny and environmental reform – those agitating in favour of public health measures were playing on opponents' fears and needs.

The campaign for free school meals

Mary Bridges Adams did not use the same language as Margaret McMillan to represent and think about the poor. She worked with a politics that did not have space for the flowery language and idealised creatures that McMillan moved into the public arena. Mary fashioned herself as the representative of organised labour on the LSB, and her identification with the working-class movement was very different. Basking in the euphoria of her election victory, the secretary of the Woolwich branch of the Labour Protection League declared that members were convinced her 'great ability and strong force of character' would 'soon gain for her an influence on the Board'.[29] Among other things, they anticipated the day when her 'strong sense of humanity' would ensure 'the feeding of the thousands of poor little children who, through circumstances over which they have no control, are now forced to attend school suffering from the pangs of hunger'.[30]

During her first months on the Board, Mary was bitter at the callous attitudes some representatives adopted towards the conditions of working-class life. 'It had been painful to her to see members who were loud in their protestations as to the necessity of religious and theological teaching exhibiting a scornful expression when the question of starving children was brought forward.'[31] In this way, she aligned herself with Father Brown (Roman Catholic member for Southwark), Frank Costelloe (one of the leaders of the Progressive Party on the LCC) and Reverend John Scott Lidgett (warden of the Wesleyan Methodist Bermondsey Settlement), who denounced the government's failure to intervene. She alienated Lyulph Stanley, however, who poured scorn on such 'loose talk' on the assumption that she 'seems to suggest that in every case where a man earned only £1 a week the Board should supplement his wages by feeding his children'.[32] In common with the majority, Stanley thought that mass feeding would undermine social Darwinist laissez-faire public policies.

Children's hunger remained a major social issue in London and campaigners kept up the pressure. In response, the School Board appointed a special subcommittee to formulate policy. Members included Bridges Adams, Father Brown, Scott Lidgett, Dr Macnamara and Honnor Morten. Inquiries suggested that around 55,000 children were in need of meals and Mary lobbied strenuously for a comprehensive measure. Her published statement to the School Board on the question of starving and underfed children underscores her conclusion that voluntary effort had been of limited value and the problem could 'only be satisfactorily dealt with by the Community as a whole'.[33]

There was clear attention to detail in her well thought-out proposals for feeding children in the ground-floor school halls, to be utilised in the short term as dining rooms. Parents who could afford to do so would obtain dinner tickets at a central office, so as to ensure that children did not know who had paid and who had not. She believed a scientific medical investigation into the health of the child population would demonstrate the need to improve nutrition and combat malnutrition. More of the electorate would then support the demand for state maintenance to ensure that the poorer classes 'will be strong in the body and sufficiently sound in mind to make a wise use of the increasing power which is falling into the hands of the democracy'.[34] Sensitive to the assumption that it is important to foster self-help, she went on: 'Few people now hold that children should suffer for their father's sins, including the unpardonable sin of poverty. But the very strong argument of parental responsibility comes in.

To this I would say, that parents who can, but will not, support their children, should be dealt with by the law'.[35] Within the sub-committee of the General Purposes Committee, there was a tension between two opposing views: those who were dissatisfied with current arrangements and those who were not. Given the basic disagreement, the sub-committee divided and the three Moderate Party members produced their own Minority Report.

Presented to the Board on 16 November 1899, the Majority Report triggered a heated debate. Frank Costelloe came from his sickbed to support the recommendations but did not manage to manipulate his School Board colleagues (he died shortly after).[36] Lyulph Stanley castigated it 'with all the vigour and sarcasm at his command: "worthless statistics", "pestilent heresy", "wild and absurd report", "irresponsible members", "wild resolutions", "sick of clap trap"'. Disheartened by the level of opposition, Mary threw caution to the wind, almost threatening members as she accused them of being 'sleek, smug, well-fed and possessing substantial banking accounts'. As she put it:

> The argument with reference to the evil of encouraging charity was the doctrine of the Devil. She warned Society that they stood upon a mine – that while they slept in smug security, quiet street-corner meetings were being held, which no reporter would think of attending, at which these very questions were discussed by men deeply touched by social evils, of which this was only one. She held that the scheme proposed was no more demoralizing than it was to steal for a starving child.[37]

This was a rebuttal of those who thought pauperism or indigence (which stood for vagrancy, promiscuity, improvidence, ignorance and insubordination) was a proper matter of regulation and who might think that to provide free meals was to relieve parents of important duties and hence to encourage irresponsibility.

Cut from very different cloth to the majority of her colleagues, Mary wanted local education authorities to provide free meals to children outside the Poor Law. In her view, there were three different ways in which to raise the money required. First, through the taxation of ground values, second, by a graduated income tax on those earning more than £300 a year, or finally, through the use of graduated death duties.[38] Nonetheless, she failed to convince her opponents, and a two-tier administrative structure was set up to organise the food supply. It was decided that there should be a central committee consisting of representatives from the London and the Rochester Diocesan Boards of Education, charity workers, school managers and members of the LSB, including Mary

Bridges Adams. In order to simulate divisional organisation, there were local committees of school managers.[39] At Putney, the sister of future Labour leader and settlement worker Clement Atlee (b. 1883) taught the youngsters to sing grace. 'He himself [Clement] brought teaspoons and small forks for the younger children because he considered those supplied too large for them, and he also trained the elder girls to cut up the meat of the little ones and to look after them.'[40]

Mary spearheaded vigorous campaigns for the health of children after the destruction of the school board system, becoming the education spokesperson for her union and her party. With the trade union movement excluding all but delegates organised in and working at their trades from its annual congress, there was no possibility for her to speak as an insider. Instead, we exhume Will Thorne's voice from the archive, the printed texts of annual congress meetings. We have but fleeting glimpses of her in the programme, acknowledgement of her service to education in the Gas Workers' quarterly balance sheets. But it is enough to convey a sense of her co-operating quite closely over the launch of the 'Children's Sunday' meetings convened by the Gas Workers at Leeds in 1904. These meetings (halted during the First World War) took place on the Sunday preceding the TUC conference and provided a political space in which to discuss questions of working-class childhood and education. She shows herself adept at building up support, getting Sir John Gorst (who had resigned from the Balfour ministry in 1902 and now sat as an independent member), to speak on the health and nutrition of schoolchildren.[41]

In January 1905, Gorst chaired a national conference on the feeding of schoolchildren, organised by the TUC, the LTC and the SDF, at the Guildhall in London. In his speech, Gorst highlighted the importance of free meals, since children were attending school undernourished and consequently unable to cope with learning. Dr Macnamara, now MP for North Camberwell, agreed with this last point but did not want to extend the provision of poor relief. Whereas he advocated a parental contribution, Mary did not. She wanted the state to provide for all the material needs of poor children. Attacking the NUT for its moderation, she concluded by asking Macnamara why he had been silent on the question of state maintenance. 'Was it a question to be forever confined to the street corner? This was the place and this was the time.'[42] Typically, Mary sought to mobilise the grass roots. Touring the country with Daisy Warwick in her patron's red motor car made Mary and Daisy vulnerable to criticism. Not a paper the Social Democrats could rely on, the *Labour Leader* likened the motor tour to a 'Prince's hunting expedition'. Its editor expostulated: 'Do they realize that it (Socialism) is to us a religion, and that the parading of wealth or vanity – or even of sympathy – is hardly less to some of us than blasphemy?'[43]

The policy voice of Mary Bridges Adams was now at its most influential in these years. In April 1906, Will Thorne presented the State Education Bill in the House of Commons. Clause 7 of the Bill would have required local education authorities to record the height, weight and chest measurements of children entering public elementary schools and to supply annual returns to the Board of Education. Clause 8 required each local education authority to appoint a medical officer or officers 'whose duty it shall be to medically examine and to test such children as the teachers may consider in need of medical advice'.[44] Much later, Mary wrote of her work on behalf of the educational programme of the TUC prior to 1914. She claimed individual responsibility for drafting resolutions on education from 1903, as well as taking the initiative for the most radical proposals contained within it. She had played a supporting role, entirely without the limelight, but she was uncompromising and must have been difficult to work with. Not only this, her independence of mind challenged every single female stereotype.

Marxists pressed the claims of city children after the passage of the Education (Provision of Meals) Act, 1906. Brian Simon is clear that whatever its shortcomings, 'the Bill introduced a new principle in social legislation – it implied acceptance by the community of responsibility for poverty'.[45] Local authorities were empowered to spend money on school feeding and, in the winter of 1907–8, the SDF organised a deputation to London's County Hall. Though the Education Committee refused to see them, it had the common-sense political tact to allow the Bermondsey doctor and settlement worker, Councillor Alfred Salter, elected as a Progressive in 1907, to present their petition. There was evidently a crusading atmosphere. *Justice* reported a mass meeting at Queen's Hall, under the headline 'Let Them Be Fed!'

> It was tactful and wise to include among the grave and reverend seigniors and young bucks of the platform the gracious presences of Lady Warwick and Mrs Bridges Adams. Not only because they gave a touch of colour to the scene, but because this meals for children is so much a question for women and mothers too, and we are quite sure that Mrs Bridges Adams was able to get to the hearts of the women in the audience – some, perhaps, cold and hostile to Socialism – in a way unknown, or impossible to the men speakers.[46]

Newly available correspondence shows that Mary also drew the physiologist and surgeon Sir Victor Horsley (b. 1857) into the Labour movement agitation. She invited him to speak on medical inspection at the 1906 Children's Sunday and successfully negotiated the hostility he expressed toward sharing the platform with the Countess of Warwick; holding office as her political secretary 'enables me to focus on building up the Educational side of the Labour movement', she wrote.[47]

Next spring, Mary addressed what *Justice* described as a 'remarkable meeting' at Canning Town, London, 'in her usual vigorous style'. She used the findings of a study carried out in Liverpool to demand free school meals. On average, the secondary school pupils were 6 1/4 inches taller and 23 1/4 pounds heavier than their counterparts at the poorer elementary schools.[48] Alluding to the fact that Britain and Germany had embarked upon a naval arms race, she said the total cost of providing free meals was £300,000, which amounted to 'one-fifth the cost of an iron clad'. She put a familiar case tersely when she urged the government to restore 'the educational endowments, by which bishops and archbishops had been educated out of funds stolen from the poor'.[49]

Bostall Wood

Weeks later, the appointment of Dr George Newman (b. 1870) as the first Chief Medical Officer at the Board of Education attracted critical attention. The response of Alfred Cox, President of the North of England branch of the British Medical Association, was typical. 'Read the *British Medical Journal* this week,' he wrote to Mary, 'there are some very straight remarks both from a correspondent and editorial on the "job" that had been worked in the new Medical Department'.[50] Cox was disgusted at the passing over of Dr James Kerr (b. 1862), who held the post of Medical Officer to the LCC Education Committee and 'was of course the man marked out for the job'. Dr Kerr had been Medical Superintendent to the Bradford School Board (from 1893, before McMillan's arrival in the city), where he carried out medical inspections though not empowered to do so. In January 1902, Mary supported his appointment as Medical Officer to the LSB and he stayed on when the Council became the education authority. The correspondent to whom Cox referred was Archibald Hogarth, one of Kerr's assistants and a past student of Newman, who, he said, 'knows nothing' of school hygiene.

Supporters were angered by the way in which Newman had been 'pitchforked into office' when Kerr had been promised 'first refusal' of the job fourteen months earlier – a clear example of recruitment by patronage. In political recruitment, the key question is whether the applicant is 'one of us'. Newman's most important qualification for the new post was his friendship with Beatrice Webb, through whom he had met Robert Morant. The Webb doctrine of 'purposeful entertaining' was pivotal here and it must have satisfied her vanity when, in September 1907, Newman wrote 'Somehow or other I connect you with this post'.[51] For certain members of the medical establishment this association prompted fears 'that a Fabian-planned school medical service would grow into a complete State health service'.[52] London radicals were suspicious also. As the Gas Workers put it in a manifesto issued in spring 1907, the Chief Medical Officer should 'be directly responsible – *not to permanent officials* – but to the Minister of Education, whom he shall advise on all matters of school hygiene' (original emphasis).[53]

One reason for the indignation of Kerr's supporters was the knowledge that he was widely regarded as the leading advocate and practitioner of school medicine in the country. However, Kerr had adopted a contrasting position to Morant's. On the one hand, he saw little point in medical inspection unless sick children received treatment. On the other, he bitterly opposed the idea that the education authority should surrender responsibility for child welfare. At loggerheads with those in government circles who favoured a universal system of medical examination, in London he put forward a modified scheme to test the opposing arguments. Under these arrangements (which the Board of Education approved) only a sample of children would be inspected in selected schools, some doctors using a simpler schedule which Kerr himself devised, others following the Board's schedule.

The Council later abandoned these proposals in favour of inspecting all the children living within easy reach of London's voluntary hospitals and sending those who required medical treatment to visit their out-patients' departments. This antagonised many of Kerr's former allies among the medical establishment, since the hospitals were in competition with doctors practising among the working classes. A warning shot came from Sir Victor Horsley, who claimed the inspections had missed large numbers of defects, a reference to the visible stigmata by which degeneracy was marked clearly on the body of its victim. His protests about inefficient classification came shortly before Morant's abrupt departure from the Board of Education in November 1911.[54] Gilbert suggests this was the moment at which Kerr's support collapsed. Under the implied threat of the subsequent withholding of government grants, the LCC bowed to pressure and committed all school medical work to the Medical Officer of Health for London County. Kerr's post of Medical Officer (General Practice) and Medical Officer (Education) disappeared.[55] Arguably, they were all trying to engineer a more efficient system managed by specialists, but the policy advocated by Morant was that which prevailed.

Shortly before the furore over Newman's appointment, Mary put forward plans to found a tuberculosis service in London. Tuberculosis was the prime cause of child deaths, at the time and children who were malnourished and debilitated were unlikely to have the physical strength successfully to resist it. Doctors claimed they could identify the type of child at risk, estimated as 10 per cent of the school population, and a new medical category of 'pre-tuberculous' children became the focus of work on the health benefits of fresh air, sunshine, healthy food and daily exercise.[56] In May 1907, Mary wrote to the RACS to ask if it would donate some of its land at Bostall Wood, Plumstead, Woolwich, to the LCC for an open-air school. She flagged the potential for coverage since the third International Conference on School Hygiene was coming up in London and Kerr had just completed a report on his visit to an open-air school set up in Berlin. She was going to Germany soon and planned to give lantern lectures about her findings in the autumn.[57] The co-operators agreed to her request, the Council accepted their offer, and the mixed school opened on 22 July, with 113 weak children.[58]

The school day started at 9 a.m. and finished at 6 p.m. on weekdays, with Saturday morning attendance as well. The daily timetable consisted of three and three quarters hours of schoolwork with physical education, and a two-hour siesta on deckchairs: treatment was fresh air and three good meals a day. That same year active trade unionists added a new clause to the TUC Education Resolution, which now called for 'the establishment under every authority of scientifically organised open-air recovery schools, the cost to be borne by the community as a whole and not in any part by charitable contributions'.[59] As Mary told a meeting organised by Chatham Trades Council, there were plenty of country estates 'where deer ran wild. They had little children who might be in those parks. The men who lived in those stately houses were merely usurpers, and they intended to dispossess those usurpers'.[60]

A close reading of the press cuttings filed by the co-operators' education committee shows 143 newspapers discussed the venture, but only *Clarion*, *Justice*, the *Lancashire Post* and the *Morning Leader* mention the involvement of Mary Bridges Adams.[61] Supporters noticed this. Under the headline 'Credit where it is not due', *Justice* accused the Tory teacher councillor Ernest Gray (b. 1857, past president of the NUT, elected to Parliament for West Ham North in 1895, re-elected 1900 but defeated in the 1906 general election) of trying to gain recognition for a scheme which was not of his making. What angered Mary was the authority's attitude to the funding, since Gray appealed for charitable donations even though the co-operators had let the Council use the land rent free. She sustained a vision of open-air recovery schools on healthy sites away from the slums, financed by a government grant. Unlike Gray, she did not worry that this would pauperise the parents of the children who attended them.

The Woolwich co-operators certainly thought highly of her. In her lifetime, they tried to redress the 'miasma of political distortion', which threatened to distort the chronicling of attempts to improve children's physical resistance against tuberculosis. After a conversation with Mary herself, this received attention in a political article first published in 1933. Its author had seen the opening of the first open-air recovery school to fight infant and child death and contagious diseases and was eager to stress Mary's role in 'calling the workers to demand democratic education which concerned the physical welfare as well as the mental equipment of their children'.[62] The years between 1907 and 1933 had seen the application of the open-air system in elementary schools. This disappointed Mary. She argued for separate facilities and became increasingly critical of the parsimonious attitudes of officials at the Board of Education.

Margaret McMillan was one of many visitors to the Bostall Wood open-air school. In an article in the *Morning Post*, she acknowledged the school's pioneer status and the role of the Woolwich Co-operative Society. The whole tone of the article was in harmony with an approach that has the commitment of the head teacher as one of the weapons in its armoury. College trained, head teacher Miss Gibbs had taught in the elementary and secondary spheres and had been involved in the concentration camp schools in South Africa. 'She is bronzed with the sun, ruddy, and walks out with a springing step that would single her out, even among modern athletic women, as possessed of a special kind of outdoor experience.'[63] Unlike the children, who returned home at night, she slept in a house nearby. 'She sees the rosy glow of the westering sun pierce the trees of this English wood, whither … she has returned to help her country people to live and think and teach "imperially".'[64]

Margaret's evocation of one 8-year-old girl, weighing barely three stone, who slept heavily on her deck chair, exemplifies her sentimentalised use of the child figure. 'Through the quivering foliage the light fell on her

5 Bostall Wood Open Air School

white, upturned face, on the colourless line of the wide open mouth, and the eyelids whose lashes fell on bluish, swollen cheeks.'[65] She hoped direct clinical intervention would be swift. Enthusiasm and inclement weather aside, the school ran for three months. Every child gained between six pounds and a stone in weight, with corresponding improvements in health.[66] The general consensus was that the experiment had been a great success, and fifty years later Elsie Lumley, one of its first admissions, wrote in very positive terms, having just completed forty years as a State Registered Nurse.[67] Nonetheless, Miss Gibbs strained relations with the RACS by her arrogant disregard for its wishes. Under her orders, the attempt to create a garden damaged the large open space in the estate woods, one of the arc lamps was broken when the caretaker climbed it to attach a flag, and she refused to stop sleeping in the camp until the intervention of London's first education officer, Robert Blair (b. 1859).[68]

The Deptford camp schools

The open-air day school at Bostall Wood predates the three camp schools Margaret McMillan set up at Deptford from 1911 to 1914. It seems plausible to suggest that the connection between the political actions of these two women was significant, albeit it has been wholly unexplored. Margaret moved south to live with her sister, Rachel, after she retired from municipal politics on grounds of ill-health. In 1904 she became a manager of three Deptford elementary schools, and the millionaire soap manufacturer Joseph Fels (b. 1854) came good on an earlier promise of financial assistance. The two approached the Moderate-controlled LCC with a proposal to help establish and equip health centres for the treatment of schoolchildren, which Fels proposed to endow with £5,000. In the event, their meeting with the Education Committee (in November 1904) did not go well and Fels withdrew his immediate and personal involvement.

Gilbert claims that McMillan's plans fell foul of the ill-feeling caused by Newman's appointment, since James Kerr declined to support her work in any way.[69] Bitterly disappointed, Margaret wrote to ask a favour of Fred Jowett (b. 1864), the first socialist elected to Bradford City Council: '*something* of my work still survives in Bradford. Could you show anything that illustrates this … to the people who will be going to you soon from Head Office? The record you sent would be damning to me'.[70] Still, she opened the first school clinic in London in the room belonging to the head teacher of the Devons Road School, Bow, in 1908. One of the reasons for its limited impact was the failure to secure local authority support, either in terms of finance or in terms of sending child patients. However, nothing could dent the enthusiasm of the two school doctors, who produced glowing accounts of its work. Privately McMillan wrote to Morant: 'Mothers go away in tears. It isn't encouraging more especially in view of the fact that thousands leaped out of their prejudices in a few years and went to welcome the new service'.[71]

The doctor–child encounter provided a wonderful opportunity to reach the working-class mother, and perhaps some resented attempts to teach them not only cleanliness but also new standards of speech, deportment and manners. In 1910, the clinic moved to Deptford to operate as the health centre for the group of schools where Margaret McMillan was manager. Her new premises were rent free and by the following year she no longer relied upon charity. Writing about these initiatives, Steedman suggests that they benefited from an unusually high level of publicity beyond the fictions of the self that Margaret was agent of, and that this included the writings of other supporters.[72] For example, the self-promoting Clara Grant (b. 1867) was headmistress of the board school that housed Margaret's first clinic, and wrote of her social action in the wake of these developments. Clara and Margaret shared strong links and ties with Froebelian networks and Toynbee Hall. Clara made contacts with Jane Addams, the founder of Hull House, while she was visiting Chicago, and Jane told her she envisaged a place for all sizes of settlement. Therefore, Clara began a small settlement of her own in a flat in the neighbourhood of her school.[73] It was named the Fern Street School Settlement and she was fortunate to receive funds from Fels, a benefactor of the McMillan sisters. Clara survived the *Titanic* disaster in 1912 and stayed in the community after she retired from teaching in 1927.

The people of Bow came to see her as the 'Farthing Bundle Woman', after her Saturday morning custom of distributing packages to local children.[74] Each child passed under an arch inscribed 'Enter now, ye children small, none can come who are too tall'. She or he paid a farthing for which they got a newspaper-wrapped package of cast-off toys, scraps and trinkets.[75] Clara Grant had little sympathy for the Labour movement and disapproved of married women working. When teacher over-supply and unemployment prompted the authority to investigate the employment of married women, she accepted an invitation to attend a meeting on the subject at County Hall. Afterwards she wrote a letter reporting common transgressions to Robert Blair, in which she argued that married women teachers were a 'danger to church and school'. Further, she claimed their employment increased the likelihood 'of the lower social type of teacher being enabled, by her salary to marry a quite uneducated type of man'.[76] Her critics included Kate Dice, married head of a Lewisham school, who many years later was dismayed when a male colleague in the National Association of Labour Teachers likened her to Grant: 'What a battle I waged with her!' she wrote, remembering Clara's expulsion from the NUT for ardently supporting the use of unqualified, low paid, 'guinea girls' (instead of properly trained teachers) introduced into the schools after the First World War.[77]

Whereas Clara Grant favoured philanthropic endeavour, the slow progress in the implementation of state reforms disappointed Mary. With the coming of the First World War, she took advantage of the unusually high level of public interest in child welfare services to coax the authorities to spend more on the care and education of working-class children. Trade and labour journals reveal that she was particularly active in the first six months of 1915.

The pursuit of social justice

On New Year's Day 1915 she appealed 'to trade unionists and all who hate child murder, whether by German bombs … or by the no less deadly disease of poverty' to champion the cause of the working-class child. Making her intentions clear, she encouraged debate on the following policy: 'That no TUBERCULOUS child under the age of 16 should be employed as wage earner until the last unemployed adult has been set to work'.[78] Writing in the *Cotton Factory Times* two weeks later, she attacked the continued use of 123 unsanitary church school buildings in London. She thought they should 'be replaced by schools well-built, well-lighted, well-ventilated, well-equipped in every way and so beautiful that the building of them shall bring to those who build, not merely wage-earning employment, but joy and hope for the better day to come'.[79] In the spring, she called for a 'national campaign demanding a childhood for the workers' children'.[80] In the summer, she provided a telling critique of the sleeping accommodation at Margaret McMillan's Deptford Centre, which consisted of an open-sided corrugated iron shed with a canvas curtain. Addressing Sylvia Pankhurst's East London Federation of Suffragettes through the *Woman's Dreadnought*, she wrote: 'Backyards in slums covered over with high canvas were no good for the treatment of consumptive children'.[81]

Speaking directly to those who worked in the textile industry in Lancashire, Mary condemned the state pension of £1,200 a year awarded a past president of the Board of Education, J.A. Pease. What were his achievements she asked? He had failed to prevent the spread of tuberculosis, the prime cause of child mortality, despite having an expert on the public treatment of consumption working with him. He had ignored the question of the conditions in the church schools that served British working-class children. She looked him up in *Who's Who* and contrasted his situation with that of the victims of the half-time system, denied educational opportunities. Pease had attended Trinity Hall, Cambridge, 'where he not only became an M.A. but must have had what schoolboys call a "rattling good time" there, for he was a member of the football team, the polo team and the Cambridge University drag hounds'. Moving on, she noted his membership of six golf clubs, Middlesex county cricket club and a local hunt. With heavy sarcasm she commented: 'The parents of consumptive children and the parents of other children who may be infected, may take what comfort they can get from the fact that Mr Pease's handsome pension will certainly provide for his dogs'.[82]

In May 1915, the Liberal Prime Minister Herbert Asquith (b. 1865) invited Labour Party general secretary Arthur Henderson (b. 1863) to join the first wartime coalition government under his leadership. Two months later, Arthur accepted the post of President of the Board of Education with a seat in the cabinet. Mary agreed with the comments of the Fabian novelist Arnold Bennett (b. 1867) on the 'stink of politics', but managed to find grounds for optimism.

> I never thought I should live to feel grateful to Mr Asquith. In this case I do. For Mr Asquith knows that there is a steadily growing working class education movement, which Mr Henderson now has it in his power to strengthen. Mr Asquith knows the strength of the forces opposed to this movement, and he knows also that in England trade unionism, having no 'lead' in matters educational from 'leaders' of social democracy will have to work out its own educational salvation. On the whole, therefore, would it not be as well for trade unionists, while emphasising more than ever the need for the absolute independence of the political Labour party, to make the best of a bad job, and show that at least THEY MEAN TO GET ALL THEY CAN FOR THE CHILDREN OUT OF THE NEW MINISTER OF EDUCATION.[83]

With the government in the throes of sending out registration papers to organise women's wartime contribution, she volunteered to organise a national system of open-air recovery schools. On 18 November 1915 she wrote to Henderson, 'This is one of the greatest scandals of the day'. Henderson arranged an interview with George Newman, who wanted to know where the public funding would come from. Her response was the Exchequer *and* income from the 'filched endowments', which she wanted to see restored to the people and publicly administered.[84] In a riposte to her critics who accused her of being unpatriotic, she claimed to have evidence of support from 'those in high places in the world of education politics who have seen fit to treat my offer of service in a totally different way'.

Politically, Mary Bridges Adams recognised that the provision of free meals was the single most important weapon at the disposal of the government to minimise the widespread unrest caused by the inflationary impact of war. The price of food was soaring and the supply chain was vanishing. Driven by the urgency of the situation, she sought to mobilise support for emergency protests to include the picketing of state schools by workers' children, as if they were factories. Thinking over the effect of food shortages on the minds of working-class mothers, she made the link with the female inmates of Norfolk County Asylum, 'brought there, mental wrecks, as a consequence of the incessant worry and strain due to their grinding poverty while bearing and bringing up their children'. Given the lack of school dining halls, she suggested central government commandeer churches and chapels. Lest anyone say 'sacrilege', she countered that sites dedicated to Christian worship would 'more consistently be used for carrying out His injunction "Feed the Lambs," than by those who, calling themselves His representatives on earth, use the sacred edifices for advocating "A fight to a finish"'.[85] Still fighting in her eighth decade, she looked to the Co-operative movement to take up the cause, answering what she considered 'the call of the child'.[86]

Between the 1880s and the 1940s, Britain evolved a set of public policies formed through a process of rejecting some alternatives and compromising over others. From the early days Mary Bridges Adams refused to behave in a way that commended itself to insiders, though she did a great deal to contribute to the climate of opinion in which that reform could take place. In contrast with Margaret McMillan, she chose not to collaborate with the traditional political leadership groups. Neither did she make use of childhood fiction and the melodramatic presentation of child deaths as an arena for political action and as a figurative device. Ahead of their time, her ideas may not have provided a legitimising framework of social thought, but she never forgot the importance of further change. In the Gramscian sense, her function was that of the organic intellectual. Her propaganda involved something akin to 'acting for and with' the poor, rather than 'acting upon' them, as the cultural elevation model suggests. It comes as no surprise, therefore, that she based her analysis and argument on the transfer of wealth, power and social esteem from the owners of capital to the working classes. As a revolutionary socialist, Mary wanted to channel discontent into outright opposition to the capitalist system.

Notes

1 M. Bridges Adams, 'When the army is disbanded', *Cotton Factory Times*, 2 April 1915, p. 1.

2 LA, Margaret McMillan Papers, A94/6, 1/63, Margaret McMillan, message to students at the Rachel McMillan Training Centre, Deptford, Christmas 1927.

3 *School Board Chronicle*, 18 December 1897, pp. 677–8.

4 C. Steedman, 'Fictions of engagement: Eleanor Marx, biographical space', in J. Stokes (ed.), *Eleanor Marx (1855–1898) life-work-contacts* (Aldershot: Ashgate, 2000), pp. 23–39.

5 This concept was developed by Donzelot, leaning heavily upon Foucault's early work: J. Donzelot, *The Policing of Families* (New York: Pantheon Books, 1979).

6 C. Steedman, *Childhood, Culture and Class in Britain: Margaret McMillan 1860–1931* (London: Virago, 1990), p. 198.
7 M. McMillan, *The Camp School* (London: George Allen & Unwin Ltd, 2nd edn, 1919), p. 85.
8 McMillan, *Camp School*, pp. 82–3.
9 McMillan, *Camp School*, p. 40.
10 The 'Famous Four' were Katherine St John Conway/Bruce Glasier, Caroline Martyn, Margaret McMillan and Enid Stacy. See J. Hannam and K. Hunt, *Socialist Women Britain, 1880s to 1920* (London and New York: Routledge, 2002), pp. 22, 24, 33.
11 Steedman, *Childhood, Culture and Class in Britain.*
12 A. Mansbridge, *Margaret McMillan: prophet and pioneer* (London and Toronto: J.M. Dent & Sons, 1932), p. 131.
13 LA, Margaret McMillan Papers, A94/6, 1/63, M. McMillan to R. Blatchford, 21 January 1929.
14 LA, Margaret McMillan Papers, A94/6, 1/99, R. Blatchford to A. Mansbridge, 18 June 1931.
15 G.A.N. Lowndes, *Margaret McMillan 'The Children's Champion'* (London: Museum Press, 1960).
16 E. Bradburn, *Margaret McMillan Framework and Expansion of Nursery Education* (Nutfield, Redhill: Denholm House Press, 1976).
17 LA, Margaret McMillan Papers, A94/6, 1/73, M. McMillan to R. Blatchford, 18 February 1929.
18 G. Searle, *The Quest for National Efficiency: a study in British political thought, 1899–1914* (London: Basil Blackwell, 1971).
19 M. McMillan, *Labour and Education* (London: Swan Sonnenschein & Co, 1907).
20 McMillan, *Labour and Education*, p. 15.
21 See, in particular, the discussion in S. Koven, *Slumming: sexual politics in Victorian London* (Princeton and Oxford: Princeton University Press, 2004) pp. 183–227.
22 Koven, *Slumming*, pp. 183–227.
23 B.B. Gilbert, *The Evolution of National Insurance in Great Britain* (London: Michael Joseph, 1966), pp. 117–18.
24 Mansbridge, *Margaret McMillan*, pp. 63–72.
25 LA, Margaret McMillan Papers, A94/6/1/8, R. Morant to M. McMillan, 26 June 1907.
26 S. Koven, 'Borderlands: women, voluntary action and child welfare in Britain, 1840 to 1914', in S. Koven and M. Michel (eds), *Mothers of a New World* (London: Routledge, 1993), pp. 119–20; Steedman presents a more nuanced account in *Childhood, Culture and Class*, pp. 54–6.
27 N.D. Daglish, 'Robert Morant's hidden agenda? The origins of the medical treatment of schoolchildren', *History of Education*, 19:2 (1990), pp. 139–48; B. Harris, *The Health of the Schoolchild* (Buckingham: Open University Press, 1995).

28 N. Rose, *The Psychological Complex: psychology, politics and society in England 1869–1939* (London: Routledge & Kegan Paul, 1985), p. 133.
29 *Kentish Mail and Greenwich Advertiser*, 3 December 1897.
30 *Kentish Mail and Greenwich Advertiser*, 3 December 1897.
31 *The Times*, 17 December 1897, p. 14.
32 *The Times*, 17 December 1897, p. 14.
33 Statement by Mrs Bridges Adams made to the London School Board on the question of starving and underfed children, printed by G.W. Giles, printer, 39 Greenwich Road, London.
34 'Underfed children attending school 1898–9', Report of the General Purposes Committee, together with the report of a special sub-committee presented to the LSB on 2 November, 1899.
35 Statement by Mrs Bridges Adams made to the London School Board on the question of starving and underfed children, printed by G.W. Giles, printer, 39 Greenwich Road, London.
36 T. Gautrey, *Lux Mihi Laus: School Board memories* (London: Link House, n.d.), p. 93.
37 *Board Teacher*, 1 December 1899, p. 285; *School Board Chronicle*, 25 November 1899.
38 Statement by Mrs Bridges Adams made to the London School Board on the question of starving and underfed children, printed by G.W. Giles, printer, 39 Greenwich Road, London.
39 School Board for London List of Members, Committees etc. reprinted from the members' pocket book for 1901.
40 C. Clemens, *The Man from Limehouse: Clement Richard Attlee* (Missouri: International Mark Twain Society, 1946), p. 7.
41 Gas Workers' and General Labourers' Union, Quarterly Balance Sheet; General Secretary's Report for quarter ending 24 September 1904, p. 5.
42 38th Annual Congress TUC, Report of the National Labour Conference on State Maintenance, p. 16.
43 M. Blunden, *The Countess of Warwick* (London: Cassell, 1983), p. 179.
44 See B. Harris, *The Health of the Schoolchild* (Buckingham: Open University Press, 1995), p. 45.
45 B. Simon, *Education and the Labour Movement 1870–1920* (London: Lawrence and Wishart, 1980), p. 282.
46 *Justice*, 25 January 1908, p. 7.
47 CUBM, Bridges Adams Papers, Mrs Bridges Adams to Sir Victor Horsley, draft (n.d.).
48 *Justice*, 11 May 1907, p. 9.
49 *Justice*, 11 May 1907, p. 9.
50 CUBM, Bridges Adams Papers, Alfred Cox to Mrs Bridges Adams, 24 September 1907.
51 Quoted in Searle, *The Quest for National Efficiency*, p. 243.
52 Gilbert, *Evolution of National Insurance*, pp. 134–5.

53 *Justice*, 20 April 1907, p. 5.
54 Harris, *Health of the Schoolchild*, pp. 59–61.
55 LMA, LCC, EO/WEL/1/1, Children's Care Organisations 1909–14, J. Kerr to R. Blair, 8 February 1911.
56 L. Bryder, 'Wonderlands of buttercup, clover and daisies: tuberculosis and the open-air school movement in Britain, 1907–39', in R. Cooter (ed.), *In the Name of the Child: health and welfare 1880–1940* (London: Routledge, 1992), p. 75.
57 *Justice*, 6 July 1907.
58 LMA, 22.53, LCC Joint Report of the Medical Officer and the Executive Officer on the Open-air School carried on in Bostall Wood, between 22 July and 19 October 1907.
59 C. Griggs, *The Trades Union Congress and the Struggle for Education 1868–1925* (Lewes: Falmer Press, 1983), p. 152.
60 *Chatham Observer*, 9 October 1907.
61 RACSP, Royal Arsenal Co-operative Society General Committee Minute Book, read letter dated 27 May from Mrs Bridges Adams; Bostall Woods open-air school press cuttings file.
62 W.J. Brown, 'Open-air recovery schools', *Comradeship and Wheatsheaf*, December 1933, p. xvi.
63 M. McMillan, 'A School in the Woods', *Morning Post*, 1 August 1907.
64 McMillan, 'A School in the Woods'.
65 McMillan, 'A School in the Woods'.
66 LMA, LCC Joint Report of the Medical Officer and the Executive Officer on the Open-air School carried on in Bostall Wood, between 22 July and 19 October 1907.
67 E.F. Jefferson, *The Woolwich Story* (Woolwich: Woolwich and District Antiquarian Society, 1970), p. 244.
68 RACSP, Royal Arsenal Co-operative Society, General Committee Minute Book, 9 August, 10 September, 12 September, 16 September, 1907.
69 Gilbert, *Evolution of National Insurance*, p. 140.
70 LA, A96, 1/2 M. McMillan to Mr Jowett, 28 November 1905.
71 LA, Margaret McMillan Archive A94/6, 1/25 M. McMillan to R. Morant, 1 November 1911.
72 Steedman, *Childhood, Culture and Class*, pp. 52–3.
73 C.E. Grant, *Farthing Bundles* (Bromley-By-Bow: Fern Street Settlement, 1929), p. 79.
74 *The Times*, 26 May 1953, p. 3; *East London History Society*, Autumn newsletter 1992, p. 1.
75 Grant, *Farthing Bundles*. p. 93.
76 LMA, EO/STA/2/12, LCC Education Officer's Department Elementary Education Branch Section No. 12 – Married Women Teachers, C. Grant to R. Blair, 7 February 1911.
77 LMA, A/NLT/1V/2,1 National Association of Labour Teachers correspondence file, K. Dice to P. Ibbotson, 20 March 1954.

78 M. Bridges Adams, 'The white scourge in schools', *Cotton Factory Times*, 1 January 1915, p. 4
79 M. Bridges Adams, 'School building "on the cheap"' (letter), *Cotton Factory Times*, 15 January 1915, p. 4.
80 M. Bridges Adams, 'When the army is disbanded', *Cotton Factory Times*, 2 April 1915, p. 1.
81 M. Bridges Adams, 'Consumption in the schools' (letter), *Woman's Dreadnought*, 31 July 1915, p. 291.
82 M. Bridges Adams, 'Government and thrift' (letter), *Cotton Factory Times*, 9 July 1915, p. 4; M. Bridges Adams, 'More thrift!', *Yorkshire Factory Times*, 12 August 1915, p. 1.
83 M. Bridges Adams, 'The minister with a mandate', *Cotton Factory Times*, 4 June 1915.
84 The National Archives, London (hereafter TNA), TNA ED 50/127 M. Bridges Adams to A. Henderson, 18 November 1915. I am indebted to Professor Roy Lowe for this reference; M. Bridges Adams, 'More thrift!', *Yorkshire Factory Times*, 12 August 1915, p. 1.
85 M. Bridges Adams, 'The war and free meals', *Yorkshire Factory Times*, 4 February 1915, p. 4.
86 W.J. Brown, 'Open-air recovery schools', p. xvi.

7

Bebel House and the political education of working women

> Miss Stacy said the old fashioned view was that a woman who took any interest in politics was a disgrace to her sex, and that she left her home duties to meddle with things that were no concern of hers. But there are women who have exceptional gifts for public life, and it is unfair for the State to be deprived of their services, just as it would be unfair to the public that Adelina Patti should only be allowed to sing to her own family circle. If a woman, by writing, or speaking, or organising can do valuable service to the State, it is her duty, as well as her privilege, to use her powers to the utmost. Many people will admit this, but urge that the ordinary woman has no place in politics. She was here to plead for the average woman, whether working in the factory or the mill, or only at home, to be allowed to take the same interest in public affairs as the ordinary man, who likewise has no special gifts. (Enid Stacy, 1900)[1]

The WEA and Ruskin College

Thus spoke high school teacher Enid Stacey to an audience of Woolwich co-operators in the winter of 1900–1. Employed by the ILP as a travelling speaker, she always tried to bring socialism and women's rights together and here she uses a household name to support her arguments for women's involvement in the formal politics of parliament and political parties. The greatest soprano of her day, Adelina Patti (b. 1843) was the most famous and highest-paid entertainer in the world. However, Enid sought to challenge any notion of the 'exceptional' and the 'average' woman as absolutely distinct categories. She portrayed political activity as something the 'ordinary' woman might fit into her life, in the same way as the 'ordinary' man. We can only speculate whether Mary Bridges Adams heard Enid speak that night, but this chapter will examine her efforts to provide an educational space for politically active working-class women akin to the Berlin party school of the German Social Democratic

Party. Bebel House was an institutional experiment designed to train a cadre of militant working women 'who will, by constructive educational work, increase working-class discontent and help to organise that discontent under the banner of organised labour'.[2] Despite her exclusion from the national power structures, I will argue that Mary's mobilisation efforts had significant implications for an intellectual culture rooted in a definite political context which played an important part in the debates and arguments within the British working-class movement at the time.

Mary was at the centre of the debate concerning the relationship between the political project of socialism and education in a broad sense at the beginning of the twentieth century. Any optimism she may have felt about 'statist' educational strategies dissipated as the expansion of popular education was interrupted by those who backed the new fee-paying grammar schools introduced by the 1902 Education Act, which provided a few free scholarship places. She preferred local control to central direction and she increasingly turned to 'substitution' as an educational strategy, at first largely refracted through a rich culture of participative reform and self-help in the South London in which she served her political apprenticeship, thereafter through a more critical tendency which offered a counter-education based on Marxist philosophy and economics.

In the summer of 1900, for example, Mary asked permission to address a meeting of the LTC on the subject of Ruskin Hall, Oxford (College from 1907), founded in 1899 as a college for working men. If a college for working men in the city of dreaming spires seemed somewhat bizarre, there was more to Mary's critique than this. As far as she was concerned, it was a mistake to assume labour might recreate Oxford, and she stressed the need for independence in working-class education as opposed to co-partnership with the church, the universities and the capitalist Board of Education. She saw education as a weapon of political struggle and did not ignore the educational problematic outlined by Antonio Gramsci: 'is it sufficient for a philosophical movement to devote itself to the development of a specialised culture for restricted groups of intellectuals or must it, in elaborating a thought which is superior to common sense and scientifically coherent, never forget to remain in contact with the "people" and, moreover, find in this contact the source of its problems to be studied and solved?'.[3] The debate about purpose had a clear effect on working-class educational politics, whether to risk the danger that a working-class elite would be assimilated by places such as Oxford, standing for the dominant national culture, or to hold firm to the belief that the Labour movement's greatest strength was its internal resources.

These positions were played out in years of friction and acrimony with individuals and organisations seemingly polarised between the WEA and the universities on the one side, and the movement for independent working-class education on the other. The controversy seeped into the work of historians, with the evidence of the relevant archives being used in theoretical debates animated by the rifts of the past. This claim was staked out by Bernard Jennings in a centenary collection on the WEA in which he comments on a 'bias and a lack of charity'[4] to be found among protagonists' accounts, and has been reworked by scholars many times since. However, in recent years the tendency has been for studies to move beyond the intrinsic limitations of either/or, showing greater sensitivity and understanding of the dynamics of specific historical situations at the local rather than the national level, where learners and tutors could and did move between the available forms of adult education. As Tom Woodin points out, 'the key distinction between radical and liberal education has a tendency to blur in today's climate where both of these approaches can be portrayed as anachronistic'.[5] It has to be remembered that both the WEA and its rivals, the Central Labour College and the Plebs League, were competing for similar students and the support of the unions. Looking at these debates again, this time from the perspective of a woman who was a participant, may serve to give a flavour of the interplay of class and gender through re-reading contemporary sources.

Mary's conception of education for the workers was rooted in the Marxist studies promoted by the earlier Socialist League slogan: educate-agitate-organise. She sometimes received less than enthusiastic backing from the established leadership of British trade unionism, but her political writings and speeches fired the imagination of another political generation who asserted the need for education funded and controlled by labour. Young, class-conscious students took up the refrain during the Ruskin College revolt in 1908, demanding an independent organisation and curriculum based on Marxism. 'Do you suffer from class consciousness? Come to Oxford and be cured', was among the pithy slogans the 'rebels' used during their dispute with the authorities.

Ruskin College provoked conflict almost from its inception. Critics included the Fabian Bernard Shaw, who declined an invitation to lecture to the students on the grounds that a working man 'will learn nothing here that he cannot learn anywhere else, except the social tone, which will be as detrimental to him as a workman as it is useful to a gentleman'.[6]

The Shoreditch branch of the SDF drew attention to the campaign for the restoration of the educational endowments as the ultimate objective. It argued that Oxford, Cambridge and all the 'other endowed seats of learning, were the rightful inheritance of the people'. Therefore, 'to attach themselves to any other educational institution would be to give their acquiescence to the deprivation of their rights'.[7] Mary criticised Ruskin's education practice, saying it was based on values such as competition rather than 'brotherhood', which made 'the system of teaching and conditions degrading to the name of "Ruskin"'.[8] Beyond a powerful undercurrent of suspicion, and ambivalence toward the liberal adult education philosophy offered by Ruskin, Mary would become the earliest, most persistent critic of the WEA. She had little time for the kind of partnership with the bourgeois state that it offered, and less for those trade unionists who advocated it.

Launched in Oxford in August 1903, the WEA institutionalised a philanthropic, humanistic and radical-liberal conception of adult education. Albert Mansbridge wanted to open up communication across class lines and the kind of alliance he advocated was captured in his claim that:

> As an organisation for education it stands unique, because it has united for the purposes of their mutual development Labour and Scholarship in and through their respective associations of Trade Unions and Universities, and because of this unity, so secured, the power of the spirit of wisdom has been increased in the affairs of men, and the building of 'Jerusalem in England's green and pleasant land' has become at least a nearer prospect.[9]

Mary's first real engagement with the WEA seems to have been at the end of 1903, when she attended an open meeting at Toynbee Hall.[10] Leaving aside her close ties with the RACS Education Committee, the *Co-operative News* claimed that the only discordant note in 'two hours of high thinking and keen talking' was sounded by a 'lady whose associations with Co-operation are rather more on the fringe than within'.[11]

Undeterred, Mary continued to participate in joint WEA/Co-operative debates, including one organised at Woolwich in February 1905. On that occasion, Robert Banner attacked Oxford University as 'the home of lost causes' and contended that all Oxbridge dons 'required educating as to the necessities of the working classes'. Drawing on past experience as secretary of Cambridge Co-operative Society Education Committee, Labour councillor Fred Chambers (b. about 1847)[12] noted how he witnessed the power of local clergy at first hand as they refused the use of church schoolrooms for public meetings. Fred was far from easy about the WEA. 'They were told that there was to be equal representation of organisation. But he would certainly not agree that to have equal numbers of university and working men was equal representation, looking at the relative numbers of University and working men in the country. He considered that the Association was one for furthering the objects of University people and not working men.' However, Marion Deans took the opposite view. In her opinion 'suspicion should be put on one side and they ought to fight unitedly against those who were their enemies in the matter of education. She did not believe that those University men who were working were tainted as had been suspected by different people'.[13]

Although Mary's words went unrecorded, that winter she spoke at another WEA/Co-operative conference at Stratford, East London, 'occasioning some amusement by announcing herself as a representative of the Gasworkers' Union' which she doubtless was.[14] The Labour movement did not have an agreed position with regard to the question of educational endowments and she wanted to rectify this. To this end, she claimed 'a balance sheet from Oxford showing how the revenues of the colleges there are obtained, and how expended, would be of more service to the working-class education movement than any number of peripatetic lectureships held by "safe" men, whose teaching in early Victorian economics, it would be hoped, might prove an antidote to the poison instilled into the working-class by wicked Socialist agitators'.[15] She believed in a common education and reiterated the point in Lancashire, at a meeting organised by the Nelson branch of the SDF, where she said 'she was just about sick of what was termed "working-class education". It was citizens' education that they wanted, and they were looking forward to the time when class would be abolished. The time was ripe for a great educational move'.[16]

Matters came to a head at a WEA conference on the topic of 'What Oxford can do for Working People' during the 1907 Summer Extension Meeting. Sharp divisions occurred, and much has been made of the contribution from Robert Morant, who promised official support for the extension classes of the universities and the WEA. However, another crucial contribution came from John Mactavish (b. 1871), a self-educated shipwright from the Portsmouth dockyards, who told a stilled audience: 'I am not here as a suppliant for my class. I decline to sit at the rich man's table praying for crumbs. I claim for my class all the best that Oxford has to give. I claim it as a right – wrongly withheld – wrong not only to us but to Oxford'.[17] Noah Ablett offered a weighty condemnation. He wanted to know 'why the Universities have so suddenly come down to help the workers to emancipate themselves'.[18] This was completely alien to the viewpoint of David Shackleton, one of those Labour leaders whom Ben Tillett described as 'softly feline in their purring to Ministers and their patronage … betrayers of the class that willingly supports them'.[19] Shackleton agreed that the working class must be educated. Indeed he told the students of Balliol that since the task of government had been 'laid upon them' they 'wanted to be taught how to do it'. But Shackleton went further: 'It will repay expenditure; for there is in their ranks some ability and some reasonableness. The best remedy against extreme views is wider views.'[20]

There were several strands to the debate, but the divided vision of workers' education in Britain, one radical and the other liberal, would pull Ruskin College in two directions. The WEA took a leading part, not least through its involvement in the influential 1908 report *Oxford and Working-Class Education*, produced with the University and Ruskin College. The emphasis on steering the new (male) working-class voter down the path of moderation, together with the appointment of Henry Sanderson Furniss (b. 1868) as a lecturer in economics, was tantamount to a red rag to bull.[21] Almost blind from birth, Furniss had virtually no teaching experience and knew little about industrial conditions or working-class life. Before going to Ruskin, he 'had hardly even spoken to a working man except gardeners, coachmen and gamekeepers'[22] and he held the Marxist theory of value to be complete nonsense. Students asked the principal, socialist clergyman Dennis Hird (b. 1850), to excuse them from attending his lectures and complained about comments like 'a jolly good essay spoilt by discussing the Marxian theory of Value'.[23] In response, Noah Ablett turned to the organisation of Marxist study groups and the Plebs League into which he soon drew many ex-students and supporters, including Mary Bridges Adams.

The League of Plebs

The League of Plebs was set up in October 1908 to organise education nationally and to promote a closer identification of Ruskin College with the Labour movement. Determined to build a working-class culture that would sustain the working class in its efforts to change society, the Plebs League made the situation clear through its motto, 'I can promise to be candid, but not impartial'. The students named their monthly journal of Marxist education the *Plebs Magazine*, to commemorate an American socialist pamphlet which drew an analogy between antiquity and the contemporary struggle between the workers and capitalist class, learning a lesson from the actions of the tribunes, who, whilst articulating some of the grievances of the plebian masses, continued to accept the basic principles on which Roman society was founded. In adopting the name 'Plebs' they were identifying themselves as revolutionary socialists, stubbornly positioning themselves in opposition to reformist Labour leaders.[24] Classes in economic and industrial history by Marxist teachers were an essential part of the wider education whose aim, as the Plebs League constitution spelt out, was 'to develop and increase the class consciousness of the workers, by propaganda and education, in order to aid them to destroy the wage-slavery and to win power'.[25]

During this tricky period the College authorities appointed a subcommittee to look into its affairs, which resulted in the dismissal of Hird for failing to maintain discipline, with six months' salary in lieu of notice and a life pension of £150 a year. In March 1909 a meeting of the students was called and the decision to strike was taken. Described as a 'seven day wonder', the boycott of official lectures and activities prompted the Ruskin executive to close the College for a fortnight. What the authorities failed to anticipate was that the militants would use the time to canvass trade union branches and Labour organisations.[26] Mary was among the two hundred members who attended the Plebs League's first annual meeting, in August 1909. Noah Ablett moved the main resolution for the principle of independence in working-class education and Mary seconded, 'and after dealing with the necessity for the principle of independence, spoke of the evil of the undemocratic system of co-option creeping into our system of government. The principle of patronised education from the wealthy classes was wrong'. The editor of the *Plebs* commended her contribution as 'a fighting speech of great power and force, the University being treated to a terrific onslaught in her inimitable style'.[27]

With support from the Amalgamated Society of Railway Servants (ASRS), the South Wales Miners' Federation (SWMF) and miscellaneous militants, the Central Labour College (CLC) was established in Oxford with Hird as principal.[28] The Plebs movement elected a Provisional Committee of thirteen, including Ablett and Bridges Adams, to govern the College, first in Oxford and then, after 1911, in the Earls Court district of London. At the Trades Union Congress of that year Mary was the only woman speaker at a meeting in support of the new institution, but there is no mention whatsoever of her role in *Justice*, only a brief insertion about her contribution to the Gas Workers' Children's Sunday. This drew a denunciation in which she expressed 'regret that in your note on the new Central Labour College, you do not state that I am a member of the Provisional Committee'.[29] David Shackleton had opposed the proposals, and it can be imagined how Albert Mansbridge and Robert Morant viewed the following: 'The Central Labour College is based on recognition of the antagonism of interests between Capital and Labour. This produced a battle of ideas. The C.L.C. seeks to make the working class conscious of this antagonism for the purpose of removing it. It teaches social science from the point of view of Labour. It believes in the independence of Labour, industrially, politically and educationally'.[30]

Caught up in these activities, Mary took a leading part before 1914. In April 1909, for example, a notice appeared in the *Clarion* newspaper announcing her willingness to lecture 'during the next two months, for out of pocket expenses, to the trade union and Socialist organisations' on 'Some Objections to the Proposals of the Joint Committee on Oxford and "Working Class" Education, with Special Reference to the Dispute at Ruskin College and the University, and Public School Endowments which have been Stolen from the Poor'.[31] One month later she wrote to say she had a few open dates for Northumberland and Durham in the middle of June and to advertise her willingness to speak to the same groups on the same subject.[32] One of her regular speaking engagements was at Stockport Labour Church. As the organisers noted in their programme for the winter of 1910, 'Mrs Bridges Adams is always sure of a large audience. We wish there were more men with the same pluck and enthusiasm'.[33]

A thorn in the side of the WEA, Mary's contribution was recorded in a rare personal tribute from George Sims (b. 1869), a carpenter from Bermondsey who attended Ruskin on a union scholarship supplemented by the patronage of Ada and Alfred Salter.[34]

> Dear Comrade – You will see this altogether meagre expression of our goodwill, gratitude and regard. You will no doubt feel a little annoyed at my presumption in writing it. Yet you will forgive me because you will understand that it is born of the desire of one who has no belief in tributes to the dead, but who, while those who are with us, of us, and for us, still pulsate with the joy of life, lays this small offering on the altar of friendship on behalf of all who have laboured in the cause.[35]

The best-known of the Ruskin strikers, Sims was Secretary of the Plebs League and the CLC. Mary continued her proselytising, trying to win support for her position within trade union circles. As Sims put it, she 'propagated and propagated and propagated, in Scotland, Wales, North, South, East and West of England' gathering in supporters and funds and helping to organise local study groups around the country.

Campaigning against the WEA

There is evidence in the WEA archive that Mary was a dissident voice who got under its founders' skin. The press cuttings files record, for example, her speeches on the misuse of educational endowments, Ruskin College, the WEA, Bebel House and the CLC, which produced defensive reactions. However, the public vitriol was especially evident in press cuttings from the *Railway Review*, perhaps because Albert Mansbridge proffered the claim that the WEA received stronger support from railway workers than from any other 'body of working men'. For example, in July 1909 Mansbridge placed an article in the *Review* to try to influence the forthcoming union conference. Alongside a flow of hostile exchanges involving Mary and a range of WEA stalwarts, a union activist who attended Ruskin on an ASRS studentship effectively sabotaged the Mansbridge line. 'If Labour was class-conscious; if it accepted the scientific theory of the class struggle … then the dangers that now beset the movement would vanish, and we should look upon all these arrangements between the class at the top and the class at the bottom as betrayals of our sacred cause, and treat those responsible for them according to their deserts.'[36]

Ultimately, despite his forthright assertion regarding railway union affiliation in almost every town where the WEA existed, Mansbridge lost the battle for the support of the NUR and the SWMF, from whose ranks several of the Plebs leaders had come. Confidential correspondence sent to organisers of the tutorial classes suggests that he feared the threat Mary posed:

> We beg to inform you that Mrs Bridges Adams, taking advantage of the strike at Ruskin College, is seeking engagements in the country, ostensibly to oppose the Report on Oxford and Working Class Education, but in reality to make bizarre mis-statements concerning the W.E.A. We shall be glad if you will inform us as to any statements she may make in your district, and if you will endeavor to arrange for an answer to be made to the same Organisation which she addresses.[37]

Speaking at a meeting organised by the Pontypool branch of the ILP on the edge of the South Wales coalfield in May 1909, Mary ridiculed the constitution of the rival organisation 'as being anti-Labour and anti-Socialist'. Would the Duke of Westminster have given his support, she asked, 'unless he was assured that the lectures to the workers were of an absolutely safe character'?[38]

What needs disentangling from the story of the Plebs League, as an educational pressure group, is Mary's ongoing campaign for an enquiry into university and public school endowments. As a letter to the Guild Socialist publication the *New Age* noted: 'within the last few days Mrs Bridges Adams has addressed a number of excellent meetings on the above subject in this locality and without doubt the South Wales miners will be prepared to give her an enthusiastic backing, now that they see the true inwardness of things'.[39] Privately, Mansbridge deplored her activities and in 1910 he wrote to Alfred Zimmern, 'the Bridges Adams opposition is more furious than ever – lies, misrepresentations, the devilments of the pit – are all brought to bear'.[40]

The link with coalfield militants is striking, for it was a direct one, but the vocabulary of demonology is missing from the public narrative. Mansbridge simply records how the WEA 'excited active opposition on the part of Mrs Bridges Adams, a well-known woman in Labour circles of the times, who, in fact regarded herself as the leader of trade union education policy'.[41] Mary Stocks (b. 1891), women's activist and college head, put it rather less charitably when she wrote the 1953 history of the WEA:

> From its earliest days there had been a rumble of thunder on the left, and when the W.E.A. had appeared to make headway in trade-union circles, Mansbridge was able to record the existence of active opposition. It came, to begin with, from the activities of a certain Mrs Bridges Adams, who professed a particular concern for trade-union education. Mrs Adams had a profound distrust of universities. They were in her opinion citadels of class-privilege whose denizens were dedicated to its preservation. If they were prepared to patronize the efforts of Mansbridge and his friends, it could only be because they hoped to divert him from uncontrolled activities which might otherwise subvert the privileged position of the rich, and to inoculate him with economic doctrines likely to render him tolerant, if not appreciative of the status quo.[42]

In 1912 Mary told a meeting at Newport town hall that she 'was not going to tell them the interests of capital and labour were identical. If she did so they would know she was "kidding" them'.[43]

The WEA insisted that it was essential to introduce students to a wide range of ideas. In contrast, Mary's radical practice proffered the keys with which activists might unlock the processes of capitalist accumulation. 'The workers had to be trained for the fight and they had to provide the armoury. Some people said, "Oh no, why don't you give them culture and the higher life". (Laughter) It was not culture and the higher life for the few. They wanted an armoury for the few so that they would become strong fighters in order to get culture and higher life for the many.' She wanted working women to be given the tools with which to work also and asked them to support the working women's college to enable 'the women of the nation to work for children of the nation'.[44]

The Working Women's College

In July 1912, an advertisement appeared on the front page of *Justice*. It contained proposals for a Working Women's College organised by Mrs Bridges Adams. The nub of Mary's scheme was to try to ensure that more working-class women got some kind of political education than previously. She wanted to empower working women so they might make their presence felt 'as propagandists, as representatives on public bodies; and as members of management committees of the trade unions in which women are organised'. At the same time, she thought that change could be achieved through the provision of 'a centre of organised working-class effort' to press the education demands of the trade union movement, which could be seen as 'a link between the Labour Movement and the most forward spirits in the Feminist Movement'. A week later she

LABOUR'S MOST VALUABLE ASSET.

6 Working Women's College, cartoon, *Railway Review*

appealed for sympathetic artists to get in touch with fellow socialist and journalist Winifred Horrabin (née Batho, b. 1887), while she tried to enlist the help of 'socialist women of leisure' to focus on building up support for the college. The aim of subsequent advertisements was to persuade others to back such a practical venture and to fundraise for her institution building. She needed 'about £1000 to buy outright the lease of a house which is available and suited for purposes of a residential college' and made overtures to 'friends of the Labour and Women's Movements' who would pledge to give a minimum of £1 per annum for five years to 'help put the Working Women's College on a satisfactory financial footing'.[45]

The *Daily Herald* also carried the story, and Mary was able to write with confidence about feminist support while pointing out that funds would no doubt follow when the vote was won. In the meantime she claimed the Duchess of Sutherland had found a cottage and her London home was, therefore, free and 'may be placed at our disposal, together with Dunrobin Castle for a summer school'.[46] The Duchess was Daisy Warwick's half-sister and Stafford House, the building to which Mary referred, was one of the most beautiful palaces in the metropolis. Dunrobin Castle, the family's ancestral seat in Scotland, was reached by means of a private railroad belonging to the Duke. In 1903 the Duchess set up Sutherland Technical Schools at Drummuie, the first school in Scotland to provide free residential education for the sons of crofters from isolated communities in the highlands and islands. How this sits with Mary's insistence on working-class independence in education is a moot point, given the purity of her critique of Albert Mansbridge's strategy of working with elite networks. Indeed, the two sisters had been among the wealthy patrons of one of her previous initiatives, to provide art for Woolwich workers in 1899.

Mary's plan was that the working women's college would be placed under the same board of management as the men's college. Members included Will Thorne, as the first treasurer, Noah Ablett, Mary Bridges Adams and George Sims. In common with the German Social Democratic Party's Berlin educational school, the intent was that whilst the women students should attend lectures at the men's college, the women's college should be run on its own lines. Jean Quataert has dealt with the educational ideal of socialist women in Imperial Germany and her research shows that German social feminists shared Mary's radical idea of creating 'revolutionary class fighters'.[47] Similarly, Mary situated the curriculum and pedagogic issues within the context of the working-class struggle. Should the model of learning be 'directed and controlled by the Trade Unions and Socialist organisations INDEPENDENTLY (according to the lead given in Denmark, Germany and other countries by the Social Democratic parties and in England by the A.S.R.S. and South Wales Miners' Unions), or in CO-PARTNERSHIP with the Church, the Universities, and the Capitalist Board of Education?' she asked in her publicity material.[48]

In another article for the *Daily Herald*, republished in the *Plebs*, she claimed 'women so trained, and understanding how the workers' children are robbed of their childhood, would, as Labour representatives on education authorities, make short work of the charity-organizers, the bureaucrats, and other superior persons, who, to the detriment of education control those bodies to-day. Such women would help to see to it that starving children should be fed, and not mocked by a cold-blooded, permissive Act.'[49] There were grounds for optimism since the response from working women and feminists had been encouraging and she was in dialogue with European socialists to forge links with Socialist Schools of Economics in other countries and to develop an International Socialist Students' Union.

Bebel House opened in the spring of 1913 in a house close to the CLC for men at London's Earls Court.[50] But the formation of a College for Working Women was not the sole aim. It was to serve essentially as both hall of residence and educational space from which to inaugurate other working women's colleges throughout the country, operating on the principle of parent-groups and worker-tutors, applied in terms of an organised educational institution. Storm Jameson took English classes and the suffragist actress Gwendolen Logan (b. about 1882), who would go on to star alongside Katharine Hepburn in the film *Christopher Strong* (1933), gave lessons in elocution and voice production.[51] At the outset attendance was weak, whether through apathy or lack of resources is unclear. There were just two students – Mary Howarth (b. about 1893, Bury Weavers Association) and Alice Pratt (née Smith, Oldham Cardroom Association), both of whom had been attending local adult education classes in Oldham, Lancashire. Mary appointed herself principal and Ethel Carnie left Manchester, where she had been living with her mother in the university settlement, and returned to London to work at Bebel House, encouraging working women to express themselves in writing.

Rebecca West (b. 1892), who had a celebrated career as a writer ahead of her, saw education such as Bebel House offered as essential to give the woman worker the self-confidence she needed 'to form the most aggressive quarter of the Trade Union Congress instead of merely the distinguished handful that now represent their sex'.[52] She commented on Mary's year of 'eager organising' and her vital role in facilitating real progress for working women. Mary was certainly a woman of immense energy but the financial position of Bebel House was by no means secure and its demise occurred fairly swiftly. The official history *The Central Labour College, 1909–29* simply notes the failure of the 'Bridges Adams foundation' as part of a wider history of unremitting financial necessity and the staff's unrelenting struggle for funds. However, an examination of the CLC papers suggests disagreement *within* the college for men as a factor prompting its closure. The minutes provide a case in point, showing that the students were worried about the money spent on staff salaries and considered a staff–student ratio of nine staff to nine students to be excessive. Perhaps Mary agreed with them. At any rate, in December 1912 she refused to loan the men's college £200 out of the £1,000 she had had placed at her disposal. The formerly cordial relations became frosty, as lecturers at the men's college stopped taking classes at Bebel House and the college's governing body authorised the establishment of a women's league with more limited fund-raising aims.

It is hardly coincidental that Winifred Horrabin and Rebecca West both worked to raise money to keep the CLC afloat and to provide scholarships to maintain women workers as students there. Winifred helped to keep the dream of independent working-class education for women alive, but tensions may have been simmering. In an otherwise favourable notice of Mary's article on 'the Last Ditch in the Co-Partnership Fraud' for the *Daily Herald*, Horrabin noted economically: 'After her telling criticism of the WEA it would have been useful to point out that a genuine working-class educational institution … is in existence – viz, the CLC … its aim is – in Mrs Bridges Adams' words – "to provide the workers with an intelligent knowledge of their position as members of an organised international working-class army arrayed against the forces of organised international capitalism".'[53] The upshot of these developments was that the resident students at Bebel House received scholarships from the CLC Women's League for full-time attendance at the men's college for the year 1913–14.[54]

Returning from London, Mary Howarth would become a full-time official of the Women's Trade Union League (in 1915), and Alice Smith took over her old adult education class, on Dietzgenite philosophic logic. The movement for independent working-class education was powerfully attracted by Joseph Dietzgen's (b. 1828) proletarian view of philosophy – unknown in the universities – with its emphasis on making students aware of the brain activities of abstracting and generalising. Dietzgen was a tanner by trade, a Marxist autodidact who spent his free time composing books and articles on philosophical questions. By the time of his death in 1888, Jonathan Rée tells us, 'he had amassed impressive credentials as the sovereign philosopher of Marxism'.[55] Not all students found it easy going, however, and Alice wrote about this in a courageous autobiographical essay for the *Plebs* magazine in which she described her own struggles and made an impassioned plea for a simplified textbook on the subject. She was a committed tutor and her class proved to be the most successful ever held in the locality. Encouraged by another student from the pre-First World War class in Oldham, Alice took on trade union work and provided articles for the *Cotton Factory Times* and *Plebs* during the interwar years.[56]

In the winter of 1913–14 Ethel Carnie set up the Bebel House Rebel Pen Club. She wanted to redress the bias in mainstream English literature, by which she meant its 'lop-sided' quality of 'dealing with life only from the standpoint of one class'. Her desire was to help 'working women who have a talent for writing and wish to turn it into account in the interests of socialism'. Her appeal generated immense interest, with upwards of one hundred manuscripts sent in for comment. All of which suggests that she provided a space for working-class voices growing out of a strong socialist culture. Meanwhile, she asked her readers all 'to try to realize that though they are not Shakespeares, they are themselves, and can write something that Shakespeare couldn't have written'.[57] For her, literary realism was an oppositional strategy in itself. This quality can be located in a set of values often at odds with most middle-class attitudes, as she wrote to Graham Wallas in a letter penned at Bebel House. 'I think that for any middle-class person to bring "concentrated criticism" to bear on working class life, in its domestic or other phases, savours of impertinence, though I know you would not mean it to be so.'[58] The purpose of education was to improve quality of life. This was the essence of her critique of the elementary school system in contributions for the *Woman Worker*. Although proud of her self-education, she regretted her own missed opportunities. For example, the influence of self-educated working people pervades an article entitled 'Factory Intelligence'. 'Oh, I grow angry when I think of the fetters they have placed upon our minds … if we had been intelligent to our own position; do you think we would have allowed them to steal these things from us? No; a thousand times no.'[59]

In common with Mary, Ethel Carnie damned the WEA for the emasculation of the working classes. Writing in the *Cotton Factory Times* she inveighed against the idea that the poor and exploited should spend their precious leisure time studying economics 'FROM EVERY POINT OF

VIEW! ... Why should I look upon the fact that I am robbed, from "every point of view"? If a robber stole something valuable from me, I should not fall into a philosophical survey of the situation, but rush upon him, provided I was armed'. This drew a sharp response from Lavina Saltonstall, a suffragette garment worker from West Yorkshire and enthusiastic supporter of the WEA who resented 'Miss Carnie's suggestion that the WEA educational policy can ever make me forget the painful history of Labour; or chloroform my senses to the miseries I see around me.'

Lavinia accused Ethel and 'those from whom she has imbibed her views' of having libelled 'the intelligence of the working classes'. It is consistent that this should have drawn a sharp denunciation from Ethel:

> Sir – Miss Saltonstall in her letter of defence of the WEA evoked by my attack, has accused me eight times of not knowing what I was talking about, and having taken my opinions at second hand ... But I note with gratitude that she is magnanimous enough to suggest the possibility that I may have written the attack myself ... I will not scruple to quote Mrs Bridges Adams in her saying that 'armoury is needed for the few in order to get culture for the many' and to get it by force from below.[60]

In fact Ethel, won a WEA scholarship which took her to one of the early summer schools in Oxford, where she met Albert Mansbridge and Margaret McMillan. In a characteristic passage, she reported having asked the latter 'if it was not an imploded idea of John Ruskin's that the salvation of the working classes would come about through the aid of the middle-classes'. Neither of them was prepared to debate the point, Ethel wrote, and when she told Albert that 'the worker had knowledge of life, of labour, he admitted that the professors etc sat humbly at the feet of working men!'[61] Significantly, Ethel explicitly mentioned her personal knowledge of Lancashire. This was the site of the pioneer WEA class in Rochdale with R.H. Tawney (b. 1880) as tutor. Already, in the winter of 1909, the Plebs League offered a direct and immediate response which brought into being successful classes, and Ethel had many friends who were past and present students of the pre-war WEA in the localities.

It is clear from a different (anonymous) letter writer that Ethel's experiential knowledge did not, of course, change all hearts and minds. 'We in the WEA don't believe in specialism which compels workers to become the twentieth parts of pins. Perhaps this standard suits Mrs Bridges Adams and her supporters, at least they argue on those lines. What they say in effect is let us learn a little of history, economics and social science and then denounce everyone who disagree with us as either "well trained lambs" or "chloroformed idiots"'. A week later Mary shot back: 'We at

Bebel House will not favour "specialism which compels the workers to become the twentieth parts of pins". In contrast to the WEA we believe in the specialization which will enable workers to become sharp stilettos directed with swift, unerring aim right at the heart of capitalism'. Ultimately it took a simple revelation to terminate the polemical warfare. 'May I suggest that Mrs Adams as a typical decent person sent her son as a child to get a good and real education? I want her to explain to the readers of the "Factory Times" why at the same time she was condemning Oxford and Cambridge she entered her own son at Worcester College, Oxford?' Bristling with condemnation, her foe showed little compassion. 'We workers like a little consistency when important matters which affect the whole of our lives are being discussed, and are not much concerned with people who "run with the hare and hunt with the hounds"'.[62]

There was no question that this opponent fiercely resented the pursuit of self-interest by one who professed to walk in the correct ideological path. I have tried to avoid the bitterness of contemporaries, but it is impossible to ignore the paradox between Mary's condemnations of class collaboration in others and her own close association with Daisy Warwick. It is also difficult to square her low opinion of Oxford University as nursery for an arrogant ruling elite and misappropriation of filched endowments with the decision to purchase privileged education for her son. William Bridges-Adams did not complete his undergraduate studies at Oxford and one cannot help thinking that his period there can't have been helped by his mother's public speaking on the subject of 'Oxford University and Working-Class Education' with special reference to the TUC's demand for the restoration of the university and public-school endowments which had been stolen from the poor.

International aspirations

In the 1920s Mary revived discussion of a new international socialist education movement. She fostered a continuing consciousness of the class struggle, combined with insistence 'on the right and duty of the organised workers to provide and control their own teaching in economic science'. An article she placed in the *A.S.E. Journal and Report* brought in Ethel Carnie, now enjoying a celebrated career as a writer, and her best-seller *Helen of Four Gates*. Unlike the wreck of the Versailles settlement, said Mary, this movement is based on four, not fourteen points, 'and as they have not been drafted by politicians and diplomats, they mean what they say, and say what they mean'.[63]

If anything, the war years strengthened Mary's commitment to internationalism and she retained the capacity to imagine an alternative to the status quo. Her educational goal remained the foundation of an International Federation of Socialist and Labour Colleges 'as are provided and controlled by working-class organisations independently and not in co-partnership with those bulwarks of capitalism, the Church and the Universities'.[64] She also planned an International Working-Class Students Union, an international system of travelling scholarships and an International Socialist Library. To evoke interest among the rank and file generally it was Ethel who launched an appeal for £2,000, while Mary dangled the promise of matched funding from sympathetic friends in the Soviet Union.

Again and again Mary pressed the case for workers' control at a time when the WEA was campaigning for reforms *within* the state. Unlike Labour reformists, she consistently linked grievances over the university and public school endowments to a revolutionary political end. In October 1912, for instance, she commented on a number of omissions to be found in a recent *Daily Herald* article on trade unionist education policy by R.H. Tawney: notably his failure to offer a full and proper explanation of the demand for a Royal Commission to inquire into the history and present value of the university and public school endowments. 'No mention is made by Mr Tawney of the Congress demand that the Commission in question shall have on it a majority of Trade Unionists elected by the trade unions and not, as your readers will note, co-opted in a minority by the favour of a Capitalist Government and of high dignitaries of the Church and Universities.' Mary recognised that this was a struggle for hegemony in relation to working-class education and politics, and once again she pleaded with Tawney to persuade the WEA to drop its non-party character. In the meantime she asked the WEA, with its powerful seal of approval from church and state, 'to accept the education programme of the Trades Union Congress, and also organise a great campaign in support of its demands. What a glorious day it would be for Trade Unionism, what a still more glorious day for the children who have been robbed of their childhood, which the filched endowments would do much to secure them'.[65]

As time went by Mary Bridges Adams would disappear from view, and while both Tawney's and the WEA's fortunes grew, hers continued to fade. There was a tendency for the 'mainstream' leadership to get its versions of events accepted, while people (especially women) positioned in a different way had difficulty gaining acceptance and were less favoured by history. Nonetheless, neglect of Mary's role in the histories of adult education can lead to underestimation of the part that female agency played in the great ideological battles of the Edwardian era. Her overriding preoccupation with independent working-class education provided a glimmer of the extension of a concept of workers' control that was designed to provide the rank and file with the experience of democracy.

Notes

1 'Women and Politics', *Comradeship*, November 1900, pp. 117–18.
2 Mrs Bridges Adams, 'Education of working women', *Cotton Factory Times*, 23 April 1913.
3 A. Gramsci quoted in: K. Worpole, 'A ghostly pavement: the political implications of local working-class history', in R. Samuel (ed.) *People's History and Socialist Theory* (London, Boston and Henley: Routledge and Kegan Paul, 1981), p. 22.
4 B. Jennings, 'The friends and enemies of the WEA', in S.K. Roberts (ed.), *A Ministry of Enthusiasm: centenary essays on the Workers' Educational Association* (London: Pluto Press, 2003), p. 106.
5 T. Woodin, 'Working-class education and social change in nineteenth and twentieth-century Britain', *History of Education*, 36:4–5 (2007), p. 488.
6 G.B. Shaw quoted in N. Kneale, '"The science and art of man-making": class and gender foundations of Ruskin Hall, Oxford, 1899', in G. Andrews, H. Kean and J. Thompson (eds), *Ruskin College Contesting Knowledge, Dissenting Politics* (London: Lawrence & Wishart, 1999), p. 8.
7 J. Rée, *Proletarian Philosophers* (Oxford: Clarendon Press, 1984), p. 19.
8 TUC Lib., London Trades Council, Minutes of delegate meeting, 12 July 1900.
9 A. Mansbridge, *An Adventure in Working-Class Education* (London: Longmans, Green and Co., 1920), p. xi.
10 'Mrs Bridges Adams to Editor Factory Times', *Cotton Factory Times*, 10 April 1914, WEA press cuttings file 1912–14.
11 *Co-operative News*, 19 December 1903.
12 'Our reformers' gallery', *Woolwich Labour Journal*, February 1903, p. 1; 'Pen pictures of Woolwich worthies: Councillor Fred Chambers', *Woolwich Pioneer*, 8 January 1909, p. 13; 1891 Channel Islands Census.
13 'Higher education of the working classes', *Woolwich Pioneer*, 24 February 1905, p. 2.
14 *Co-operative News*, 19 November 1904.
15 *Justice*, 16 November 1907, p. 1.
16 *Nelson Leader*, 8 January 1909.
17 Quoted in T. Mooney, *J.M. Mactavish General Secretary of the W.E.A. 1916–1927: the man and his ideas* (Liverpool: Workers' Educational Association, 1979), pp. 13–14.

18 Quoted in L. Goldman, *Dons and Workers: Oxford and adult education since 1850* (Oxford: Clarendon Press, 1995), p. 121.
19 Quoted in K.D. Brown, 'Shackleton, Sir David James (1863–1938)', *Oxford Dictionary of National Biography* (Oxford: Oxford University Press, 2004; online edn, Jan 2008) [www.oxforddnb.com/view/article/36033, accessed 19 March 2008].
20 Goldman, *Dons and Workers*, pp. 120–1.
21 B. Simon, 'The struggle for hegemony, 1920–1926', in B. Simon (ed.), *The Search for Enlightenment: the working class and adult education in the twentieth century* (London: Lawrence and Wishart, 1990), pp. 18–19; Goldman, *Dons and Workers*, pp. 126–7.
22 H. Sanderson Furniss, *Memories of Sixty Years* (New York: D. Appleton and Co., 1931), p. 94.
23 W.J. Edwards, *From the Valley I Came* (Sydney and London: Angus and Robertson, 1957), p. 168.
24 J.P.M. Millar, *The Labour College Movement* (London: N.C.L.C. Publishing Society, 1979), p. 7.
25 'The constitution of the Plebs League', *Plebs*, April 1909, p. 44.
26 S. Rees, 'The Ruskin strike in 1909', *Plebs*, February 1959, p. 37.
27 TUC Lib., WEA press cuttings file 1909/10, *Railway Review*, 6 August 1909; *Plebs*, August 1909, p. 174.
28 *Plebs*, October 1909, p. 185; *Justice*, 21 August 1909.
29 *Justice*, 21 August 1909.
30 Cited in F. Moxley, 'Railwaymen and working-class education', Appendix A in P.S. Bagwell, *The Railwaymen* (London: George Allen & Unwin, 1963), p. 678.
31 'Notice: Ruskin College and Oxford University', *Clarion*, 16 April 1909.
32 'Notice: Oxford and "Working Class" Education', *Clarion*, 28 May 1909.
33 CUBM, Stockport Labour Church, 'Our winter work, being a syllabus arranged by the Stockport Labour Church for the session September 5, 1909 to April 24, 1910'.
34 'In memoriam – G.F. Sims', *Plebs*, June 1943, p. 126.
35 'A tribute', *Plebs*, July 1912, pp. 131–2.
36 TUC Lib., WEA press cuttings file 1909/10; F. Moxley, 'Railwaymen and working-class education', p. 676.
37 TUC Lib., A. Mansbridge to 'Dear Sir', 20 April 1910.
38 TUC Lib., WEA press cuttings file 1909/10, 'Higher education of the working classes', *Railway Review*, 20 May 1909.
39 *New Age*, 3 June 1909.
40 A. Mansbridge to A.E. Zimmern, n.d. [May 1910] quoted in B. Jennings, *Knowledge is Power. A short history of the WEA 1903–78*, Newland Papers No. 1 (Hull: University of Hull Department of Adult Education, 1979), p. 20.
41 A. Mansbridge, *The Trodden Road* (London: J.M. Dent and Sons, 1940), p. 63.
42 M. Stocks, *The WEA* (London: George Allen & Unwin, 1953), p. 48.
43 TUC Lib., WEA press cuttings file 1912/14.

44 TUC Lib., WEA press cuttings file 1912/14, *Newport Post*, 7 September 1912.
45 *Justice*, 20 July, 27 July, 3 August 1912.
46 TUC Lib., WEA press cuttings file 1912/14, *Daily Herald*, 8 July 1912.
47 J.H. Quataert, *Reluctant Feminists in German Social Democracy, 1885–1917* (Princeton: Princeton University Press, 1979), pp. 189–205.
48 'Working Women's College (in connection with the Central Labour College for Men)', Hon. Organiser: Mrs Bridges Adams, 64 Prince of Wales Mansions, Battersea Park, personal papers in possession of Mrs J. Bridges-Adams.
49 'New college scheme for training working women', by Mrs Bridges Adams, *Plebs*, August 1912, pp. 163–4.
50 W.W. Craik, *The Central Labour College* (London: Lawrence and Wishart, 1964), p. 103; 'Proposed working women's labour college', *Plebs*, September 1912, pp. 176–7; Mrs Bridges Adams, Working Women's College, appeal for funds, printed by the Utopia Press, London.
51 Mrs Bridges Adams, 'Education of working women', *Cotton Factory Times*, 23 April 1913.
52 'News in brief', *The Times*, 10 July 1912, p. 10; R. West, 'A training in truculence', *Clarion*, 14 February 1913, in: J. Marcus (ed.) *The Young Rebecca: writings of Rebecca West 1911–17* (London: Macmillan, 1982), pp. 154–7.
53 TUC Lib., WEA press cuttings file 1912–14, 'Workers' education', *Daily Herald*, 10 June 1913.
54 TUC Lib., Central Labour College, Board of Management Minutes, 21 June 1913; Craik, *Central Labour College*, pp. 102–3; R. West, 'The Working Women's College', *Clarion*, 14 February 1913.
55 J. Rée, *Proletarian Philosophers* (Oxford: Clarendon Press, 1984), p. 28.
56 E. Frow and R. Frow 'The spark of independent working-class education: Lancashire, 1909–1930', in B. Simon (ed.), *The Search for Enlightenment: the working class and adult education in the twentieth century* (London: Lawrence and Wishart, 1990), pp. 73–4; Rée, *Proletarian Philosophers*, pp. 33–4.
57 'Rebel pen club of working women', *Christian Science Monitor*, 10 January 1914, p. 31.
58 BLPES, Graham Wallas Papers October–December 1913, Wallas/1/52, Ethel Carnie to Mr Wallas, 22 November 1913.
59 'Pictures, poverty and prigs', *Woman Worker*, 5 May 1909, p. 414; 'Factory intelligence', *Woman Worker*, 10 March 1909, p. 219.
60 Ethel Carnie, Lavina Saltonstall, letters to *Cotton Factory Times*, 20 March 1914; 3, 10, 17 April 1914.
61 E. Carnie, 'Which way in education? Miss Carnie replies to Miss Saltonstall' (letter), *Cotton Factory Times*, 3 April 1914, WEA press cuttings file 1912/14.
62 Mrs Bridges Adams, C.H. Pearce, letters to *Cotton Factory Times*, 3, 10, 17 April 1914.
63 E. Carnie Holdsworth, *Helen of the Four Gates* (London: Jenkins, 1917); M. Bridges Adams, 'Education and the youth of the Red International', *A.S.E. Monthly Journal and Report*, March 1920.

64 M. Bridges Adams, 'Education and the youth of the Red International', *A.S.E. Monthly Journal and Report*, March 1920.
65 Mrs Bridges Adams, 'Stolen endowments – the education policy of the TUC', *Daily Herald*, 19 October 1914, WEA press cuttings file 1912–14.

8

Revolutionary politics and the First World War

> Therefore, being one of those individuals who have a trick of gravitating towards a minority, I find myself doing my little best in the direction of inducing British trade unionists to help their suffering comrades in Russia. Difficult though, at this terrible time, the task may be, I am encouraged by the thought that this organised British working class movement for their relief will help to strengthen that world-wide solidarity of Labour – the one great weapon with which the workers in any country can effectively wage war against the menace of the world-wide reaction which now confronts the workers of the world. (Mary Bridges Adams, 1915)[1]

Socialist reactions to war

Mary's left opposition aroused strong emotions during the First World War and this was how she explained herself to 'N.D.', a hostile correspondent to the *Cotton Factory Times*. Earlier in the same letter, Mary adopted the language of social maternalism to rebut the highly emotional attack her opponent made on her, which included the accusation of being impervious to mass murder. 'No women are indifferent to human slaughter, least of all the mothers of the race – those who in pain and anguish have – in the words of Olive Schreiner – "LEARNT THE PRICE OF HUMAN FLESH".'[2] Even before 1914, she experienced the hardening of attitudes which comes from finding yourself in a disliked minority, at odds with the pro-war wing of the BSP, strongly represented by Will Thorne and the Countess of Warwick, who had supported the frenetic build-up of arms during the pre-war years. This chapter gives an account of her political practice in a very specific historical moment when old alliances were shaken up and new ones forged. The campaign she mounted to force the British authorities to preserve the right of asylum and stop their repressive measures against the activity of the Clydeside revolutionary John Maclean carried implications which have a continuing relevance. Before looking in detail at her struggles, let us take a general view of socialist reactions to the declaration of war on 4 August 1914, situated in the battle for control between the pro-war and anti-war factions of the BSP.

Mary spoke against militarism and imperialism during the Second Anglo-Boer War. As we have seen, she was vilified by opponents and subjected to physical attack, when the windows of her home were smashed on Mafeking night. The experience did not disillusion her. During the war years, 1914–18, there was a tendency for political parties to try to co-operate but she maintained the opposition to which she had given voice in journals and meetings. There was a coalition government from 1915, at first under the leadership of Herbert Asquith and later, from 1916, under Lloyd George (b. 1863). Nonetheless, Mary maintained her offensive. With great courage and consistency, she criticised the government's actions and attacked everything from child labour to state education, wartime industrial legislation, conscription and the war itself. Education and propaganda were all-important. The task was to raise socialist consciousness so as to ensure that this really would be a war to end wars. At Christmas 1915, for example, she was still expressing other possibilities. 'Let our hearts go out in deepest sympathy with the brave Socialist minorities in other lands who, against tremendous odds, are struggling to hold aloft the banner of international working-class solidarity,' she urged her readers. 'To those who say "the international working class movement is dead" let us reply, "Long live the international solidarity of Labour," which alone can bring peace on earth, goodwill to all men.'[3] Whether or not such an aspiration was realistic, she still believed that if the proletariat knew the facts and could make its wishes felt, workers would refuse to support the machinations of self-interested elites. In the name of the Socialist International, she did not endorse the views of the patriots in the BSP who believed the war against Germany was just.

Those who had opposed rearmament represented the anti-war movement and attacked the Hyndmanite right wing from within the party. Numerically they became a majority on the Executive Committee in October 1914 and established their own journal, *The Call*, edited by E.C. Fairchild (b. 1874), as a vehicle for building up support. Born in London and apprenticed as a bookbinder, Fairchild went on to become a workshop manager before devoting himself to full-time political activity.[4] Starting as a member of the ILP, he joined the SDF in 1895. Elected to Hackney Borough Council in 1903, he became the party's London organiser in 1910. A leading figure in the opposition to the leadership of H.M. Hyndman, he used his influence on the Executive Committee of the BSP.

At the annual conference in April 1916 delegates adopted Fairchild's views as official party policy. They also voted in favour of the Zimmerwald demand for working-class action to end the war, passed at an international socialist conference held in Switzerland from 5 to 8 September 1915. Appalled, Hyndman led those siding with him in a breakaway, forming the National Socialist Party, which later readopted the name of Social Democratic Federation. His opponents gained control of the BSP, but not of the party newspaper, *Justice*, since that belonged to the Twentieth Century Press, most of whose shareholders backed Hyndman. Mary was equally resolved to adopt an unequivocal anti-war stance, and her association with clandestine opposition to the war can be illustrated from the war-time history of her sister-in-law, Hope Adams Lehmann.

Hope arrived in London days after the fighting began. Having got a passport in her maiden name, she stayed with Mary at Bebel House and immediately made contact with British anti-war networks. It was a dangerous move for both women but Hope was anxious to disseminate the peace proposals drafted and agreed upon by the Munich branch of the German Social Democratic Party, which put the emphasis on the need for a peace settlement on terms designed to heal wounds, both old and new, and give lasting security. For the Munich socialists, international peace was inextricably bound to the success or failure of a federalised Europe, made up of democratic nation-states with adequate machinery to ensure democratic control of foreign policy and armaments. The voluntary nature of Hope's stay changed when she came under suspicion of being a German spy, and she remained in the country until 7 January 1915. Leaving England for what would be the last time, she smuggled out press cuttings to aid the anti-war German socialists, at a time when the British authorities were searching people's clothing for hidden contraband. Back in Germany, Hope wrote a paper about her experiences in England in which she spoke of a 'half-metre' file in the British Home Office about her activities. She included sixteen articles by English peace campaigners in a pamphlet she edited, entitled *Kriegsgegner in England*, organised around the question of how to make a lasting peace.[5]

The views of the Union for Democratic Control featured prominently. Set up by a group of active politicians including Ramsay MacDonald and Charles Trevelyan (b. 1870), who resigned as Parliamentary Secretary of the Board of Education because he disagreed with the way that Herbert Asquith and his government were dealing with the crisis in Europe, the Union emerged as the most important of all the anti-war organisations in Britain. Its object was not to oppose the war. It was intended to preserve clarity of thought on the problems of international relations, with an aim of working towards a just resolution in the interests of world peace.[6] Hope and Mary agreed with the Union and its associates about the need for public opinion to be educated. Thus, Mary recommended that people read *International Socialism and the War* by A.W. Humphrey, which expounded the views of the peace-making leaders of the International. Also published in 1915, it contained the Munich peace proposals and distinguished between German militarism and the German people. The argument was that the latter had been misled by their leaders into seeing the war as a just war, fought to protect Europe from Russian despotism.[7]

British socialists who publicised their continuing opposition to war had good cause to fear the state's more sinister side. The Defence of the Realm Act (DORA) was to give the government wide-ranging powers during the war period, including censorship of journalism and of letters coming home from the front line. At home, the flying of kites was banned, as was lighting a bonfire (which could attract Zeppelins), buying binoculars, feeding bread to wild animals, discussing naval or military matters and buying alcohol on public transport. On the one hand, British liberal opinion protested. On the other, surveillance intensified. There was panic about German spies, and moral outrage against 'alien' shirkers and 'alien' job-snatchers was whipped up. The sinking of the *Lusitania* in April 1915 triggered a wave of anti-alien and anti-Semitic protest, which a spate of summer air raids did nothing to appease. Prejudice and discrimination spilled over into open hostility, with numerous and continuing assaults on individuals and on property. Meanwhile the British government was fast reaching the conclusion that voluntary recruitment was insufficient and two Military Service Acts in 1916 introduced conscription. Initially this applied to single men only, but its scope rapidly expanded so as to call up all able-bodied men except those who were exempt because they were working on munitions, railway work or other jobs essential to the war effort. A clamour about what to do with immigrants who refused to enlist grew to a crescendo.

The Prisoners' Committee

Thus, the idea of an English committee for assisting Russian political prisoners and exiles emerged. George Chicherin met with representatives of various Russian groups in London to set up the organisation and invited Mary to become his assistant. The priority was to prevent the introduction of an Anglo-Russian convention on conscription which would offer refugees the choice of enlistment in the British army or deportation, and Mary allowed Bebel House to become the committee's headquarters. Raymond Challinor suggests its choice of assistant 'was wise'. The community of Russian émigrés established in London in the 1880s both liked and admired Mary, and her long-standing participation in a heady and vigorous radical culture had given her extensive contacts among suffragettes, trade unionists and socialists as well as émigrés. Not only had she taught English to foreigners for a long while, but many 'refugees in difficulties had acquired the habit of turning to her for advice and assistance'.[8]

Under Mary's guidance, the committee chose to concentrate on influencing the Labour movement through union and trade journals. She was a prolific publicist. N.D. was predictably venomous:

> It is depressing to note the topics, and still more the tone, which some of your contributors favour at this momentous crisis. One could have wished to see all classes working together in harmony, trusting their leaders, sinking their differences, and placing the interests of their country before all other considerations. It is evident, however, that Mrs Bridges Adams thinks differently, for she writes as though the times were ripe for slinging mud at political opponents, and for setting one class against another.[9]

While admitting her unease at the depth and ferocity of the attacks, Mary challenged N.D. to let her know who 'he is'.[10] In the winter of 1915–16 she gave more encouragement to the idea of international rank-and-file movements, advocating that British and Russian workers unite. 'Even in my girlhood', she wrote, 'the struggles of the Russian people against oppression stirred my sympathies and it was with deep veneration that I looked upon those Russians who, while born to high privilege, gave up all for the cause of the oppressed.'[11] At this point she must have had her friends George Chicherin, Alexandra Kollontai and Peter Kropotkin in mind.

Ivan Maisky writes of this campaign in his autobiography. It had, he wrote, been Chicherin's wish to set up a British arm of the international movement for providing financial assistance to the victims of Tsarist oppression who were imprisoned in the hard labour prisons or in exile in Siberia for claiming the right of political and industrial organisation. In a fragment of autobiographical notes, Mary applauded Chicherin's faith in British trade unionists, 'of whose growing strength not only in the political and industrial fields, but also in the KEY department of Education' he was fully aware. She went on:

> Wishing to have an active connecting link between his committee and the organised working-class movement he sought my help – this because of a footing I had gained in the Trade Union Movement by long years of service in its educational side, both as for six years the only Labour member on the late London School Board, and also as a propagandist on behalf of the pre-war education demands of the Trades Union Congress, in support of which I had frequently written in Trade Union journals.[12]

Maisky says that Mary 'became the moving spirit on the committee'.[13] In practical terms, her house became the committee's headquarters and reprints of Chicherin's articles in the *A.S.E. Journal and Report*, the *Cotton Factory Times*, the *Railway Review* and the *Yorkshire Factory Times* provided the basis of their official literature. She provided Chicherin's contacts in the British Labour movement, including the RACS and the Woolwich Trades Council. William Barefoot offered to help their work and Chicherin was advised to make a 'formal application for assistance to the Trades Council', being sure to give 'special mention' to the question of 'getting the books into the Arsenal'.[14]

By autumn 1915, the Prisoners' Committee had an extensive network of collectors countrywide, particularly among branches of the ILP, the BSP, the ASE and NUR as well as local Trades Councils. As Mary's writings make clear, it was in fact fear of a move against the right of asylum for political refugees which prompted her to contact Lyulph Stanley, now Lord Sheffield. It was more than coincidence that shortly after the committee was established the offices of the Russian Seamen's Union and the Central Bureau of the Foreign Committee of the Russian Social Democratic Labour Party were raided. Mary needed others' support and recruited liberal-minded parliamentarians who equated such measures with repression, as well as members of the Society of Friends of Russian Freedom, like émigré David Soskice (b. 1866), who organised campaigns against the Russian Tsarist government.[15]

In December 1915 the Metropolitan Police raided the office of D. Anichken, Secretary of the Russian Seaman's Union. Outlawed in Russia itself, the Union was established first at Constantinople and then in Egypt.[16] Each time, the Russian government took a hand in getting the Union offices closed down. On the second occasion, the authorities deported the Union's president to Russia. Put on trial, he received a sentence of transportation for life to Siberia, but the residue of the Union found their way to Antwerp, and thence to London following the German invasion of Belgium. Further police raids on Anichken's lodgings, Bebel House and Chicherin's flat warned of stormy times ahead. Reporting the incidents in the *Cotton Factory Times*, Mary wrote that the confiscated papers included a list of Russian refugees, mostly very poor, who donated money to help fund raising.

Taking up the case in the House of Lords, Lord Sheffield explained that there was going to be a conference of English trade unions on 6 January and Mary had helped the secretary of the Russian union to prepare what was called an Open Letter to the Organised Workers of England. This was an appeal to British trade unionists 'to protect their comrades in Russia in the right of association to defend the claims of labour and also to stand by them if the right of asylum was invaded by the English government'.[17] However, between five and six hundred copies of the offending literature were seized during a police raid on Bebel House on 5 January, although interested parties managed to get copies sent to individual trade unions. Weeks later, Anichken answered a police summons to Scotland Yard. The police could find no fault with his papers, which they returned, and the Prisoners' Committee was free to continue its work.[18]

Shortly after, Ivan Maisky was threatened with arrest and reported that his mail was being intercepted. The man in command of interception was Sir Basil Thomson (b. 1861), the son of the Archbishop of York, who became assistant commissioner of the Metropolitan Police and head of the Criminal Investigation Department at New Scotland Yard in June 1913. Charged with investigating espionage, sabotage and subversion, the police and Special Branch under Captain Vernon Kell (b. 1873) worked as one unit throughout the war. As an aspect of their national security role, Kell and Thomson created a card index system on all potential subversives and allegedly had details of fourteen thousand people. For the first time the system included the surveillance of the socialist movement as a whole, as well as Irish political groups, foreign immigrant groups and the suffragettes.[19] In 1916 the Ministry of Munitions asked Thomson to organise an intelligence operation to report on industrial unrest. The arrest and imprisonment of revolutionary socialist and anti-war campaigner Alice Wheeldon (b. 1866) for allegedly plotting to assassinate Prime Minister David Lloyd George with a poison dart while out walking on a Surrey golf course provides a case in point. Sheila Rowbotham tells a story of spies infiltrating socialist meetings and conferences, desperate to round up people operating within various kinds of protest movement.[20]

Mary had found a space in which to express her views and continued to do so, using her position as a journalist writing for the *Cotton Factory Times* to place on record her discomfort at the 'vituperation' N.D. still 'pours forth' and anticipate her own arrest and trial. Skilled in engaging with the emotions of her readers, she presented what she called 'rough notes of a speech for the defence', since she believed N.D. to have connections 'with those in high places'. Underlying her wartime propaganda was her fear of all that would follow in the war's train. Therefore, she 'concentrated on matters bearing on the well-being of the children in our elementary schools' and declared that:

> It would be an interesting example of the ironies of the Labour movement if a government, having in it three leading Trade Unionists … were to show 'justice', rather than mercy to a woman who has been responsible for providing a standard by which Labour 'leaders' of to-day will at the bar of history be judged on the question 'What did they do for the children of the class to which they themselves once belonged?'[21]

Mary disapproved of what she saw as 'opportunism' on the part of men like Arthur Henderson, who took over as leader of the Labour Party when Ramsay MacDonald temporarily withdrew from the leadership and joined the War Cabinet. Her unease at his position was all the more acute since he reached Parliament largely on education principles, having been completely opposed to the events of 1902/3. Now she thought his accession to the Cabinet as Minister of Education had gone 'hand in hand' with 'a meek acceptance of the consolidation of that legislation'. Moving on to the question of the need to mobilise the Labour movement, she criticised the equivocation of Hyndman and his circle on the issues of militarism and internationalism. Capitalism crossed international borders, so teaching and propaganda functions were all-important:

> In all that I have written I have urged the need of intelligent study of these great capitalist alliances, and also of the movements for peace, which are growing among the workers of the various countries of the world. But this work 'N.D.' declares to be 'traitorous scheming,' while I submit that it is work needed in the organised working class movement, and as 'N.D.' knows no 'lead' on those questions of vital international importance – has been given to the trade unions by the 'leaders' even of the organisation which in Britain claims to represent International Social Democracy.[22]

The tone is polemical and Mary denounced the misguided patriotic zeal of the BSP under Hyndman's leadership. Over the course of the Second Boer War and immediately before and during the First World War, *Justice* adopted a blatantly anti-Semitic tone. Julia Bush and others suggest Jewish influence was very strong among those who began to show a determined resistance to Hyndman. For example, there was evidence of this in the *Call*, which immediately took up cudgels in defence of the right of asylum.[23] Whereas Hyndman had supported the build-up of the British navy because he believed Germany sought war and world dominance, Mary clung firmly to the position of the Zimmerwald Conference of socialists opposed to the war and reaffirmed her belief in, and commitment to, internationalism.

Mary situated her pronouncements in the context of the industrial unrest on the Clyde. Behind all this could be seen the recent detention of the Marxist émigrés Peter Petroff and his wife, Irma Gellrich (b. 1891), which led Mary to comment on 'the manner in which "His Majesty's Advisers" have on the Clyde shown their "toleration" towards those whose views are similar to those laid down in my contributions to the "Cotton Factory Times"'.[24] This was not simple paranoia. Refugee clubs and cafés came under surveillance from the later 1880s, and it was common practice for police to use disguises to gain entry to refugee meetings and the homes of the most prominent exiles too. Agent provocateur Alex Gordon was active in the London area and later admitted that his visit to the Communist Club in Charlotte Street – an address well known to foreign exiles – had been a 'prelude' to police raids.[25] Basil Thomson's wartime diary contained the following entry for 30 June 1916: 'Yesterday there was a meeting of the Central "Stop the War" Committee. The only attendants were two lady police spies, who entered into conversation, neither knowing the other's occupation. At a subsequent election for vacancies on the committee both these ladies were elected, so I shall not be without information!'[26]

Born into a Jewish family near Odessa, Peter Petroff joined the Russian Social Democratic Labour Party in 1901. At the time of the 1905 Revolution he held the post of party organiser and during the fighting he had led three workers' battalions, been severely wounded, imprisoned and sent into exile in Siberia. After serving two years he escaped and fled to England in 1908. Having reached the Scottish port of Leith, he made himself known to members of the SDF, who put him in touch with John Maclean in Glasgow. He lived at John's house for about two months before he went to London and became an active member of the Kentish Town branch of the SDP. Together with Fred Knee, Petroff helped to shape the London Labour Party in 1914. Described by Mary as a 'self-educated worker', before the war he made a 'modest living' as a journalist and procuring scientific apparatus for educational bodies in Russia. Later she wrote:

> He and I had much in common. He was strongly internationalist and we were in absolute agreement as to the necessity for a Socialist movement providing for its younger members systematic instruction in Socialist

> principles … also agreed that the Social Democratic movement in Britain will continue to be a failure unless it gives to the rest of the working-class movement here an intelligent, well-thought out lead in fighting the great forces of reaction which now hold the education of the workers and their children in their grip.[27]

Originally, Peter met German-born Irma Gellrich at a socialist Sunday school in Hampstead in 1911. Irma's parents died when she was a child and she received a secondary education in Breslau before working as a clerk and typist. She later attended the Social Democratic Party's Berlin educational school and returned to England in March 1913. The couple were 'married' on May Day, though without undergoing a legal process.

Irma became a London correspondent for the German social democratic press, but her nationality made her particularly vulnerable once war had broken out. Brought back to Scotland by invitation of the Glasgow branch of the BSP, the couple lived on £1 a week and joined the anti-war propaganda. Maclean especially valued Petroff's 'all-round' talents as propagandist, writer and authority on international socialism and had hopes of offering the couple greater protection from official harassment amid a mounting tempo of industrial and political militancy.[28] Consequently, he took Petroff to meetings of the Clyde Workers' Committee, then leading the opposition to the introduction of the Munitions Act in June 1915, which rendered strikes in the munitions industries illegal and encouraged the 'dilution' of skilled by unskilled labour.

For the authorities, desperate to reduce costs and increase production, the objective was clear. Opposition had to be smashed, and this meant testing the water on Clydeside. Intelligence reports advised action against John Maclean and Peter Petroff to undermine the militants and see if it provoked any serious reaction from the rank and file. Splits within the BSP came to an ugly head and on 23 December 1915 Peter was subjected to what Mary described as 'an exceedingly vicious' personal attack in the columns of *Justice*. The article in question, 'Who and what is Peter Petroff?' drew a denunciation from Chicherin, who pointed out the threat it posed to Petroff's freedom. There was thus built-in suspicion of fellow socialists, exacerbated by the timing of the raids both on Chicherin's lodgings and on the offices of the Russian Seamen's Union. Sure enough, the Petroffs' arrest, imprisonment and subsequent internment followed.

That Yuletide, Lloyd George and Arthur Henderson travelled to Glasgow to pacify the Clydeside engineers. The mission did not succeed and the authorities took the decision to censor press reports but failed to communicate this to the Glasgow branch of the ILP, whose *Forward* newspaper carried the story on New Year's Day 1916. Therefore, the police raided its offices and its printing presses and confiscated both the offending copy and proofs of John Maclean's *Vanguard*. In early February, the authorities arrested John Maclean. They held him in Edinburgh Castle for a week before charging him of various offences, including incitement to strike against conscription, which fell within the amended regulation to DORA dealing with the offence of inducing others to obstruct the war effort. A month later, the authorities deported other leading figures from the Clyde Workers' Committee, and B.J. Ripley and J. McHugh suggest that the 'militant wave ebbed away'.[29] When comrades James Maxton (b. 1885) and James MacDougall (b. about 1890) tried to provoke a general strike they, too, found themselves under arrest.

Most press attention revolved around the case of John Maclean. Mary concluded that there was a consciousness on Clydeside that went beyond industrial discontent and attributed it to the workers' educational classes associated with Maclean. Therefore, she asked readers of the *Cotton Factory Times* to note the names and whereabouts of five people: James Maxton (Duke Street Prison, Glasgow), James MacDougall (Duke Street Prison, Glasgow), John Maclean (at home awaiting trial), Irma and Peter Petroff (internment camp).[30] 'The list is worth studying,' she said. 'Not one is a "limelighter", not one would be of use to "draw" large crowds, to cheer at an Albert Hall meeting the vague generalities of demagogues, who stimulate in the mob a species of frothy revolt, which it is not difficult to show works out in the end as a powerful asset to reaction.'[31]

Born into a teaching family, James Maxton met Maclean as a fellow student at Glasgow University. At the time of his arrest and detention, Maxton was a leading member of the ILP, an active member of the Socialist Teachers' Society and secretary of the Glasgow Branch of the Teachers' Federation. Employed originally as a bank clerk, James MacDougall was Maclean's political protégé: an active member of the Co-operative movement, Scottish organiser of the BSP and by 1914 a member of the Eastwood School Board. Willie Gallacher (b. 1881), chairman of the Clyde Workers' Committee, was another close associate of Maclean's at this time. A fellow member of the anti-war section of the British Socialist Party, Gallacher wrote in his biography that 'Maclean had become a national figure known to everyone by 1915',[32] but this was an exaggeration. Only after his trial in April 1916 and exemplary sentence of three years' penal servitude did he receive a dramatic elevation of status as Britain's most important political prisoner, excluding Sinn Feiners.

Mary was outraged at the travesty of justice meted out to 'one of the best men'[33] she had known. She drew attention to the failure of Labour parliamentarians to come forward, but reserved her special condemnation for Henry Hyndman, Daisy Warwick 'and their aristocratic ecclesiastical association in the Church of the Resurrection', who remained silent on the suffering of their former political comrade.[34] Nonetheless, she remained upbeat. 'We shall win and my assurance is based on experience, as for many years past I have spent much time and energy in propagating the principle that the teaching in social science must be provided and controlled by the working-class organisations – independently – and not in co-partnership with capital and its bulwarks the Church, the universities and the Board of Education.'[35] In Mary's view, there were two distinct currents within the organised labour movement. Those whom she termed the 'servants of the Plutocracy' advocated a respectable path to social reform. Others who, in common with her and Maclean, were working to build the movement on strong independent class lines opposed them.[36] In May 1916 Mary published a letter from Maclean's wife written shortly after a visit to her husband. Conditions at Peterhead prison were described as 'most degrading and injurious to health. The feeding is very poor, about one hour is allowed for exercise daily, the rest of his time is filled up in doing prison work picking oakum. He is allowed to read … but no newspapers, no contact with the outside world at all. I do not know how he will stand that for so long. He is not allowed to write or see me for another seven months'.[37]

Police raids against Mary

Thus, Mary was involved in the public side of the anti-war movement. She tried to unite anti-militarism with the class struggle and this gave her a much greater significance to the authorities than local anti-war work would merit. Two further police raids afford us a glimpse of her impact. The first took place on 30 June 1916. On that day, the Home Office instructed the City Police to seize a leaflet entitled 'The Right of Asylum' and to arrest any person found distributing it. Once again, this literature was due to be communicated to a trade union congress meeting at the Memorial Hall in London's Farringdon Street. Some time earlier Mary had placed an order for five thousand copies, which she collected from the printers that very morning. At five o'clock she and a helper, 'Miss D.', were surrounded by plain-clothed policemen on Farringdon Street and picked up under the amended regulation of the DORA.

Both women were taken to Snow Hill police station, where they were searched and their keys taken from them. The police then went to their respective homes and raided them in their absence. Mary was detained for twenty-six hours, until seven o'clock on the evening of 1 July. She remembered what followed as the worst moment of all:

> 'As for you, Mrs Adams' said the Inspector, 'the military authorities will not charge you because you are not worth it; you are not worth powder and shot'. Miss D went home. I went at once to report myself to friends whom I had expected at my house on the previous evening … Later I went home. And then all the fire in my Welsh blood blazed forth when I saw what had been done in my absence … for the first time in my life I FELT I HAD NO HOME; for at every turn the spirits of evil had left traces of their presence.[38]

Pictures that had belonged to her father-in-law's second wife, Sarah Flower, had been mishandled. Unused writing paper, circulars, private letters, documents and press cuttings lay in miscellaneous heaps in her sitting room. Elsewhere police had wiped their dirty hands on a clean table cloth and stubbed out cigarettes on her bedroom floor. 'At the same time', she sardonically pointed out, 'it is only fair to add that the wallpaper had not been torn from the walls.' The Home Office file on Chicherin reveals that 'Miss D.' was, in fact, a Miss Lilian Lewis, who had moved into Bebel House but was then living in Tottenham Court Road.[39]

In July 1916 Mary used the columns of the *Cotton Factory Times* to inform readers that she might go to America to advise people of the threat to civil liberties in Britain.[40] She also wrote to the Home Secretary to demand the return of her papers. Her case was taken up by Joseph King (b. 1860), a radical Liberal who opposed Lloyd George and was equally hostile to the state intelligence networks. In August, Mary commented on the support she had received from Lord Sheffield and the *Manchester Guardian*. Indeed, her old friend from happier times had spoken strongly against the action of the Home Office during a debate in the House of Lords on the question of Russian refugees and military service.

In the first place, Lord Sheffield wanted to know whether police pressure had been put on Russian subjects in this country to return to Russia, and second, if 'Russian and other alien friends' had been told they were under no obligation to return to their country of origin. Third, if the right of asylum had been abandoned, whether persons who refused military service might choose where to go from 'the countries that do not close their doors to political refugees'. Drawing on past experience as a member of the LSB to consider the contribution of East End Jews, he continued, 'they have been industrious, sober, fond of their families, and anxious to get on'. He equated these interventions with repression and suggested the government was offering a 'sort of pirate's alternative, "Either be killed by me on deck or walk the plank." There is very little difference between that alternative and saying to these people that they must either be deported to Russia or join the British Army.'[41]

That autumn, Mary went to the Midlands to attend the annual Congress of the TUC, as she usually did. The leadership was rather lukewarm in its attitude toward the issue of the right of asylum, but her object was to influence the thinking of the delegates. Nevertheless, her request to make information on the aliens question available was ignored and on arrival she was told not to leave pamphlets on tables. Meanwhile, two uniformed policemen followed her into a crowded restaurant where she was having lunch and demanded to know the whereabouts of a suitcase in which she had brought pamphlets to Birmingham. Without arousing the suspicion of the authorities, she had already hit upon what she later described as 'a very clever ruse.'[42] Earlier that morning she had gone back to the train station, collected the parcels and hailed a taxi, which took her to Birmingham town hall, where she deposited the package in a committee room.

Mary stayed at the Hurst Street Domestic Mission, a Unitarian institution which combined humanitarian and educational work with the aim of helping the poor. That night, the Birmingham police seized two thousand copies of an abridged form of the Right of Asylum leaflet, together with the reprint of an article from the *A.S.E. Journal and Report* entitled 'The Unsanitary Denominational Schools of London' and a pamphlet with a cartoon by Walter Crane which had appeared in 1912 and contained the trade union educational policy. More dramatically, they captured her host's son, who was a war resister, and turned him over to the military authorities.[43]

Support came from the rank and file. In November 1916 Mary, while admitting that the 'police did not like it', wrote that 'friends among the miners guarded my big portmanteau' so she could distribute reprints of the House of Lords debate on Russian refugees and military service at a rally in London. Yet there was silence on the part of Free Church leaders, the TUC, the Labour Party bureaucracy and prominent Labour women like Margaret Bondfield (b. 1873), who declared the Right of Asylum no concern of the Women's International League.[44] Once again it came about that Lord Sheffield intervened, explaining his position to the House of Lords and moving that the increased powers of surveillance and security 'be used strictly for the defence of the Realm, and not strained so as to interfere unduly with civil liberty or to deprive those living in this country of their constitutional safeguards'. Sheffield's criticisms had a strong libertarian element to them. He expressed both shame and anger at Mary's treatment, observing that the majority of the papers seized 'show the extreme, I might say, imbecility of the officials employed to make the raid'. Beside the documents described earlier, another was a three months' financial statement of the receipts and expenditure of the Russian Political Prisoners and Exiles' Relief Committee.[45]

Lord Derby, the Secretary of State for War, disagreed with Sheffield's interpretation of events, relating that the authorities first started tracking Mary's activities because of a letter printed in *Labour Leader* in November 1915 in which she publicised the formation of the Prisoners' Committee. The spies did not consider this a 'perfectly harmless' body and the Secretary of State agreed with the basis of their assessments. Mary had close links with Petroff and Maclean and a London correspondent of *Vorwarts*, organ of the German Social Democratic Party, now interned.

> If people like to keep the company that this Mrs Bridges Adams does, they must expect to come under suspicion. I am all for keeping strictly within the law, but I am all for exercising the law in this respect to the fullest of the powers that it gives to us. I agree that supervision must be kept by those in authority over their subordinates, but I believe in prevention being better than cure, and if a person gives rise to suspicion as Mrs Bridges Adams undoubtedly did, I hold that the authorities are perfectly right in taking steps to prevent her from doing illegal action before she has done that illegal action rather than try afterwards to punish her for so doing.[46]

The file on Chicherin corroborates this, showing that the authorities thought its 'true purpose the incitement of rebellion against the British Government'. For example, spies were able to infiltrate a meeting at London's East End on 31 October 1915 which Mary addressed on the topic of the Russian political prisoners, speaking of her long-standing interest in the Russian socialist movement and past membership of the LSB. The agents reported her as saying that she 'had met many influential Russian socialists especially during a residence in Paris ... when on an important mission she was arrested at Stuttgart and very carefully searched, but she and her friends were too clever to be caught with incriminating documents ... and she believed that when we had a "shooting democracy" we should have an intelligent democracy'.[47]

Looking back, Mary struggled to express the debt she owed Lord Sheffield. She said it had been difficult to convince him that the Right of Asylum was under threat, but once convinced, 'the grand old hero' put up a great fight.[48] 'When Labour & Socialist "Leaders" forsake me', she wrote later, on her reprint of the parliamentary debates, 'the Lords will take me up'.[49]

Irish connection and Russian comrades

However, Mary had another unnamed association and that was with the Sinn Feiners and the struggle in Ireland. In an article for the *Cotton Factory Times*, she protested the brutal murder of Francis (Frank) Sheehy Skeffington (b. 1878) during the Easter-week rising in Dublin in 1916. Sheehy Skeffington, the son of a school inspector, was pro-feminist and pacifist. He was educated at University College Dublin, and Irish novelist James Joyce (b. 1882) commended him as the cleverest person he had met. Five feet four and half inches tall, with a high-pitched voice and red beard, he always wore tweed knickerbockers, long socks and boots. Joyce called him 'hairy Jaysus'.[50] Frank supported Mary's desire to found travel scholarships for working-class women to study the social and industrial conditions in other countries because he thought it might further the establishment of a strong working women's peace movement. Both were 'agreed as to the necessity of educating young men and women members of the trade unions in the principles of International Labour Solidarity'. Something else he and Mary had in common was a lack of interest in material goods. In Mary's opinion, a fine epitaph would be for socialists to show 'that the "CAUSE goes marching on" and the way must be led by the organised working women, and by such of the younger generation of trade unionists as have the courage – I am almost tempted to say rashness, to remain in Britain "after the war"'.[51]

On the second day of the Rising, Frank Skeffington walked to the centre of Dublin with his wife, Hanna (b. 1877). Whereas she made her way straight to the General Post Office, headquarters of the insurgents, to deliver much-needed supplies of food, he spent the day putting up notices, signed by him alone, against the looting of shops. In late afternoon the couple met at the rooms of the Irish Women's Franchise League, and since they were both anxious about their young son, Owen (b. 1909), Hanna decided she had better go home. Setting off in the early evening, Frank was arrested and brought into Portobello Barracks. Nothing incriminating was found but he was the perfect hostage for a raiding party organised by Captain J.C. Bowen-Colthurst. With his hands tied behind his back Frank was taken on a patrol where Bowen-Colthurst shot dead one 17-year-old boy and captured two male journalists who were sheltering in a tobacconist's shop. The next morning the three men were marched into the prison yard and a firing party was given the order by Bowen-Colthurst to shoot them dead. Later, Frank's leg was noticed to be still moving and another volley was fired into his body to finish him off.

In the aftermath of the tragedy Mary wrote to Hanna, whom she tried to offer consolation: 'what can I say that you do not already know? That the hearts of thousands have gone out to you in your great sorrow. You know too that many British born men and women are feeling with a bitterness which no words can express the shame and humiliation of the recent events in Ireland'. She remembered her own shock of bereavement after Walter's death in 1900: 'In time you will find solace in working for the causes he loved'. She admired Hanna's courage: 'You are splendid to go on working as you are doing and you will inspire others. The Cotton Factory Times is a good paper to write in,' Mary concluded, stating of her experience: 'I am pegging away' in Lancashire as three-quarters of all trade unionists in the textile industries are women workers. 'It is hard work, but will *tell* in time – is telling already'.[52] Finally, Mary promised to do all she could to bring pressure to bear until justice had been achieved. In the event, one English officer refused to go along with a cover-up of the arbitrary execution. Court-martialled and found 'guilty but insane', Bowen-Colthurst spent twenty months in Broadmoor before his release on 'retired pay', which he continued to receive until his death in 1965.[53]

Mary shared the delight of many on hearing news of the Russian Revolution in February/March 1917. The joy is vividly conveyed in her description of her own reactions at a rally organised by Russian socialist groups: 'it was a soul stirring experience to be part of that great mass of people who had learnt to think in terms of the international working-class movement … I came away hoping with all my heart that the rank and file of the trade unionists of Britain will … secure in their branches close study and intelligent discussion of the real meaning of the revolution'.[54] On 10 August 1917, however, the police warned George Chicherin of his impending arrest. Days later, he languished in Brixton prison charged with 'hostile associations' with Germans and pro-Germans at the Communist Club and the danger he represented to the British secret service. Among those named was Alexandra Kollontai, described as 'an exceedingly beautiful and fascinating woman'.

Mary said the Russian government had entrusted Chicherin with papers seized from the archives of the Tsarist secret police in Petrograd and asked that he investigate the collaboration, which undoubtedly took place, between the British and the Russian secret police. Then she spelt out what happened next. 'It was arranged that I should visit him, attend to his private business, and purchase the food he was allowed to provide for himself. I paid one visit during which in the presence of a police officer he requested that in any effort made on his behalf I would lay emphasis not on his work in connection with the secret agent investigation but on the question "is internationalism pro-Germanism?"'[55] During his internment, Chicherin was refused any further visits from Mary because MI5 was 'strongly of the opinion that she should neither visit not correspond with any 14.B. prisoners'. In April 1917, her visiting rights to Irma and Peter Petroff were withdrawn completely. Prison authorities in the camp known as 'The Institute', Islington, censored Peter's letters to Mary, though Irma seems to have retained her writing privileges. In the House of Commons, Irma's treatment at Aylesbury Camp, Buckinghamshire was the subject of a parliamentary question, to investigate allegations that she had been forced to bathe with women who had syphilis, and she also told visitors that a fellow prisoner attacked her.[56]

The eventual decision to repatriate the Petroffs, with George Chicherin, was the culmination of two months of diplomatic negotiations conducted between the British government and the newly established Bolshevik government in Russia. It was Trotsky, as Commissar of Foreign Affairs, who took up the case. It led him to threaten the arrest and internment of all British subjects in Russia unless the three prisoners were released. Thus, the Petroffs and Chicherin returned to Russia in January 1918. Mary's story was that a visitor knocked at her door in the late afternoon on New Year's Day, with the news of Chicherin's deportation the following night. In the morning she visited an old school friend of Chicherin's, the ex-Tsarist consul general, and begged him to use his influence to get her a visiting permit. He phoned immediately, but failed to get the desired response.

Ironically, it was Mary's wartime foe, Arthur Henderson, a personal stranger, who got to pay a last-minute visit to Brixton jail. It was thus that Mary travelled to the train station hoping to 'catch a glimpse' of her political friend. Fortuitously, she entered the platform café by one door just as Chicherin and his police escort entered by another. Seated at adjoining tables, they snatched a few words and Mary wrote 'poor Tchitcherine's last meal in Britain was eaten in "hostile association" with myself!' As Chicherin boarded his train, the Petroffs pulled up, reunited minutes before 'in a taxi with two police officers present'. Chicherin subsequently thanked Lord Sheffield for his role in events with characteristic brevity: 'Much appreciation of enlightened support.' In Mary's opinion, someone like Chicherin who was 'no generator of hot air', valued this kind of support most.[57]

Once back in Russia, the Petroffs would face more surveillance and harassment. Peter fell out of favour and left the Russian Communist Party in 1925, when attached to the Russian Trade Mission in Berlin. In the early 1930s, concern at German fascism and possible threats from Stalin's agents led him to seek permanent refuge in Britain for himself, Irma and their two young daughters. Prominent Labour movement figures backed his efforts but the Home Office rejected their requests, as did the Jewish Refugee Committee in London. The family spent time on the run, but everything changed when the Paris passport control office decided to issue entry visas to the Petroff children. Sylvia Pankhurst made arrangements for their education and James Maxton added his weight to the campaign to grant the Petroffs a two-month visa to visit their children and publisher.

The couple wished to arrange publication of an English edition of a book that they had written on the causes of Hitler's rise to power in Germany. Eventually, when George Lansbury intervened, the Home Office agreed to his request and the Petroffs returned to Britain. On three separate occasions, the Home Office extended the visas until the autumn of 1936, when the Home Secretary communicated to the General Secretary of the TUC that the Petroffs could stay without limit. How Irma and Peter must have celebrated with their comrade Mary, now sharing her home with them. The Home Office file on Peter Petroff reveals that they were living at Bebel House and had been there ever since they departed Newhaven ferry port in early December 1933.[58]

Working-class feminism

Mary remained a militant socialist for the remainder of her life. Strong Labour movement ties were crucial to her activities on behalf of the Russian Political Prisoners and Exiles' Relief Committee and her old friend Lord Sheffield endorsed her well-publicised views on issues of surveillance and security in Parliament. On the case of Peter Petroff, John McHugh concludes that 'such publicity may have prevented' his 'deportation to Russia and possible execution and contributed to the relatively relaxed condition of his internment'.[59] Throughout it all, Mary's was a resolute voice castigating complacency. Influenced by syndicalist emphasis on rank-and-file workplace action and distrust of leaders, she was suspicious of the encroachment of the employers' control in conditions of wartime repression. She did not believe the interventions were for the duration of the war only and feared 'workers may be kept hard at it for many years on the NEGATIVE task of winning back pre-war conditions'.[60] Her long-term goal was rather different. She was convinced that when working women had political power, the world would be better.

As peace approached, Mary's writings consistently advocated women's self-organisation within the socialist movement. She acknowledged the need for social reconstruction and urged working-class women to play their part. 'The work they are now called upon to face is too vital to their class to be delegated to middle-class women as "leaders", however well meaning and however democratic such women may be.' Once again, she challenged them to work 'shoulder to shoulder with working men', just as she had when she rallied around the engineers' struggle for the eight-hour day during the national lockout of 1897. This would demonstrate a 'great truth' to influential and well-placed women in the peace movement. It would show them that 'the fight for a world peace can only be effective, will only be feared by the great forces which make wars when it goes hand in hand with the fight for the full emancipation of Labour from Capitalist domination'.[61]

Half the leading women in the British suffrage movement opposed the war, and they joined female suffragists from all over Europe and America to press for a negotiated peace. Unlike most of them, Mary connected feminism and pacifism with workers' control.

> If the new working-class international is to be a force for ending wars and is not itself to be destroyed by future Imperial wars, then the organised working women of Britain and other countries must be in that International. Their inclusion must be real and not fictitious. They must, through mandates from the rank and file, have a voice in that international, and must not be content to be led like sheep, with Labour bureaucracies or self-appointed caucuses of Socialist intellectuals speaking in their name … and thus let the diplomats know that a new force will for the future have to be reckoned with in international politics.[62]

The years had not diminished the revolutionary intensity of Mary's utopian vision. Now she wanted to find a space in which working-class women might contribute to the advance of socialism.

In the context of the war, a new generation of women became involved in socialist, suffrage and peace politics and the following vignette illustrates this. In the summer of 1917, fellow socialist Agnes Dollan (b. 1887), one of eleven children of a blacksmith and associate of Harry McShane, helped to launch the Women's Peace Crusade in Glasgow. Yes, she was working alongside her friend Helen Crawfurd (b. 1877) the daughter of a prosperous master baker, but Agnes, who had worked in a factory and as a telephone operator, had found a political voice just as Mary would have wanted.[63]

Notes

1 M. Bridges Adams, 'Why political prisoners?', *Cotton Factory Times*, 29 October 1915, p. 2.
2 M. Bridges Adams, 'Why political prisoners?', p. 2.
3 Mrs Bridges Adams, 'Towards peace on earth', *Cotton Factory Times*, 24 December 1915.
4 M. Crick, *The History of the Social Democratic Federation* (Keele: Ryburn Publishing, 1994), p. 303.
5 H. Adams Lehmann (ed.), *Kriegsgegner in England* (München: Druck and Verlag von G. Birk & Co.m.b.H., 1915).
6 M. Howard, *War and the Liberal Conscience* (Oxford: Oxford University Press, 1981), pp. 75–84.
7 Mrs Bridges Adams, 'Towards peace on earth', *Cotton Factory Times*, 24 December 1915; Mrs Bridges Adams, 'Internationalism and the child', *Cotton Factory Times*, 5 March 1915; A.W. Humphrey, *International Socialism and the War* (London: P.S. King and Son, 1915), pp. 61–2, and personal information from Dr Marita Krauss.
8 R. Challinor, *The Origins of British Bolshevism* (London: Croom Helm, 1977), p. 185.
9 N.D. 'Attitude to the war' (letter), *Cotton Factory Times*, 16 July 1915.
10 M. Bridges Adams, 'Political Prisoners and Exiles Relief Committee' (letter), *Cotton Factory Times*, 30 July 1915, 5.
11 M. Bridges Adams, 'British and Russian workers unite!' *Cotton Factory Times*, 17 December 1915, 6.
12 M. Bridges Adams, 'Memoirs', p. 2.
13 I. Maisky, *Journey into the Past*, translated from the Russian by Felix Holt (London: Hutchinson, 1962), p. 75.
14 CUBM, Bridges Adams Papers, correspondence with individuals, J.D. Lawrence to G.V. Chicherin, 5 September 1915.
15 HL, Soskice Papers M. Bridges Adams to David Soskice, 12 August 1915.
16 Constantinople was renamed Istanbul after the fall of the Ottoman Empire.
17 Parliamentary Debates, House of Lords, Wednesday 7 March 1917, extract from Vol. 24, No. II, Official Report (unrevised) Defence of the Realm Acts, p. 404.
18 M. Bridges Adams, 'Raid on Russian refugees' (letter), *Cotton Factory Times*, 7 January 1916; M. Bridges Adams, 'Another police raid: Mrs Bridges Adams's house searched' (letter), *Cotton Factory Times*, 14 January 1916.
19 T. Bunyan, *The History and Practice of the Political Police in Britain* (London: Quartet Books, 1977).

20 S. Rowbotham, *Friends of Alice Wheeldon* (London: Pluto Press, 1986).
21 Mrs Bridges Adams, 'In defence of my propaganda – dangers of reaction during the war – reply to "N.D."', *Cotton Factory Times*, 25 February 1916, p. 4.
22 Mrs Bridges Adams, 'In defence of my propaganda – dangers of reaction during the war – reply to "N.D."', *Cotton Factory Times*, 25 February 1916, p. 4.
23 J. Bush, *Behind the Lines: East London labour 1914–1919* (London: Merlin Press, 1984), pp. 176–7.
24 Bush, *Behind the Lines*, pp. 176–7.
25 K. Weller, *'Don't be a Soldier!' The radical anti-war movement in north London 1914–1918* (London: Journeyman Press Limited and the London History Workshop Centre, 1985), p. 64.
26 B. Thomson, *The Scene Changes* (London: Collins, 1939), p. 297.
27 M. Bridges Adams, 'The extradition laws and the case of Peter Petroff', *Yorkshire Factory Times*, 30 March 1916, p. 1.
28 N. Milton, *John Maclean* (Bristol: Pluto Press, 1973), pp. 37, 108–9.
29 B.J. Ripley and J. McHugh, *John Maclean* (Manchester: Manchester University Press, 1989), pp. 90–4.
30 Mrs Bridges Adams, 'The arrests on the Clyde', *Cotton Factory Times*, 14 April 1916.
31 Mrs Bridges Adams, 'The arrests on the Clyde', *Cotton Factory Times*, 14 April 1916.
32 W. Gallacher, *Revolt on the Clyde* (London: Lawrence and Wishart, 1980), p. 67.
33 Mrs Bridges Adams, 'The release of Maclean', *Cotton Factory Times*, 30 June 1916.
34 Mrs Bridges Adams 'The Approach of the Iron Heel: democracy swept back by tide of war', *Cotton Factory Times*, 28 April 1916.
35 Mrs Bridges Adams, 'The sentence of John Maclean: significance of attacks on educationalists', *Cotton Factory Times*, 21April 1916.
36 Mrs Bridges Adams, 'The approach of the iron heel: democracy swept back by war', *Cotton Factory Times*, 28 April 1916.
37 Mrs Bridges Adams, 'The ground we are losing', *Cotton Factory Times*, 12 May 1916.
38 Mrs Bridges Adams, 'The right of asylum', *Cotton Factory Times*, 21 July 1916; Mrs Bridges Adams, 'Smashing right of asylum', *Cotton Factory Times*, 4 August 1916; Mrs Bridges Adams, 'Congress and right of asylum', *Cotton Factory Times*, 22 October 1916.
39 TNA, Home Office Papers, Chicherin file, HO.144/2158/C329891.
40 Mrs Bridges Adams, 'The right of asylum', *Cotton Factory Times*, 21 July 1916.
41 Parliamentary Debates, House of Lords, 'Russian refugees and military service', Thursday 27 July 1916, pp. 987–8.
42 Mrs Bridges Adams, 'Congress and right of asylum: adventures with leaflets at Birmingham', *Cotton Factory Times*, 22 October 1916.
43 'New minister at the Hurst Street Mission', *Newspaper Cuttings Birmingham*

Biography Volume 9, 1914–16, p. 100; Hurst Street Domestic Mission, Reports 1914–16; Parliamentary Debates, House of Lords, Wednesday 7 March 1917, extract from Vol. 24, No. II, Official Report (unrevised) Defence of the Realm Acts, pp. 406–7.

44 Mrs Bridges Adams, 'A great tradition in peril', *Cotton Factory Times*, 29 September 1916; Mrs Bridges Adams, 'The right of asylum', *Cotton Factory Times*, 17 November 1916.

45 Parliamentary Debates, House of Lords, Wednesday 7 March 1917, extract from Vol. 24, No. II, Official Report (unrevised) Defence of the Realm Acts, pp. 406–7.

46 Parliamentary Debates, House of Lords, 7 March 1917, Vol. 24, No. II, p. 411.

47 TNA, Home Office Papers, Chicherin file, HO.144/2158/C329891.

48 M. Bridges Adams, 'Memoirs', p. 4.

49 These were the words Mary wrote on the front of her copy of a reprint of a parliamentary debate in the House of Lords, 'Defence of the Realm Acts', Parliamentary Debates, House of Lords, Wednesday 7 March 1917, extract from Vol. 24, No. II, Official Report (unrevised) Defence of the Realm Acts, pp. 403–24.

50 M. Ward, *Hanna Sheehy Skeffington: a life* (Cork: Attic Press, 1997), pp. 19–20.

51 Mrs Bridges Adams, 'For the period of the war', *Cotton Factory Times*, 19 May 1916.

52 NLI, Sheehy Skeffington Papers, Ii3, MS 33,605 (5), MS 33,605 (6), M. Bridges Adams to Mrs Skeffington, 6 June, 18 June, n.d. [June] 1916.

53 Ward, *Hanna Sheehy Skeffington*, pp. 155–65.

54 Mrs Bridges Adams, 'A great Russian socialist meeting in London', *Yorkshire Factory Times*, 5 April 1917.

55 M. Bridges Adams, 'Memoirs', p. 5.

56 TNA, Home Office Papers, Petroff file HO.144/17485/306431; HO.144/17486/306431.

57 M. Bridges Adams, 'Memoirs', pp. 7–9.

58 TNA, Home Office Papers, Petroff file HO.144/17487/306431/208; 144/17487/306431/209; 144/17487/306431/213; 144/17487/306431/218; 144/17487/306431/219; 144/17487/306431/220; 144/17487/306431/221; 144/17487/306431/222; 144/17487/306431/223; 144/17487/306431/224; 144/17487/306431/225.

59 J. McHugh, 'Peter Petroff: the view from the Home Office file', *Scottish Labour History*, 35 (2000), p. 27.

60 Mrs Bridges Adams, 'The ground we are losing', *Cotton Factory Times*, 12 May 1916.

61 Mrs Bridges Adams, 'Towards peace and after', *Cotton Factory Times*, 5 May 1916.

62 Mrs Bridges Adams, 'Towards peace and after'.

63 Helen Corr, 'Dollan, Agnes Johnston, Lady Dolan (1887–1966)', *Oxford Dictionary of National Biography* (Oxford: Oxford University Press, 2004; online

edn, May 2007) [http://www.oxforddnb.com/view/article/54395, accessed 24 April 2008]; H. Corr, 'Crawfurd [née Jack; other married name Anderson], Helen (1877–1954), *Oxford Dictionary of National Biography* (Oxford: Oxford University Press, 2004; online edn, May 2007) [http://www.oxforddnb.com/view/article/40301, accessed 24 April 2008].

9

Reflections, connections and Utopian visions

> To have become a Socialist is to have learnt something, to have made an intellectual and a moral step, to have discovered a general purpose in life and a new meaning in duty and brotherhood. (H.G. Wells, 1909)[1]

> In my mother's eyes, inspired by the Socialist ideal, undimmed by cynicism, alight with faith in our common labours, despite all her troubles, disappointments, and unceasing poverty, were shining hope, belief, and the purpose of a better future. (Margaret McCarthy, 1953)[2]

The first quotation comes from *New Worlds for Old*, the last of H.G. Wells' quartet of books on the socialist future. Making socialists meant helping people to change, and Wells expressed the emerging consensus when he wrote that 'the Socialist movement *is* teaching, and the most important people in the world from the Socialist's point of view are those who teach'.[3] In the second quotation, former Communist, ex-trade unionist and Labour parliamentarian Margaret McKay (née McCarthy, b. 1911) portrayed her mother's politics as strengthened through suffering. Mary lived the same kind of politics in the same period and her face could have told the same kind of story of hardships endured for the class struggle. She persisted in the promotion of socialism's promise of a new way of life, eventually charting her course beyond the Labour Party's main strategies of reform through the National Labour Education League with movements of independent working-class education, the Russian question and, by the 1920s, self-identity as an 'unattached Communist'.[4] By exploring Mary's politics and politicisation, I have shown the workings of a political life at local level in the context of war and peace. This socialist woman had first-hand experience of inequality and was determined to produce a fairer world.

Looking across Labour's first century, Jon Lawrence shows the importance of party mythology in the construction of political identities within the twentieth-century Labour Party. However, Mary's activism is quite lost to historical view in the popular histories, the 'myths' that Labour Party activists have internalised about their party's past. The context for her story is the 'foundation myths' about the 'early days', although her involvement in the struggle to 'make socialists' does not feature in Labour's life story. To revisit the notion of parties as discursive 'sites', Mary is part of the ebbs and flows of the extra-parliamentary Left, for whom parliamentary politics has always been of secondary importance. She, like the Labour Left, never came near to capturing the movement's commanding heights. Hers, as the preceding chapters make clear, is a story that highlights complex disagreements over policy and ideology, a story that highlights what Lawrence calls the 'myths of political division'. Amid the feuding that beset different social and political groupings, Mary's preference was to use the language of ideology in adversity, whereas others like N.D. (the protagonist she addressed in the quotation at the start of chapter 1) chose to use the language of personalities.

Always in a minority, Mary tried to push the Parliamentary Labour Party into accepting more radical policies and programmes, in response to challenges from Labour's opponents. Indeed, the party's early strength built upon the welfare issues she raised as an elected member of the LSB, as a trade unionist and as education spokesperson for the SDF. Losses like the Education Acts of 1902/3 were punctuated by developments in social policy at national level, the conversion of 'Comrade Warwick' and the election of Victor Grayson at Colne Valley in 1907. For socialists of Mary's generation, the choice between revision and revolution was real, as was the possibility of creating a radicalised class through a sustained campaign of education and propaganda.

Before 1910, Labour behaved in the House of Commons much less like an opposition party than as a pressure group, and to an important extent the introduction of free school meals for the poorest schoolchildren in 1906, and compulsory medical inspection in state schools a year later, originated in Mary's work. With the benefit of hindsight, both she and others greatly overestimated the chances of revolutionary success, but if a member of the landed aristocracy could be persuaded, why not others? In founding Bebel House, she aimed to create an informed minority of working women, a layer of the working class, capable of utilising their implacably class-conscious insights in the struggle for political power. Grass-roots enthusiasts with fervent energy anticipated a new dawn when Labour would stand for socialism in practice, rather than 'the historic coalition of socialists and social reformers' that Ralph Miliband subsequently defined as labourism.[5]

The political scene was stormy in the years 1910–18 and economic militancy intensified, but it was by no means a foregone conclusion that the possibilities of their ideas and activities would be lost. They risked all. Take the heart-wrenching political oratory of John Maclean to evoke the drama of the time as he spoke from the dock of a Scottish courtroom in July 1918: 'I wish no harm to any human being, but I, as one man, am going to exercise my freedom of speech. No human being on the face of the earth, no government is going to take from me my right to speak, my right to protest against wrong, my right to everything that is for the benefit for mankind. I am not here, then, as the accused; *I am here as the accuser of capitalism dripping with blood from head to foot.*'[6] This was a powerful force rooted in action, totally convinced of the justice of his cause. Remarkably constant over the political prosecutions in wartime, Mary conducted a campaign on his behalf and that of the Russians in the columns of the *Cotton Factory Times*. 'I was the only one of our party who was arrested and the prosecution was dropped', she remembered in 1924.[7]

Mary was consistent in the way in which she told the story of what attracted her to socialism. She always stressed the influence of William Morris, and she had a vision that socialism would end the poverty and suffering that working people faced, especially working-class children. Following the pathway Morris laid out in *News from Nowhere*, his English Utopia published in 1890, she remained convinced that his was a vision, not a dream.[8] Her focus on education never wavered and her ideas were more complex than her later writings, with their emphasis on producing cadres for the revolution, would imply. There is a sense that she wants working-class people to have a good, classless education because that is what will empower them, despite the stress on lessons in Marxist economics and the social sciences. This may have been a reflection of her social background and teaching experience, as well as her personal struggle to secure access to elite knowledge as an adult. We can only surmise the impact of her relations with the Adamses after Walter's death, her sense of her ambiguous class position.

During her Woolwich activism, there are shades of the ethical reformer who believed that art should be a central concern of education for all and wanted to change the workers' outlook to ensure they were better prepared for Utopia. Mary worked practically to ameliorate conditions, offering a radical response at a crucial turning point in English education. The policies she favoured were local control and 'common schools' rather than the workable 'ladder of opportunity' that Robert Morant and

Sidney Webb put into operation. The effects of the educational settlement of 1902/3 were just as she anticipated. On the one hand, the abolition of the school board system distanced teachers and working people from popular politics. On the other, the exclusive element in the legislation drove a wedge between the two school systems, and teachers and pupils keenly felt this.[9]

After the school board period, there was a shift of rhetoric and emphasis in Mary's political practice. The Taff Vale Judgment in 1901 (when the House of Lords penalised trade unions for losses caused by strike action), changes in the organisation of the local educational state, as well as the 1905 Russian Revolution, consolidated the leftward trend in her views. She believed the First World War was the result of imperialist rivalries, which the working-class movements on either side had no cause to support.

Politics was not 'the art of the possible', in Mary's case. In the war years, her language became much more radicalised and she redoubled her efforts to attract working-class women to socialist politics.

> Middle class women have shewn us what women can endure for the vote. I believe I may reasonably hope to live to see the day when the organized working-class women (among whom are many who, because they love children, have not dared to bring children into the world to be doomed to a life of poverty), will shew what motherhood actual and suppressed is capable of in the first place on behalf of the children of their class, and in the second place for the building up of industrial organizations, in which as women's education increases they will see the greatest instrument in securing the emancipation of the children.[10]

As we follow Mary's ardent appeals, we see and record her disappointment with Labour leaders. Discontent with the politics of manoeuvre and compromise added to disillusion with the pro-war stance of erstwhile allies like Henry Hyndman, Will Thorne, Ben Tillett and her old patron Daisy Warwick. As she put it in 1916:

> Once more, I say it is time that organised Labour took stock of its position. There are many men now who, too old now to join the Army to fight for our 'liberties' in the battlefield, were prior to 1906 young enough to feel enthusiastic in that fight against the forces of reaction which resulted in the return of a substantial Labour party in the House of Commons. That fight was against militarism, imperialism, and tariffs, and in the field of education politics declared emphatically against the clerical education legislation of 1902 and 1903. All that Labour fought against IS HERE![11]

Mary collapsed from nervous strain after Chicherin's departure, which stilled her voice for a while, although we still hear it in the interwar years. She continued to raise the issues of Russian political prisoners, independent working-class education, church schools and child welfare.

In the summer of 1920, for example, Mary reiterated her support for education that is 'provided and controlled by the working-class organisations INDEPENDENTLY, without any kind of association with that clerical-capitalist-lion-and-lamb-ultra-coalitionist organisation known as the Workers' Educational Association'. She reminded readers of the *Socialist* of the 'bed-rock' principle at stake, 'That it is the duty of the working-class organisations to provide for their members the education necessary to an intelligent understanding of their position AS WORKERS, and that such education should be controlled by the organisations INDEPENDENTLY and not in co-PARTNERSHIP or COALITION with such capitalist forces as the Church, the Universities, and the Board of Education'.[12]

Four years later, she positioned herself as the voice of experience after the fall of the first minority Labour government. She advised an open response to strong anti-Soviet propaganda, drawing on her involvement in the fight for the right of asylum, which taught her 'very, very much. I paid a heavier price for my lessons than my Lancashire friends have yet learned,' she wrote in a letter to the editor of the *Cotton Factory Times*. After all, she concluded, 'I have earned the right to say that my work for distressed Russians in pre and post revolution days, even in the difficult days of the war, proved conclusively that there is no need, no room, in the British Labour movement for "secret", "illegal," "underground" movements'.[13] Perhaps comrade 'Mazeppa' felt some sympathy with her position. Five years previously, he had allied himself with her in the opinions that he rehearsed. 'My efforts are as nothing to those of Mrs Adams who for four years has been endeavouring to place before your readers the real feelings of the Russian masses,' he wrote. 'Is it "playing the game" to leave all the work to a mere woman like Mrs Adams … Is official Labour in this year of grace 1919 again to relapse into such a state of hide-bound inaction?'[14]

In her writing, Mary created her own history. From 1914 onwards, she mobilised her past in the many articles she wrote for the *Cotton Factory Times* and its sister paper, the *Yorkshire Factory Times*, consciously recording her campaigns in her own history-making activities. Her later reminiscences would emphasise three things. First of all, the support she received from William Morris; second, her role as an elected representative on the LSB, which she could and did interpret as evidence that she was regarded as an expert on educational matters; third, her courageous opposition in the First World War and the hostility she experienced for daring to stand out against the jingo tide. Therefore, she collated an archive of press cuttings 'for future use', presumably with the intent of writing her own autobiography.[15]

For Mary, caught up in the dissension following Sylvia Pankhurst's expulsion from the newly formed British Communist Party (CP) in 1921, it was preferable to think 'in terms of principles rather than of personalities'. To her way of thinking, personal attacks played into the enemies' hands by 'bolstering up the fetish of leadership' and 'keeping the idea of the movement in the background'.[16] Stung by an allegation of ignorance regarding the socialist movement in which, were she better informed, she might find 'Heartbreak House', she made the content of a letter from Chicherin widely available:

> It is just one year since we exist. Our Committee has decided on this occasion to express to you our warmest, most warm appreciation of the enormous, exceptionally great, and important work you have done, in connection with our Committee, for the defence of the Right of Asylum, and for the development of the principle of Internationality. Your work belongs to those pivots, around which the movement for the development of the new International is proceeding.[17]

Undaunted by the attempts of a younger political generation to undermine her authoritative voice, she brought up the question of Russian influence on the organisation of the infant CP. To begin with, she said she was pleased to say that Lenin agreed with her view. Indeed, she supplied a quotation from a speech he had made to the 1922 meeting of the Third International. Clear evidence, she said, of his having 'come round to the view of Rosa Luxemburg, when she said, "The danger comes when they (the Russian Bolsheviks) make a virtue of their necessity, and lay down their tactics as the universally correct ones, and hold them up as an example to the International proletariat"'.[18]

Verve and plain speaking spatters Mary's last known article written for the *Cotton Factory Times*, in the summer of 1932. Her hostility to armaments and war becomes visible, as do her antipathy toward policies of cautious expediency and pragmatism espoused by 'experts' who were, in her view, 'talking piffle'. Writing in the wake of a disarmament conference at Geneva, she proposed a change of location to help focus the mind. Instead of beautiful lake and mountain scenery, she suggested a camp built next 'to a war cemetery in France, with temporary huts for working, sleeping and eating, the windows all facing the cemetery'.[19] Perhaps this would help the 'experts' to decide whether or not an armoured tank constitutes an offensive or a defensive weapon. The obstacle was weight: whereas Britain took the view that all tanks weighing more than twenty-five tons were offensive, France insisted that tanks only fell into that category when they weighed more than seventy tons.

From 1918, it seems likely that she would have agreed with Ralph Miliband's analysis as summed up in *Parliamentary Socialism*, which he completed at the end of 1960.[20] The point that he develops, two decades on from Mary's death, is that the Labour Party as a whole subordinated revolutionary socialism to the dictates of the parliamentary road, thereby wasting the potential of those who came to identify with it, and so thwarting the possibility of socialist advance. Therefore, the Labour Party stood merely for social reform rather than for socialism. Mary wanted to play a part in changing the world and her resistances, initiatives and socio-political strategies fit into a larger history of popular struggles which, as the Education Group at the Centre for Contemporary Cultural Studies, emulating E.P. Thompson, put it, may be presented as 'actually constitutive of state policies and state forms'.[21] Mary tried to unify the Labour movement on education principles and pushed education as a crucial weapon in the class struggle. It does seem accurate to say that her endorsement of a more 'activist' model of socialism and growing recognition of the shortcomings of a leadership temperamentally inclined toward piecemeal change supports Miliband's thesis that the British Labour Party was never a socialist one.

From the Milibandian perspective, Mary's defeats become another yardstick against which labourism might be compared and found wanting. Inspired by the mercurial promise of Victor Grayson, she belongs to a more general militant and anti-capitalist subterranean tradition, which remained alien to the mainstream of the Labour movement.[22] As Stuart Macintyre suggests,[23] it might almost seem to define itself against the discourse of respectability lampooned by Noah Ablett when he caricatured 'Gentleman' Bowerman's dress code at the 1911 Trades Union Congress: 'Black broadcloth, three-quarter tail coat, semi-top-hat to match, with an air of refinement, silky voice, and deprecatory manner'.[24] Charles Bowerman (b. 1851) was one of the Lib-Lab parliamentarians who had to face a barrage of criticism, largely from grass-roots socialists who opposed the Parliamentary Labour Party's commitment to support of the Liberal government. Notwithstanding the passage of time since Mary and Noah were active forces, the arguments of Miliband and Marcel Liebman in 'Beyond Social Democracy' would probably ring true: 'the notion that very large parts of "the electorate", and notably the working class, is [*sic*] bound to reject radical programmes is a convenient alibi, but nothing else. The real point, which is crucial, is that such programmes and policies need to be defended and propagated with the utmost determination and vigour by leaders totally convinced of the justice of their cause'.[25]

We can only speculate about Mary's personal motivation. It has not been possible to discover either the inner detail of her politicisation or whether a tradition of political radicalism within her family influenced her. However, there is little doubt that her Celtic origins and sense of belonging to the pioneering generation played a central part in the construction of her political identity. In the Edwardian era, working women were often represented not as independent and assertive, but as the downtrodden victims of an exploitative system. Mary Bridges Adams showed that this need not be so and offered a challenge to Labour's traditional and patriarchal conceptions of domesticity. By the late 1920s, moving with the grain of those who saw 'the danger to the future of the Parliamentary Labour Party which lies in the growing tendency of the local Labour parties to choose as candidates aristocratic and other socially well-placed "intellectuals"', Mary handed down the endless struggle to a female successor. She chose elementary school teacher Jennie Lee (b. 1904), the daughter of a Scots miner, who climbed the scholarship ladder to tread a path denied her mentor, through secondary education to university, to Westminster. In Mary's opinion, the support of an organic intellectual like Jennie would make more possible the restoration of the 'filched educational endowments' to the children of the poor.[26]

Doer *and* dreamer, Mary made varied political choices through a lifetime of activism. The way in which she expressed her notion of education made ever-greater concession to propaganda rather than improvement and the politics of place situate her in the 'Little Moscows' of the South Wales coalfield, with strong links to the North-East Lancashire protest tradition. London was the setting in which she would bear witness to the fact that the world did not go her way, of course. Earlier analyses of the labour theory of value, which took a moral position on productive and unproductive labour, disappeared from view, as did perspectives which echoed a concern voiced among radical educator activists. It would seem that the idea of 'really useful knowledge', as a definitive core of a socialist education philosophy, got buried beneath Tawney's consistent advocacy of 'secondary education for all', which he failed to rethink in terms other than the grammar school, with its existing traditional curriculum. As detailed in chapters 4 and 5, in the 1890s and early 1900s Mary pursued two somewhat paradoxical strategies of education reform. The first touched on progressive education as practised in Bedales School, which she wanted to see transferred into state schools, and the second, equal opportunity, entailed an attack on educational institutions seen to be bastions of privilege.

Political influence is notoriously hard to measure and it depends where one is looking. By profiling Mary's life of campaigning, we see the transformative aspects of female agency. The radicalised rhetoric underpinning her assault on class injustice shows a deep moral commitment and disgust at a capitalist system, which deprived people of opportunity, enlightenment, pleasure and beauty. While the attempt to create a fusion between the working class and socialism cannot be reduced to the work of a single individual, her viewpoint may be seen in Labour Party policy and identity with regard to welfare issues in the 1920s and beyond. Mary's legacy is there in the socialist alternatives articulated by radical education organisations like the Teachers' Labour League in the interwar years; it is there in the feminist politics underpinning the peace movement that the women's protest at Greenham Common gave rise to in the 1980s.[27]

Mary Bridges Adams represents the common, unnamed socialist woman who was anxious to identify herself with the cause of the working class. She did not set aside her militancy, whereas others, including leaders like Margaret McMillan, did. Yet, her story is also uncommon and remarkably unique. The experience of war did not dent her belief in the principle of internationalism, neither did she give away her faith in the contested terrain of working-class education which she had worked so hard to shape. Consequently, when hostilities ceased, she urged that 'older Socialists must, in the years remaining to us, strive to bring together the youth of various countries … We must bring the young men, and the mothers, actual and potential, together under the banner of International Socialism.'[28] Communicating with fellow travellers across the borders of European states, Mary never lost faith in the vision of a global socialist Utopia and was a strong advocate of International Socialist Summer Schools in association with an International Working-Class Students' Union, while identifying with her sex.[29] She justified her social existence through 'making socialists', but looked to other working women to continue the taste for contention through protest and political activity in the central and local state. For her, education was the path to a new social order.

Notes

1 H.G. Wells, *New Worlds for Old* (New York: Macmillan, 1909), pp. 323–3.
2 M. McCarthy, *Generation in Revolt* (London: William Heinemann Ltd., 1953), p. 276.
3 Wells, *New Worlds for Old*, p. 265.
4 M. Bridges Adams, 'The Communists: wanted, post-Revolution information', *Cotton Factory Times*, 21 September 1923, p. 2.
5 M. Newman, 'Ralph Miliband and the Labour Party: from *Parliamentary Socialism* to "Bennism"', in J. Callaghan, S. Fielding and S. Ludlam (eds), *Interpreting the Labour Party* (Manchester: Manchester University Press, 2003), p. 59.
6 John Maclean Internet Archive, www.marxist.org/archive/maclean/works/1918-dock.htm, J. Maclean, 'Speech from the dock', 9 May 1918.
7 M. Bridges Adams, 'Political prosecutions' (letter), *Cotton Factory Times*, 19 December 1924, p. 4.
8 W. Morris, *News from Nowhere* (Oxford: Oxford University Press, 2003 edition).
9 G. Grace, 'Teachers and the state in Britain: a changing relation', in M. Lawn and G. Grace (eds), *Teachers: the culture and politics of work* (Lewes: Falmer, 1987), pp. 193–203.
10 M. Bridges Adams, 'The solidarity of working class motherhood and rural child labour', *Yorkshire Factory Times*, 11 February 1915, p. 5.
11 M. Bridges Adams, 'Looking beyond the war: development of capitalist imperialist policy', *Cotton Factory Times*, 11 February 1916, p. 4.
12 Mrs Bridges Adams, 'Independent working-class education Britain and the Communist Young International', *Socialist*, 19 August 1920, leader article.
13 M. Bridges Adams, 'Political prosecutions' (letter), *Cotton Factory Times*, 19 December 1924, p. 4.
14 Mazeppa, 'Views about Russia' (letter), *Cotton Factory Times*, 28 March 1919, p. 4.
15 M. Bridges Adams, 'Propaganda and "Russian Gold"' (letter), *Socialist*, 12 January 1922, p. 16.
16 M. Bridges Adams, 'Propaganda and "Russian Gold"'.
17 M. Bridges Adams, 'The Irish Labour movement and independent working class education', *Socialist*, 23 February 1922, p. 61.
18 M. Bridges Adams, 'The Communists', *Cotton Factory Times*, 21 September 1923, p. 2.
19 M. Bridges Adams, 'The war experts and Geneva', *Cotton Factory Times*, 15 July 1932, p. 4.
20 R. Miliband, *Parliamentary Socialism* (London: Merlin Press, 1979).
21 Centre for Contemporary Cultural Studies, *Unpopular Education: schooling and social democracy in England since 1944* (London: Hutchinson, 1981), p. 16.

22 See, for example, B. Barker, 'The anatomy of reformism: the social and political ideas of the Labour leadership in Yorkshire', *International Review of Social History*, Volume 17 (1973) Part 1, pp. 1–27.
23 S. Macintyre, *A Proletarian Science: Marxism in Britain, 1917–1933* (London: Lawrence and Wishart, 1980).
24 'At Newcastle', *Plebs*, November 1911, p. 236.
25 R. Miliband and M. Liebman, 'Beyond social democracy', in R. Miliband, J. Saville, M. Liebman and L. Panitch (eds), *The Socialist Register 1985–86* cited in: D. Coates and L. Panitch, 'The continuing relevance of the Milibandian perspective', in J. Callaghan, S. Fielding and S. Ludlam (eds), *Interpreting the Labour Party* (Manchester: Manchester University Press, 2003), p. 75.
26 M. Bridges Adams, 'A lass o'pairts', *Cotton Factory Times*, 15 February 1929, p. 4.
27 K. Jones, *Beyond Progressive Education* (London and Basingstoke: Macmillan, 1983), p. 97; M. Lawn, *Modern Times? Work, professionalism and citizenship in teaching* (London: Falmer, 1996).
28 M. Bridges Adams, 'Education and the New International' (letter), *Yorkshire Factory Times*, 14 November 1918, p. 2.
29 M. Bridges Adams, 'Education and the youth of the Red International', *A.S.E. Monthly Journal and Report*, March 1920, p. 59.

APPENDIX 1

The Daltry family tree

- William Daltry, d. 1894, m. 1) Margaret Jones, d. 1858, 2) Margaret Thomas, d. 1907
  - Thomas, 1845–1890, m. Maria Matthews
    - William, b. 1882
    - Robert, b. 1884
  - Mary, 1855–1939, m. Walter Bridges Adams, 1858–1900
    - William, 1889–1965, m. 1) Muriel Pratt, 2) Marguerite Coote
      - Nicholas, 1930–1998
  - Benjamin, d. 1858

APPENDIX 2

The Adams family tree

William Bridges Adams 1797–1872 m. 1) Betsy Place 2) Sarah Flower 1805–1848 3) Ellen Rendall d. 1898

Child of William Bridges Adams and 1) Betsy Place:

William Alexander 1821–1896

Children of William Bridges Adams and 3) Ellen Rendall:

Hope 1855–1916 m. 1) Otto Walther 2) Carl Lehmann d. 1915

Mary Daltry 1855–1939 m. Walter 1858–1900

Child of Mary Daltry and Walter:

William 1889–1965

APPENDIX 3

Mary Bridges Adams (née Daltry) time-line

1855	Born Maesycwimmer, South Wales
1871	Pupil teacher, Newcastle
1887	Marries Walter Bridges Adams
1889	Gives birth to her only child, William
1894	Unsuccessful in the elections to represent Greenwich on the London School Board
1897	Becomes Labour member for Greenwich on the London School Board
1900	Re-elected Labour member for Greenwich on the London School Board
1901	Formation of the National Labour Education League
1903/4	Becomes Lady Warwick's secretary and collaborator
1904	Abolition of the London School Board
1907	Helps set up Bostall Wood Open-Air School
1909	Joins the Plebs League
1912	Foundation of the College for Working Women, Bebel House
1915	Becomes secretary of the Committee of Delegates of Russian Socialist Groups
1939	Dies at Princess Beatrice Hospital, London

APPENDIX 4

Biographical notes

These notes cover some of the major figures discussed in the text but not covered in the biographical chapters. Information comes from a variety of sources, notably the *Dictionary of Labour Biography*, the *New Oxford Dictionary of National Biography*, the local and Socialist press, autobiographies, biographies and memoirs.

Charles William Bowerman, 1851?–1947
Charles was the son of a tinplate worker. He attended a national school until the age of 12, became an apprentice printer and continued his self-education. After his apprenticeship, he joined the staff of a daily paper called the *Hour*, before moving on to the *Daily Telegraph*. In 1873 he joined the London Society of Compositors. Active in seeking to improve working conditions in the highly competitive London newspaper market, Charles became general secretary of the union in 1892. His political attitudes were of the radical Liberal kind. In the 1890s, he joined the TUC's parliamentary committee, sat on the LCC, and won the parliamentary seat of Deptford for the LRC in 1906. Associated with Ruskin College from its foundation until his death, he opposed the Ruskin College strike and the establishment of the Central Labour College.

Katharine Bruce Glasier (née St John Conway), 1867–1950
The daughter of a Congregational minister, Katharine was born into a wealthy family. Educated at Hackney High School for Girls, she studied Classics at Newnham College, Cambridge, with a scholarship. She became a socialist as a teacher at Redland High School in Bristol, after seeing a demonstration by striking female cotton workers. She lost her job and joined the socialist lecture tour as a Fabian and founding member of the ILP. She sat on the ILP executive and married fellow ILPer John Bruce Glasier in 1893.

Sir John Eldon Gorst, 1835–1916
Educated at Cambridge, John spent three and half years in New Zealand before returning to England and being called to the Bar. He became a MP in 1866 and was thereafter in the House of Commons for twenty-five years on and off. In the 1870s he helped to reorganise Conservative Central Office and played a major role in the unexpected Tory election victory in 1874. Later on, he became a driving force

behind the maverick parliamentary grouping known as the Fourth Party. In the 1890s he served on the Royal Commission on Labour, a government inquiry into London's poor-law schools, and became associated with Toynbee Hall. He held office as Solicitor-General, Financial Secretary to the Treasury and Vice-president of the Committee of Council on Education, but resigned in July 1902, since he was not to have charge of the Education Bill. Free of office, he campaigned for social reform, especially the health and nutrition of schoolchildren. He received a knighthood in 1886.

James Keir Hardie, 1856–1915
The illegitimate son of a Scottish servant, Keir Hardie grew up in poverty. Having left school at the age of 6 to work as an errand boy, by the age of 11 he was working down the pits of Lanarkshire. He began the process of self-education down the pit, set up a union at the colliery where he worked and subsequently moved to Ayrshire to become a journalist, having been victimised for his union activities. Originally a supporter of the Liberal Party, he became a founder member and leader of the ILP, editor of the *Labour Leader*, member of the Fabian Society and MP for West Ham South in 1892. He lost the seat in 1895. In 1900 he fought Merthyr Tydfil and Aberdare in the South Wales valleys under the auspices of the LRC, which he would represent for the rest of his life.

Stuart Headlam, 1847–1924
Educated at Eton and Cambridge, Stuart became a Church of England clergyman and Christian Socialist. He had considerable private means, which enabled him to ride out years without church employment, owing to his radical views, and to subsidise his varied religious and political activities. For example, he founded the Church and Stage Guild (in 1879), stood bail for Oscar Wilde (in 1895), served on the Fabian Society executive and led the Guild of St Matthew, an association for high-church laity and clergy sympathetic to socialist ideals. He sat on the LSB from 1882 until its abolition in 1904, taking an active role in the promotion of evening classes for adults, especially as chair of the Evening Continuation Schools Committee from 1897. He opposed the 1902 Education Act. Elected to the LCC for the Progressive Party in 1907, he served until his death.

Arthur Henderson, 1863–1935
The son of a Glasgow labourer, who died when Arthur was 9, he left school at 12 and became an apprentice iron moulder. In 1883 he joined the Friendly Society of Iron Founders. A successful local politician and trade unionist, in 1896 he accepted the full-time position of Liberal agent to the MP for Barnard Castle and fought the seat under the auspices of the LRC in 1903, which he would represent until 1918. During the First World War he became chair of the War Emergency Workers' National Committee, joining the Liberal cabinet as President of the Board of Education. In the 1920s he built and extended the party organisation, holding office as Home Secretary, Labour Chief Whip and Foreign Secretary.

Sir Victor Horsley, 1857–1916

From a medical background, Victor studied medicine at University College Hospital medical school, where he became house surgeon and surgical registrar. As professor-superintendent to the Brown Institution (University of London), he founded in Britain the modern study of the thyroid gland and became the only representative and interpreter of Pasteur's preventative treatment of rabies in Britain. He established an international reputation in the field of cerebral surgery and received a knighthood for his contributions to medicine in 1902. Victor was active in the politics of his profession and an ardent supporter of women's suffrage.

Henry Myers Hyndman, 1842–1921

Born to a wealthy family with colonial connections, Henry studied for the Bar after a Cambridge education. As a young man, he was a good cricketer and played for the Sussex County eleven. Having decided law was not for him, he became a journalist on the staff of the *Pall Mall Gazette*. Under the influence of Karl Marx, he founded the Democratic Federation in 1881, but the two fell out over his failure to acknowledge Marx's work in his booklet *England for All*. Prominent in the unrest among the London unemployed in the late 1880s, he went on to fight four unsuccessful parliamentary contests for the SDF in Burnley. In 1916 he and his followers left the anti-war BSP and formed a National Socialist Party. This resumed its old name, the SDF, in 1920.

Dr James Kerr, b. 1862

As Bradford's School Medical Officer, James carried out the first medical inspections of elementary schoolchildren in Britain. His studies helped to evolve a medicalised view of working-class childhood, based on a professional understanding that took dirt and disease, spread in overcrowded and poorly ventilated classrooms, to be the indices of deprivation and poverty. He took up the post of School Medical Officer to the LSB in 1902, was active in the politics of his profession and co-editor of the journal *School Hygiene*.

Rosa Luxemburg, 1871–1919

A Polish-born revolutionary, in 1889 Rosa fled to Zurich in Switzerland to escape arrest and was persecuted thereafter. In 1898 she left Zurich for Berlin, where she joined the German Social Democratic Party. Among the minority who opposed Germany's entry into war in 1914, she and Karl Liebknecht formed the Spartacus League but were imprisoned for their political activities. Released from prison in 1918, she co-founded the German Communist Party. In January 1919 she was murdered by the right-wing Freikorps.

James Ramsay MacDonald, 1866–1937

The illegitimate son of a farm servant and a ploughman, James grew up in north-east Scotland. After an education at the local parish school, he became a pupil teacher. He moved to London in the mid 1880s and became politically active in the ILP and the Fabian Society. After his marriage he was financially secure and his position as secretary of the LRC gave him a key role in party management and electoral strategy. He was elected to Parliament in 1906. In 1914 his anti-war stance caused a breach with the pro-war majority in the Labour Party, but he fought his way back to Labour's inner circle, becoming MP for Aberafan in 1922. He became the first Labour prime minister after a surprise general election in November 1923, holding the office once more after Labour won power in 1929. Huge cuts in public spending played a key role in the formation of a National Government in 1931, over which he also presided. Expelled from the Labour Party, he spent the remainder of his life in a social and political wilderness, shunned by past friends and allies.

Albert Mansbridge, 1876–1952
Albert was already familiar with the Co-operative movement through his mother's involvement with the WCG and it was as a co-operator that he first approached the question of adult education. Both he and his wife taught in church Sunday Schools and he taught evening classes for the LSB. Albert founded the WEA in 1903, international branches followed in Australia in 1913, and later in Canada and New Zealand. In the early part of the twentieth century he served as a member of numerous government committees of education, including the Consultative Committee of the Board of Education from 1906 to 1912 and from 1924 to 1939.

Caroline Martyn, 1867–96
The daughter of a Lincolnshire clergyman, Caroline was a well-known socialist lecturer until her premature death. She had to earn her living from socialism and journalism and was the editor of the *Christian World*. The first Clarion women's van was named after her. Female volunteers toured the countryside in horse-drawn caravans, holding open-air meetings, selling socialist literature and handing out leaflets.

Eleanor Marx, 1855–98
The youngest child of Karl and Jenny Marx, Eleanor was expensively educated. She showed an early talent for drama and languages, besides developing a taste for politics and literature. As a young woman she became involved with the Fenian Society supporting Home Rule for Ireland. She had a long, unhappy relationship with fellow socialist Edward Aveling. The two worked together in the organised labour movement, supporting the formation of trade unions, including the first women's branch of the National Union of Gasworkers and General Labourers.

Margaret McMillan, 1860–1931
Margaret spent her early years in America but her mother returned to Scotland in 1865. Margaret and her sister, Rachel, were expensively educated and Margaret became a teacher. Recruited to the ILP in 1893, she moved to Bradford to teach adult education classes and became a successful candidate for the School Board, winning elections in 1894, 1897 and 1900. She quickly established herself as a local

educational expert, engaging in heavy programmes of lecturing and writing for the socialist press. In 1902, she rejoined Rachel, a health visitor for Kent County Council, and they laid plans for the establishment of experimental school clinics/ open-air centres. The first opened at Bow in 1908, followed by the Deptford Clinic and the open-air nursery school that developed out of it after 1910.

Hannah Mitchell (née Webster), 1871–1956
Growing up on a small farm in Derbyshire's Peak District, Hannah had only two weeks' formal schooling in her entire life. Her mother was very harsh and Hannah ran away from home at the age of 14. Having found work as a dressmaker, she continued her self-education and became deeply involved in the socialist and suffrage movements. In 1895 she married a socialist, Gibbon Mitchell, a tailor's cutter. The couple had one son. During the First World War she worked for the Women's Peace Council and by the 1930s she was an established public figure in Manchester, as city councillor and magistrate.

Sir Robert Laurie Morant, 1863–1920
Educated at Winchester College and Oxford, he moved to Siam in 1886 after a short spell as a preparatory school teacher. As tutor to the crown prince, he involved himself in the reconstruction of the Siamese educational system, stressing English educational values and concentrating on the needs of the ruling elite and of secondary education and teacher training. He returned to England in 1894, took up both residence and a staff appointment at Toynbee Hall, and pursued a career in the civil service. In 1899 he became Gorst's private secretary and became the Acting Permanent Secretary of the Board of Education in 1902. Important in the role of adviser at the time of the 1902 Education Act, he reorganised the Board of Education into an effective central instrument for the implementation of the Act.

William Morris, 1834–96
Educated at Marlborough and Oxford, William came from a wealthy family. He was an English architect, designer, printer, poet, novelist and social reformer, a man who made his own furniture, wallpaper, textiles, ceramics and stained glass, inspired by a profound reverence for the craftsman of the pre-industrial past. An important figure in the pioneering days of British socialism, he founded the Socialist League in 1884, working directly with Eleanor Marx, among others, and founding a new organ, *Commonweal*. For many years, he held an anti Parliamentary position, but towards the end of his life he worked for socialist unity.

Sir George Newman, 1870–1948
Born to a Quaker family, George began his education at a local dame school, before attending boarding school and studying medicine at Edinburgh University. In 1892 he became assistant physician to the London Medical Mission but public health work attracted him. In 1900 he secured his first permanent full-time position as medical office of health to Finsbury. For him, infectious diseases were as

much an index of moral as of physical ill-health. His solution would combine moral education with medical intervention. Beatrice Webb contacted him in 1906 and he subsequently met her friend and ally, Robert Morant. In 1907 he secured the new post of chief medical officer to the Board of Education, with responsibility for setting up a new school medical service.

Ada Salter (nee Brown), 1866–1942

Ada grew up in Northamptonshire but left her comfortable home to join the West London Mission. Subsequently, she took up residence at the nonconformist Bermondsey Settlement, taking charge of the Girls' Club. A founder member of Bermondsey ILP, in 1909 she became the first woman borough councillor in London and, in 1922, London's first woman mayor and the first woman Labour mayor in Britain. She represented Bermondsey on the LCC from 1925 to 1941 and made a significant contribution to the life and welfare of the area.

Dr Alfred Salter, 1873–1945

Born into a nonconformist family of modest means, Alfred grew up in south London. Under the influence of his mother, he became a fervent Christian. In 1898 he took up residence at Bermondsey Settlement – where he met Ada Brown – rejecting a promising research career for general practice in Bermondsey. A Progressive member of Bermondsey Borough Council (1903–10) and the LCC (1906–10), he resigned from the Liberal Party in 1908 and helped to set up the Bermondsey branch of the ILP. Alfred represented West Bermondsey in Parliament from 1922 to 1945. The Salters wanted to rebuild Bermondsey on garden city lines. In 1925 it became the first constituency in Britain to achieve 100 per cent socialist representation – holding the parliamentary seat, the two LCC seats, every seat on the Borough Council and the Board of Guardians.

David Shackleton, 1863–1938

Born in Lancashire, the only surviving child of a power-loom weaver and his wife, David was educated at a dame school, followed by Wesleyan and Anglican day schools. He began work at the age of 9 as a half-timer, becoming a full-time worker at the age of 13. A cotton union leader, he was active in municipal politics before winning the parliamentary seat of Clitheroe for the LRC in 1902. A keen supporter of the WEA, he was chair of the north-western district in the early 1900s.

George Sims, 1867–1943

A Cockney carpenter from Rotherhithe, George started work at the age of 8, and taught himself to read, moving from religion to socialism via Marx. He fought in the Second Boer War and was later active in the SDF/SDP, and simultaneously the ILP. He entered Ruskin College in 1908, becoming a strike leader and one of the best-known pedagogues identified with independent working-class education in its early years: secretary of the CLC from its inception and the first general secretary of the NCLC. He fought in the First World War, becoming secretary of the Plebs League in 1922. Possibly addicted to gambling, he was involved in the misappropriation of CLC funds and died in poverty and obscurity.

Enid Stacy, 1868–1903

The daughter of an artist, Enid spent her early years in the seaside town of Weston-super-Mare, in Somerset. In 1881 the family moved to Bristol; she attended a local high school and stayed on as a student teacher, gaining an external London degree in 1890. A founding member of the ILP, she quickly became a sought-after platform speaker, averaging two hundred meetings a year. She was fearless when speaking. For example, when the police harassed her in Liverpool, she jumped on an open-topped tram and addressed the crowd from on high.

John Stokes

A member of the BSP, secretary of the London Glassblowers' Union, he took over from Harry Quelch as chair of the LTC in 1913. In this capacity, he played a key role in the formation of the London Labour Party, working closely with Fred Knee.

Ben Tillett, 1860–1943

Ben was the son of a labourer. His mother died when he was small and he had only a few days' formal schooling at a local National School. At the age of 6 he worked in a brickyard, and joined the circus at 8 and the Royal Navy at 13. He could hardly read until he was 17 years old, when he attended Bow and Bromley Institute Evening Classes. A prominent agitator in the 1889 London Dock Strike, he became General Secretary of the Dockers' Union. A member of the Fabian Society and ILP, he grew increasingly critical of the Labour leadership and joined the SDF in 1908. He fully supported Britain's involvement in the First World War and became Independent MP for North Salford in 1917. In the 1918 general election he contested the seat for Labour and was a Labour Member of Parliament until he retired in 1931.

Graham Wallas, 1858–1932

Graham grew up in a clerical household in Barnstaple, Devon. Educated in the Classics at Shrewsbury and Oxford, he became a Classics schoolmaster. He joined the Fabian Society in 1886 and served on its executive from 1888 to 1895, leaving the Society in 1904 over disagreements with Fabian education policy. From 1894 to 1904 he was a member of the LSB and from 1897 to 1904 chair of its School Management Committee. From 1898 to 1904 he was a member of the London TEB. Having declined the offer of the post of director of the newly established London School of Economics, he agreed to teach there, becoming Professor of Politics in 1914.

Sidney Webb, Baron Passfield, 1859–1947

The son of a radical accountant, Sidney became a clerk in the City of London at the age of 16, educating himself by evening classes. He took an external Law degree at London and was called to the Bar in 1885–86. A founder member of the Fabian Society, he married Beatrice Potter in 1892, and her private income enabled him to give up his clerical work. They formed a personal and political partnership, in which they devoted their lives to the cause of social reform and education. Among other things, in 1895 they founded the London School of Economics. Sidney sat on the LCC from 1892 to 1910 and became chair of the Technical Education Committee. He was a Labour Member of Parliament from 1922 to 1929, President of the Board of Trade in 1924, Dominions Secretary 1929–30, Colonial Secretary 1929–31, and was created Baron Passfield in 1929.

Alex Wilkie, b. 1850

An orphan by the age of 10, Alex received a sound elementary education and won school prizes. He left school at the age of 12, at 13 he became an apprentice in the ship-building yards. In 1881 he became general secretary of the Shipwrights' Union, and was active in both municipal politics and trade unionism. Serving as a member of Newcastle School Board and subsequently the Education Committee of Newcastle City Council, in 1897 he joined the TUC Parliamentary Committee. He contested Sunderland for Labour in the 1900 general election; six years later he won the Parliamentary seat of Dundee.

Bibliography

Archival sources

Birmingham City Archives, Central Library
Hurst Street Domestic Mission, Annual reports 1890–1915

Monthly Record, 1914–21
Newspaper cuttings, Birmingham biography
School Board for Birmingham, Minutes, 1871–1890

British Library of Political and Economic Science, London School of Economics
Fabian Society Papers
George Lansbury Papers
Graham Wallas Papers

Calgary University, Alberta, Special Collections/Archives
William Bridges-Adams Papers

Columbia University, New York, Bakhmeteff Materials
Bridges Adams Papers

Greenwich Heritage Centre, London
'Vincent's Cuttings'

Greenwich University, London
Woolwich Polytechnic Archive

House of Lords Record Office, London
Soskice Papers

Hull University Archives, Brynmor Jones Library
Archives of the Dictionary of Labour Biography
DLB/6/1 1915–1939
DLB/6/2 1901–1979

Labour Party Archives, National Museum of Labour History, Manchester
Letter, M. Bridges Adams to J.R. MacDonald, 12 May 1903

Lewisham Local History and Archives Centre, Lewisham Library
Margaret McMillan papers

London Metropolitan Archive
LCC Children's Care Organisation 1909–14
LCC Joint Report of the Medical Officer and the Executive Officer on the Open-air School carried on in Bostall Wood, between 22 July and 19 October 1907
LCC Education Officer's Department Elementary Education Branch Section No. 12 – Married Women Teachers, letter C. Grant to R. Blair, 7 February 1911
National Association of Labour Teachers correspondence file
School Board for London, Minutes, 1870–1904
School Board for London, Meals for School Children, Report of a Special Committee of the General Purposes Committee, 1899
School Board for London List of Members, Committees etc reprinted from the members' pocket book for 1901
Women's Local Government Society papers

The National Archives, Kew
Home Office files on George Chicherin
Home Office files on Peter Petroff

National Library of Ireland, Dublin
Sheehy Skeffington Papers

Northamptonshire County Record Office
Diary of Lady Louisa Knightley of Fawsley, Northamptonshire County Record Office

Royal Arsenal Co-operative Society Papers, Woolwich, London
Bostall Woods open-air school press cuttings file
General Committee Minute Book, 1890–1914
Royal Arsenal Co-operative Society Reports, 1890–1914

Royal Holloway, University of London Archives
Bedford College Records

Senate House Library, University of London
University Register

TUC Library Collection, London Metropolitan University
Central Labour College, Board of Management Minute Book
London Trades Council, Minute Books, 1890–1910
Tuckwell Collection
WEA press cuttings 1909/14

Tyne and Wear Archives Service
Newcastle school records
Records relating to Armstrong's Elswick Works

School Board for Gateshead, Minutes, 1871–1890
School Board for Newcastle, Minutes, 1871–1890

University College London, Special Collections
William Adams, 'The Record of a Busy Life', 1891

Working Class Movement Library, Salford
Gas Workers' and General Labourers' Union, Quarterly Balance Sheets, 1890–1914

Government publications

Morant, R.L., 'The national organisation of education of all grades as practised in Switzerland', Education Department Special Reports on Educational Subjects, Vol. III, *Parliamentary Papers*, XXV (1898) [C.8988], p. 24.
Department for Education and Skills (2004) *Five Year Strategy for Teachers and Learners* (London: HMSO).

Newspapers and periodicals of the period

A.S.E. Monthly Journal and Report
Board Teacher
The Call
Chatham Observer
Christian Science Monitor
Clarion
Commonweal
Comradeship and Wheatsheaf
Co-operative News
Cotton Factory Times
Greenwich and Deptford Observer
Justice
Labour Leader
The Link
Kentish Independent
Kentish Mail and Deptford and Greenwich Observer
Kentish Mercury
Manchester Guardian
The Millgate
Plebs
Railway Review
School Board Chronicle
Shafts
The Socialist

The Times
Woman Worker
Woolwich and District Labour Notes
Woolwich Gazette and Kentish Advertiser
Woolwich Labour Journal
Woolwich Pioneer
Yorkshire Factory Times

Books and articles published before 1950

Aberdeen, I. (ed.), *Women in Education. Transactions of the Educational Section of the International Congress of Women* (London: T. Fisher Unwin, 1899).

Adams Lehmann, H. (ed.), *Kriegsgegner in England* (München: Druck and Verlag von G. Birk & Co.m.b.H., 1915).

Badley, J.H., *Bedales School: outlook of its aims and system* (Cambridge: Cambridge University Press, 1900).

Badley, J.H., *Bedales: a pioneer school* (London: Methuen & Co. Ltd, 1923).

Barefoot, W., *Twenty-five Years of the Woolwich Labour Party, 1903–1928* (Woolwich: Woolwich Labour Party, 1928).

Bettany, F.G., *Stewart Headlam: a biography* (London: John Murray, 1926).

Bridges Adams, W., *The Rights of Morality: state of society in England* (London, 1832).

Bryher, S., *An Account of the Labour and Socialism Movement in Bristol Part Three* (Bristol: Bristol Labour Weekly, 1931).

Clayton, J., *The Rise and Fall of Socialism in Britain 1884–1924* (London: Fale & Guryer, 1926).

Clemens, C., *The Man from Limehouse: Clement Richard Attlee* (Missouri: International Mark Twain Society, 1946).

Clynes, J.R., *Memoirs 1869–1924* (London: Hutchinson, 1937).

Cole, M., *Women of To-day* (London: Thomas Nelson and Sons, 1948 edition).

Gautrey, T., *Lux Mihi Laus: School Board memories* (London: Link House, n.d.).

Grant, C.E., *Farthing Bundles* (Bromley-By-Bow: Fern Street Settlement, 1929).

Hall, J.R., *The Elswick Works Schools 1869–1871: some recollections and impressions* (Newcastle-upon-Tyne: Privately printed by the Schools Committee, 1912).

Humphrey, A.W., *International Socialism and the War* (London: P.S. King and Son, 1915).

Hyndman, H.M., *Further Reminiscences* (London: Macmillan & Co., 1912).

Jamieson, J., *Northumberland at the Opening of the Twentieth Century* (London: W.T. Pike and Co., 1905).

Mansbridge, A., *An Adventure in Working-Class Education* (London: Longmans, Green & Co., 1920).

Mansbridge, A., *Margaret McMillan: prophet and pioneer* (London and Toronto: J.M. Dent & Sons, 1932).

Mansbridge, A., *The Trodden Road* (London: J.M. Dent and Sons, 1940).

McMillan, M., *Labour and Education* (London: Swan Sonnenschein & Co., 1907).

McMillan, M., *The Camp School* (London: George Allen & Unwin Ltd, 2nd edn, 1919).

Montefiore, D.B., *From a Victorian to a Modern* (London: Edward Elgar, 1927).

Quin, M., *Memoirs of a Positivist* (London: George Allen & Unwin, 1924).

The Reformers' Year Book (formerly the *Labour Annual*) (Manchester, Labour Press Society; London, The Clarion and the New Age Press, 1897–1910).

Richardson, J., *How It Can Be Done; or constructive socialism* (London: Twentieth Century Press, 1898 edition).

Richardson, J., *The Education Problem and Its Solution. Being seven chapters from "How It Can Be Done"* (London: The Twentieth Century Press, 1898 edition).

Sanders, W.S., *Early Socialist Days* (London: 1927).

Sanderson Furniss, H., *Memories of Sixty Years* (New York: D. Appleton and Co., 1931).

Snell, Lord *Men, Movements and Myself* (London: J.M. Dent & Sons Ltd, 1936).

Spencer, F.H., *An Inspector's Testament* (London: English Universities Press Ltd, 1938).

Thomson, B., *The Scene Changes* (London: Collins, 1939).

Thorne, W., *My Life's Battles* (London: George Newnes, Ltd, 1926).

Tuke, M., *A History of Bedford College for Women* (Oxford: Oxford University Press, 1939).

Vincent, W.T., *The Records of the Woolwich District* (London: J.S. Virtue and Company Ltd, 1890).

Wallas, G., *Men and Ideas* (London: George Allen and Unwin, 1940).

Wells, H.G., *New Worlds for Old* (New York: Macmillan, 1909).

Williams, M., *John Wilson of Woolwich* (London: Marshall, Morgan and Scott Ltd, 1937).

Books, book chapters and articles published after 1950

Albisetti, J.C., *Schooling German Girls and Women* (Princeton: Princeton University Press, 1988).

Anand, S., *Daisy: the Life and Loves of the Countess of Warwick* (London: Piatkus, 2008).

Attfield, J., *With Light of Knowledge: a hundred years of education in the Royal Arsenal Co-operative Society, 1877–1977* (London: The Journeyman Press, 1981).

Barker, B., 'Anatomy of reformism: the social and political ideas of the Labour leadership in Yorkshire', *International Review of Social History*, 18:1 (1973), pp. 1–27.

Bellamy, J.M. and Saville, J. (eds), *Dictionary of Labour Biography* (Macmillan: Basingstoke, 1987).

Benwell Community Project *The Making of a Ruling Class*, Final Report No 6, (Newcastle Upon Tyne: Benwell Community Project, 1978).
Berger, J., *About Looking* (London: Writers and Readers, 1980).
Betts, P.Y., *People Who Say Goodbye: memories of childhood* (London: Futura, 1991).
Betts, R., *Dr Macnamara 1861–1931* (Liverpool: Liverpool University Press, 1999).
Blunden, M., *The Countess of Warwick* (London: Cassell, 1983).
Bourdieu, P., *Practical Reason* (Cambridge: Polity Press, 1998).
Bradburn, E., *Margaret McMillan Framework and Expansion of Nursery Education* (Nutfield, Redhill: Denholm House Press, 1976).
Brockway, F., *Bermondsey Story: the life of Alfred Salter* (London: Stephen Humphrey, 1995).
Bryder, L., 'Wonderlands of buttercup, clover and daisies: tuberculosis and the open-air school movement in Britain, 1907–39', in R. Cooter (ed.), *In the Name of the Child: health and welfare 1880–1940* (London: Routledge, 1992), p. 75.
Bunyan, T., *The History and Practice of the Political Police in Britain* (London: Quartet Books, 1977).
Bush, J., *Behind the Lines: East London labour 1914–1919* (London: Merlin Press, 1984).
Carnie Holdsworth, E., *Helen of the Four Gates* (London: Jenkins, 1917).
Carr, E.H., *What Is History?* (Harmondsworth: Penguin, 1987 edition).
Centre for Contemporary Cultural Studies, *Unpopular Education: schooling and social democracy in England since 1944* (London: Hutchinson, 1981).
Challinor, R., *The Origins of British Bolshevism* (London: Croom Helm, 1977).
Chase, M., *Chartism a New History* (Manchester: Manchester University Press, 2007).
Clark, D., *Victor Grayson: Labour's lost leader* (London: Quartet Books, 1985).
Coates, D. and Panitch, L., 'The continuing relevance of the Milibandian perspective', in J. Callaghan, S. Fielding and S. Ludlam (eds), *Interpreting the Labour Party* (Manchester: Manchester University Press, 2003), pp. 71–85.
Common, J., *Kiddar's Luck* (Newcastle-Upon-Tyne: Bloodaxe Books, 1991).
Craik, W.W., *The Central Labour College* (London: Lawrence and Wishart, 1964).
Crick, M., *The History of the Social Democratic Federation* (Keele: Ryburn Publishing, 1994).
Cunningham, P. and Gardner, P., *Becoming Teachers: texts and testimonies 1907–1950* (London: Woburn Press, 2004).
Daglish, N.D., 'Robert Morant's hidden agenda? The origins of the medical treatment of schoolchildren', *History of Education*, 19:2 (1990), pp. 139–48.
Davidoff, L. and Hall, C., *Family Fortunes: men and women of the English middle class 1780–1850* (London: Hutchinson, 1987).
Davies, M.L., (ed.), *Life As We Have Known It By Co-operative Working Women* (London: Virago, 1984).

Denzin, N.K., *Interpretive Biography* (Newbury Park: Sage, 1989).
Donzelot, J., *The Policing of Families* (New York: Pantheon Books, 1979).
Dyhouse, C., *No Distinction of Sex? Women in British universities 1870–1939* (London: UCL Press, 1995).
East London History Society, Autumn newsletter 1992.
Edwards, W.J., *From the Valley I Came* (Sydney and London: Angus and Robertson, 1957).
Englander, D., *The Diary of Fred Knee* (Warwick: Society for the Study of Labour History, 1977).
Erben, M. (ed.), *Biography and Education: a reader* (London: Falmer Press, 1998).
Finkelstein, B., 'Revealing human agency: the uses of biography in the study of educational history', in C. Kridel (ed.), *Writing Educational Biography: explorations in qualitative research* (New York: Garland Publishing, 1998), pp. 45–59.
Flett, K., *Chartism after 1848* (Monmouth: The Merlin Press, 2006).
Foote, G., *The Labour Party's Political Thought* (Basingstoke: Macmillan, 1997).
Fox, P., *Class Fictions: shame and resistance in the British working class novel, 1890–1945* (Durham and London: Duke University Press, 1994).
Frow, E. and Frow, R., 'Ethel Carnie: writer, feminist and socialist', in H. Gustav Klaus (ed.), *The Rise of Socialist Fiction 1880–1914* (Sussex: Harvester Press, 1987), pp. 251–66.
Frow, E. and Frow, R., 'The spark of independent working-class education: Lancashire, 1909–1930', in B. Simon (ed.), *The Search for Enlightenment: the working class and adult education in the twentieth century* (London: Lawrence and Wishart, 1990), pp. 71–104.
Gaffin, J. and Thoms, D., *Caring and Sharing: the centenary history of the Co-operative Women's Guild* (Manchester: Co-operative Union Ltd, 1983).
Gallacher, W., *Revolt on the Clyde* (London: Lawrence and Wishart, 1980).
Gareth Evans, D., *A History of Wales 1815–1906* (Cardiff: University of Wales Press, 1989).
Gilbert, B.B., *The Evolution of National Insurance in Great Britain* (London: Michael Joseph, 1966).
Goldman, L., *Dons and Workers: Oxford and adult education since 1850* (Oxford: Clarendon Press, 1995).
Goodman, J., 'Women school board members and women school managers: the structuring of educational authority in Manchester and Liverpool, 1870–1903', in J. Goodman and S. Harrop (eds), *Women, Educational Policy-Making and Administration in England* (London: Routledge, 2000), pp. 59–77.
Grace, G., 'Teachers and the state in Britain: a changing relation', in M. Lawn and G. Grace (eds), *Teachers: the culture and politics of work* (Lewes: Falmer, 1987), pp. 193–203.
Gramsci, A., *Selections from Prison Notebooks*, edited/translated by Q. Hoare and G. Nowell-Smith (London: Lawrence and Wishart, 1971).
Grant, R., 'G.V. Chicherin and the Russian Revolutionary Cause in Great Britain', in J. Slatter (ed.), *From the Other Shore: Russian political emigrants in Britain,*

1880–1917 (London: Frank Cass, 1984), pp. 117–40.
Griggs, C., *The Trades Union Congress and the Struggle for Education 1868–1925* (Lewes: Falmer Press, 1983).
Groves, R., *The Strange Case of Victor Grayson* (London: Pluto Press, 1975).
Hannam, J. and Hunt, K., *Socialist Women Britain, 1880s to 1920s* (London: Routledge, 2002).
Harris, B., *The Health of the Schoolchild* (Buckingham: Open University Press, 1995).
Harrison, R.J., *The Life and Times of Sidney and Beatrice Webb 1858–1905: the formative years* (Basingstoke: Palgrave, 2001).
Hennessy, R., *Materialist Feminism and the Politics of Discourse* (New York: Routledge, 1993).
Hollis, P., *Ladies Elect: women in English local government 1865–1914* (Oxford: Clarendon Press, 1989).
Holton, S.S., 'The suffragist and the "average woman"', *Women's History Review*, 1:1 (1992), pp. 9–24.
Howard, M., *War and the Liberal Conscience* (Oxford: Oxford University Press, 1981).
Howell, D., *British Workers and the Independent Labour Party 1888–1906* (Manchester: Manchester University Press, 1983).
Humphries, S., *Hooligans or Rebels?* (Oxford: Basil Blackwell, 1981).
Hunt, F., *Gender and Policy in English Education 1902–1944* (London: Harvester Wheatsheaf, 1991).
Jacobs, J., *London Trades Council 1860–1950* (London: Lawrence and Wishart, 1950).
Jameson, S., *Journey from the North Vol. 1* (London: Virago, 1984).
Jefferson, E.F., *The Woolwich Story 1890–1969* (Woolwich: Woolwich and District Antiquarian Society, 1970).
Jennings, B., *Knowledge is Power. A short history of the WEA 1903–78*, Newland Papers Number One (Hull: University of Hull Department of Adult Education, 1979).
Jennings, B., 'The friends and enemies of the WEA', in S.K. Roberts (ed.), *A Ministry of Enthusiasm: centenary essays on the Workers' Educational Association* (London: Pluto Press, 2003), pp. 97–110.
Johnson, R., '"Really useful knowledge": radical education and working-class culture', in J. Clarke, C. Critcher and R. Johnson (eds), *Working Class Culture* (London: Hutchinson, 2nd edn, 1980), pp. 75–102.
Jones, A.W., *Lyulph Stanley: a study in educational politics* (Waterloo, Ontario: Wilfred Laurier Press, 1979).
Jones, G.S., *Languages of Class: studies in English working-class history, 1832–1982* (Cambridge: Cambridge University Press, 1983).
Jones, K., *Beyond Progressive Education* (London and Basingstoke: Macmillan, 1983).
Kapp, Y., *Eleanor Marx Family Life 1855–1883* (London: Virago, 1979).

Kean, H., *Challenging the State? The socialist and feminist educational experience, 1900–1930* (Lewes: Falmer Press, 1990).

Kean, H., 'The place of Ruskin in its own history', in G. Andrews, H. Kean and J. Thompson (eds), *Ruskin College Contesting Knowledge, Dissenting Politics* (London: Lawrence & Wishart, 1999), pp. 167–83.

Kneale, N., '"The science and art of man-making": class and gender foundations of Ruskin Hall, Oxford, 1899', in G. Andrews, H. Kean and J. Thompson (eds), *Ruskin College Contesting Knowledge, Dissenting Politics* (London: Lawrence & Wishart, 1999), pp. 5–34.

Koven, S., 'Borderlands: women, voluntary action and child welfare in Britain, 1840 to 1914', in Koven, S. and Michel, M. (eds), *Mothers of a New World* (London: Routledge, 1993), pp. 119–20.

Koven, S., *Slumming: sexual politics in Victorian London* (Princeton and Oxford: Princeton University Press, 2004).

Krauss, M., *Die Frau der Zukunft* (München: Buchendorfer Verlag, 2002).

Lawn, M., *Modern Times? Work, professionalism and citizenship in teaching* (London: Falmer, 1996).

Lawn, M. and Grace, G. (eds), *Teachers: the culture and politics of work* (Lewes: Falmer, 1987).

Lawrence, J., 'Labour – the myths it has lived by', in D. Tanner, P. Thane, N. Tiratsoo (eds), *Labour's First Century* (Cambridge: Cambridge University Press, 2000), pp. 341–66.

Lawton, D., *Education and Labour Party Ideologies 1900–2001 and Beyond* (London and New York: RoutledgeFalmer, 2005).

Levy, C., 'Education and self-education: staffing the early ILP', in C. Levy (ed.), *Socialism and the Intelligentsia 1880–1914* (London: Routledge & Kegan Paul, 1987), pp. 135–210.

Linklater, A., *An Unhusbanded Life* (London: Hutchinson, 1980).

Lowndes, G.A.N., *Margaret McMillan 'The Children's Champion'* (London: Museum Press, 1960).

McCarthy, M., *Generation in Revolt* (London: William Heinemann Ltd., 1953).

McCord, N., *North East England* (London: Batsford, 1979).

MacDougall, I., *Militant Miners* (Edinburgh, Polygon: 1981).

McDowell, L., *Gender, Identity and Place. Understanding feminist geographies* (Cambridge: Polity Press, 1999).

McHugh, J., 'Peter Petroff: the view from the Home Office file', *Scottish Labour History*, 35 (2000), pp. 25–32.

Macintyre, S., *A Proletarian Science. Marxism in Britain, 1917–1933* (London: Lawrence and Wishart, 1986).

Mackail, J.W., *The Life of William Morris* (New York and London: Benjamin Bloom, 1968 edition).

MacKenzie, N. and MacKenzie, J. (eds), *The Diary of Beatrice Webb, Volume Two 1892–1905* (London: Virago, 1986).

Maclure, S., *A History of Education in London 1870–1990* (London: Allen Lane, 1990).

McShane, H. and Smith, J., *Harry McShane: no mean fighter* (London: Pluto Press, 1977).

Maisky, I., *Journey into the Past*, translated from the Russian by Felix Holt (London: Hutchinson, 1962).

Malmstad, J.E. and Bogomolov, N., *Mikhail Kuzmin: a life in art* (Harvard: Harvard University Press, 1999).

Mannheim, K., 'The problem of generations', in M. Hardy (ed.), *Studying Aging and Social Change* (London: Sage, 1997), pp. 22–65.

Manton, K., *Socialism and Education in Britain 1883–1902* (London: Woburn Press, 2001).

Marcus, J., (ed.), *The Young Rebecca: writings of Rebecca West 1911–17* (London: Macmillan, 1982).

Marquand, D., *Ramsay MacDonald: a biography* (London: Jonathan Cape, 1977).

Martin, J., *Women and the Politics of Schooling in Victorian and Edwardian England* (London: Leicester University Press, 1999).

Martin, J., 'London women and the 1902 Education Act', in J. Goodman and S. Harrop (eds), *Women, Educational Policy-Making and Administration in England* (London: Routledge, 2000), pp. 87–91.

Martin, J., 'Working for the people? Mrs Bridges Adams and the London School Board, 1897–1904', *History of Education*, 29:1 (2000), pp. 49–62.

Martin, J., 'Gender, the city and the politics of schooling: towards a collective biography of women "doing good" as public moralists in Victorian London', *Gender and Education*, 17:2 (2005), pp. 143–63.

Miliband, R., *Parliamentary Socialism* (London: Merlin Press, 3rd impression, 1979).

Millar, J.P.M., *The Labour College Movement* (London: N.C.L.C. Publishing Society, 1979).

Miller, J., *School for Women* (London: Virago, 1996).

Milton, N., *John Maclean* (Bristol: Pluto Press, 1973).

Mitchell, H., *The Hard Way Up* (London: Virago, 1977).

Moi, T., *What is a Woman? and Other Essays* (Oxford: Oxford University Press, 1999).

Mooney, T., *J.M. Mactavish General Secretary of the W.E.A. 1916–1927: the man and his ideas* (Liverpool: Workers' Educational Association, 1979).

Morris, W., *News from Nowhere* (Oxford: Oxford University Press, 2003 edition).

Moxley, F., 'Railwaymen and working-class education', Appendix A in P.S. Bagwell, *The Railwaymen* (London: George Allen & Unwin, 1963).

Müller, D., Ringer, F. and Simon, B. (eds), *The Rise of the Modern Educational System: social change and cultural reproduction, 1870–1920* (Cambridge: Cambridge University Press, 1989).

Newman, M., 'Ralph Miliband and the Labour Party: from *Parliamentary Socialism* to "Bennism"', in J. Callaghan, S. Fielding and S. Ludlam (eds), *Interpreting the Labour Party* (Manchester: Manchester University Press, 2003), pp. 57–70.

Page Arnot, R., *William Morris: the man and the myth* (London: Lawrence and Wishart, 1964).

Pankhurst, S., *The Suffragette Movement* (London: Virago, 1977 edition).

Pearson, G., *Hooligan: a history of respectable fears* (London and Basingstoke: Macmillan, 1983).

Porter, C., *Alexandra Kollontai: a biography* (London: Virago, 1980).

Quataert, J.H., *Reluctant Feminists in German Social Democracy, 1885–1917* (Princeton: Princeton University Press, 1979).

Radice, E.A. and Radice, G.H., *Will Thorne: constructive militant* (London: George Allen & Unwin Ltd, 1974).

Ratcliffe, S.K., *The Story of South Place* (London: Watts & Co., 1955).

Rée, J., *Proletarian Philosophers* (Oxford: Clarendon Press, 1984).

Rhodes, R., *An Arsenal for Labour* (Manchester: Holyoake Books, 1998).

Ripley, B.J. and McHugh, J., *John Maclean* (Manchester: Manchester University Press, 1989).

Rose, J., *The Intellectual Life of the British Working Classes* (New Haven and London: Yale Nota Bena, 2002).

Rose, N., *The Psychological Complex: psychology, politics and society in England 1869–1939* (London: Routledge & Kegan Paul, 1985).

Rosen, H., *Speaking from Memory: the study of autobiographical discourse* (Stoke-on-Trent: Trentham Books, 1998).

Rowbotham, S., *Friends of Alice Wheeldon* (London: Pluto Press, 1986).

Samuel, R., *The Lost World of British Communism* (London: Verso, 2006).

Savage, M., *The Dynamics of Working-Class Politics: the Labour movement in Preston, 1880–1940* (Cambridge: Cambridge University Press, 1987).

Saville, J. and Bellamy, J. (eds) *Dictionary of Labour Biography* (Cambridge: Cambridge University Press, 1982).

Scott, G., *Feminism and the Politics of Working Women* (London: UCL Press, 1998).

Scott, G., '"As a war-horse to the beat of drums": representations of working-class femininity in the Women's Co-operative Guild, 1880s to the Second World War', in E.J. Yeo (ed.), *Radical Femininity. Women's self-representation in the public sphere* (Manchester: Manchester University Press, 1998), pp. 196–219.

Scott, J., *Gender and the Politics of History* (New York: Columbia University Press, revised edition, 1999).

Searle, G., *The Quest for National Efficiency: a study in British political thought, 1899–1914* (London: Basil Blackwell, 1971).

Simon, B., *Education and the Labour Movement 1870–1920* (London: Lawrence and Wishart, 1980 edition).

Simon, B., 'The struggle for hegemony, 1920–1926', in B. Simon (ed.), *The Search for Enlightenment: the working class and adult education in the twentieth century* (London: Lawrence and Wishart, 1990), pp. 15–70.

Smith, D., *Aneurin Bevan and the World of South Wales* (Cardiff: University of Wales Press, 1993).

Smyth, J. and Rodgers, M., 'Peter Petroff and the socialist movement in Britain, 1907–18', in J. Slatter (ed.), *From the Other Shore: Russian political emigrants in Britain, 1880–1917* (London: Frank Cass, 1984), pp. 100–16.

Speight, R. (ed.), *A Bridges-Adams Letter Book* (London: The Society for Theatre Research, 1971).

Stanley, L., *The Auto/biographical 'I': the theory and practice of feminist auto/biography* (Manchester: Manchester University Press, 1992).

Stedman Jones, G., *Languages of Class: studies in English working class history 1832–1982* (Cambridge: Cambridge University Press, 1996 edition).

Steedman, C., *Landscape for a Good Woman* (London: Virago, 1986).

Steedman, C., *Childhood, Culture and Class in Britain: Margaret McMillan 1860–1931* (London: Virago, 1990).

Steedman, C., 'Fictions of engagement: Eleanor Marx, biographical space', in John Stokes (ed.), *Eleanor Marx (1855–1898) life-work-contacts* (Aldershot: Ashgate, 2000), pp. 23–39.

Steedman, C., *Dust* (Manchester: Manchester University Press, 2001).

Stocks, M., *The WEA* (London: George Allen & Unwin, 1953).

Stuart, D., *Dear Duchess: Millicent, Duchess of Sutherland* (Littlehampton: Littlehampton Book Services, 1982).

Taylor, B., *Eve and the New Jerusalem* (London: Virago, 1983).

Thompson, E.P., *The Making of the English Working Class* (London: Victor Gollancz, 1963).

Thompson, E.P., *William Morris: from romantic to revolutionary* (London: Merlin Press, 1977).

Thompson, L., *The Enthusiasts: a biography of John and Katherine Bruce Glasier* (London: Victor Gollancz Limited, 1971).

Thompson, P., *Socialists, Liberals and Labour: the struggle for London 1885–1914* (London: Routledge & Kegan Paul, 1967).

Thompson, P., *The Edwardians* (London: Routledge, 1975).

Torr, D., *Tom Mann and his Times 1856–90* (London: Lawrence and Wishart, 1956).

Turnbull, A., 'So extremely like Parliament: the work of the women members of the London School Board, 1870–1904', in The London Feminist History Group (eds), *The Sexual Dynamics of History* (London: Pluto Press, 1983), pp. 120–33.

Tyler, P., *Labour's Lost Leader: the life and politics of Will Crooks* (London: I.B. Tauris Ltd, 2007).

Usborne, C., *Cultures of Abortion in Weimar Germany* (New York and Oxford: Berghahn Books, 2007).

Vlaeminke, M., *The English Higher Grade Schools* (London: Woburn Press, 2000).

Wake, R. and Denton, P., *Bedales School 1893–1993* (London: Haggerston Press, 1993).

Ward, M., *Hanna Sheehy Skeffington: a life* (Cork: Attic Press, 1997).

Watts, R., *Gender, Power and the Unitarians in England 1760–1860* (Harlow: Longman, 1998).

Weller, K., *'Don't be a Soldier!' The radical anti-war movement in north London 1914–1918* (London: Journeyman Press Limited and the London History Workshop Centre, 1985).

Wilson, A.N., *Incline Our Hearts* (Harmondsworth: Penguin, 1988).

Woodin, T., 'Working-class education and social change in nineteenth and twentieth-century Britain', *History of Education*, 38:4–5 (2007), pp. 483–96.

Worpole, K., 'A ghostly pavement: the political implications of local working-class history', in R. Samuel (ed.) *People's History and Socialist Theory* (London, Boston and Henley: Routledge and Kegan Paul, 1981) pp. 22–32.

Yeo, S., 'A new life: the religion of socialism in Britain, 1883–1896', *History Workshop*, 4 (1977), pp. 5–56.

Yoonak Stenberg, K., 'Working-class women in London local politics, 1894–1914', *Twentieth Century British History*, 9:3 (1998), pp. 323–49.

Unpublished theses

McCann, W.P., 'Trade unionist, co-operative and socialist organisations in relation to popular education 1870–1902' (University of Manchester PhD, 1960).

Smalley, R., 'The life and work of Ethel Carnie Holdsworth with particular reference to the period 1907 to 1931' (University of Lancashire PhD, 2006).

Internet and web-based sources

Census records

Oxford Dictionary of National Biography (Oxford: Oxford University Press, 2004).

Index

CPSIA information can be obtained at www.ICGtesting.com
Printed in the USA
LVOW06s0259010214

371909LV00007B/121/P

9 780719 089947